Medical Culture
in Revolutionary
America

Medical Culture in Revolutionary America

Feuds, Duels, and a Court-Martial

Linda Myrsiades

Madison • Teaneck
Fairleigh Dickinson University Press

Associated University Presses
2010 Eastpark Boulevard
Cranbury, NJ 08512

The paper used in this publication meets the requirements of the American National Standard for Permanence of Paper for Printed Library Materials Z39.48-1984.

Library of Congress Cataloging-in-Publication Data

Myrsiades, Linda S.
Medical culture in revolutionary America : feuds, duels, and a court-martial / Linda Myrsiades.
    p. ; cm.
Includes bibliographical references and index.
ISBN 978-0-8386-4190-3 (alk. paper)
    1. Medicine—United States—History—18th century.   I. Title.
[DNLM: 1. History of Medicine—United States.   2. American Revolution—United States.   3. Dissection—history—United States.   4. History, 18th Century—United States.   5. Military Medicine—history—United States.
6. Quackery—history—United States.   WZ 70 AA1 M998m 2009]
R152.M97   2009
610—dc22   2008029494

Contents

Acknowledgments

The author is indebted to the libraries of the Historical Society of Pennsylvania, the College of Physicians of Philadelphia, and the Library Company for their fine collections of eighteenth-century material and their cooperation in assisting with my research. I very much appreciate not only the generosity of Pennsylvania Hospital for its permission to reprint photographs of the hospital but for the inspiration it provides through its preservation of the original eighteenth-century hospital building with its unique library and operating theater. The city of Philadelphia has been a wonderful site to conduct this study, with its fine period homes, churches, cemeteries, and courthouses, for the preservation of which we must all be grateful. Finally, and perhaps most importantly, I can never express sufficiently my appreciation to West Chester University, which has been most generous in making available a most talented and energetic staff of librarians, as well as various small grants that have managed to keep this study going.

This book is for my grandchildren, whose noisy energy is both my blessing and my burden.

Introduction

THIS STUDY TAKES PLACE AT A TIME WHEN AMERICAN MEDICINE FOUND itself caught in a liminal zone of change that forced it to explore where it had been and where it was heading. It examines eighteenth-century doctors' feuds and duels—with a focus on Philadelphia—trials by press, issues of medical malpractice, antimedical riots, and a court-martial of the medical director of the army hospitals during the Revolutionary War. The theory chapter gives us a means of modeling the ways in which medicine organized itself, offering an understanding of what the past, present, and future offered as medicine moved from within a nonlegal to within a legal order along a continuum of change. The discussion of theory provides an overarching template that establishes the importance of reputation and honor and locates the venues and the processes in which and by means of which the medico-legal interface and its changes would occur.

The sections on medicine provide an understanding of those elements that combine or can be combined to create storied constructions of medical discourse. They provide the material of stories that reflect a process of choices made under conditions not of one's own choosing, as Marx would have expressed it.[1] Narrative constructivism offers us a way to capitalize on accounts of the actors themselves, institutional and professional medical discourses, and interactions between practitioners and competitors to tell the story of medicine. We see how actors make meaning in their social and professional spaces, how they contest the meaning-making of others, and how language is used to construct reality, both privately and publicly. At the same time, we recognize that the history of medicine identifies themes and perspectives that inform as well as constrain the roles that medicine performs and the direction of changes that will occur. Taking an interdisciplinary perspective, we discover that religious, economic, and political perspectives on healing and the medical marketplace are as important to the self-presentation of medicine in a time of crucial turnaround as are the narratives constructed of medical practice and the medical profession, its institutions, and roles that tell the story of medicine struggling in the young nation to create a new identity.

In tracing the constructions of medicine that informed its development in the eighteenth century, the study provides two extended cases treating medico-legal events that frame our understanding of institutional medicine and medical feuds in eighteenth-century America. We see them work themselves out not only as a test of the principles of social theory, but in terms of a larger social narrative in which they test the building of a nation and of a profession essential to that nation's survival. Self-organizing rules and norms create order by means of which doctors deal with conflict, and they establish the parameters within which physicians undermine or develop professional status. William Shippen's feud with John Morgan and Benjamin Rush bursts out of a world of feuds and duels of a nonlegal order as large-scale conflicts that push into a new legal order.

This study covers three areas: theory, medical history, and cases. Chapter 1 looks at theories of norms and values by means of which law, medicine, and social reality make themselves and then operate. It provides a background for the study that considers the continuum that runs from nonlegal to legal order, that establishes the importance of honor and reputation on the nonlegal end of that continuum, and that contrasts French game theory to English and American socioeconomic theory as alternate theoretical frameworks by means of which to access the nonlegal order of feuding. In the process, the chapter identifies the conditions within which norms operate—the interests they serve, the rules they follow, the moves they invent—and their progress from a nonlegal order of feuding to a legal order that is exemplified in its early stages in a court martial. Reputation is discussed as a form of symbolic capital that constitutes a way of producing and being produced. By this argument, honor has economic power with social utility. As medicine develops into a profession, it generates agreed-upon norms to bind its group members together as well as to resolve conflicts and distribute justice. Tests of reputation and sanctions to prevent violations of honor enforce the norms as parts of an unofficial system to achieve order.

The model of an unofficial order based on norms can be applied to the world of feuds, duels, and trial by press that emerged in the medical wars of the second half of the eighteenth century. The leaching of feuds into duels and the magnification and spread of press libels led to a move from an unofficial order based on social norms to a greater use of litigation in formal court settings. As part of this movement, honor and the value of reputation were gradually trumped by justice and official order as explanatory concepts so that conflict resolution changed its venue, content, and its dynamic, transitioning from a nonlegal to a legal order. Agreed-upon norms became codified as rules of evidence and due process and were less likely to be negotiated than adjudicated as immediate parties with personal stakes, a private form of resolution, were replaced by neutral, objective experts in a third-party public form of resolution. French game theory and English and American socioeconomic theory offer two ways of theorizing these events, using psychological and rational explanations, respectively.

Chapter 2 provides background to a period that had yet to free itself from a medical tradition that dated back to 800 BCE. Nor had it availed itself of emerging scientific thinking that would move medicine away from abstract theorizing toward empirical and experimental findings. The physician Benjamin Rush's medical lectures at the University of Pennsylvania Medical School, dating from the first decade of the nineteenth century, provide unique insights into how medicine figured itself as one of the three professional "crafts" of the period—law and religion being the other two—how physicians accessed medical knowledge, how they set up to practice medicine as a business, and their relation to religious healing. This chapter considers eighteenth-century medicine in terms of the three stories that permeate the century: the residual religious story, the dominant professional story, and the emerging scientific story.

To understand medicine in eighteenth-century America, it is important to understand the marketplace issues that emanated from the battle between irregulars and regulars and the struggle to gain public acceptance of the study of anatomy and the dissecting of human bodies. Chapter 3 focuses on the roles played by quacks and by cadaver, or resurrection, riots (public demonstrations against dissection) in the formative years of American scientific development. The competition between quacks and regular physicians, as well as the overlap between those who saw medicine as a business and those who sponsored new discoveries in medicine, allows us to explore the open medical marketplace in a period of protocapitalism. Competitive practices aggravated existing feuds and created new areas of disagreement within an already contentious profession. Patients accrued greater value through a balance of power, their willingness to purchase services, and their loyalty to a given physician's practice.

Their greater value led to innovations in medicine at the same time that they sponsored hypochondria and over-consumption.

Medicine was not going to transition into a specialized, professionalized field until it gained command of anatomy. Nor was society itself likely to be medicalized absent the kind of knowledge that could only be made available by dissection. But the promise of progress offered by anatomy and dissection required corpses, and corpses implied body-snatching. Whose body, from what source, and how it was to be provided became the looming questions around cadavers, leading to the questionable procurement of corpses of women and children, whites, and the middle class while permitting the use of bodies of executed criminals, the poor, people of color, immigrants, and strangers. Christian burials and graveyard thefts were off limits whereas the gallows and almshouses as sources of corpses were well within what would be officially tolerated. Having failed to consider the sentiments of the lower classes, however, meant that popular riots would attend efforts by medical schools to gain access to bodies, either independently or from a proliferating underground industry that grew up to supply them. At the same time, medical schools had to address the value placed on death in the eighteenth century. Social as well as fashionable rituals had developed around the dead body to create a sentiment that placed a premium on a "beautiful death" even as residual customs still focused on superstitious reverence of the dead tied to sin, guilt, redemption, and even worship of the dead.

The final part of the book is made up of two cases that allow us to fully flesh out issues related to nonlegal and legal order as they were experienced through feuds that led to the development of professionalism in medicine. Chapter 4 takes up medical feuds in eighteenth-century Philadelphia and chapter 5 the Revolutionary War court-martial of William Shippen, involving John Morgan and Benjamin Rush, taking into account in both chapters these three preeminent physicians of eighteenth-century Philadelphia. Even before yellow fever epidemics of the 1790s turned Philadelphia into a crucible testing residual and emerging medical theories and therapeutics, physicians had an uneasy professional history of unstable alliances and networks. Doctors established themselves through discoveries or inventions with which they were identified, as well as by commanding their share of rewards in terms of patients, pupils, and appointments to a medical association, hospital, dispensary, or medical school. Each of these endeavors required a competition, a jealous regard for one's reputation, and the accumulation of symbolic capital, cultural, reputational, or otherwise, and each led to endemic and long-lasting feuds. The feud of feuds appears to have been that between William Shippen and John Morgan over the founding in 1765 of the College of Philadelphia Medical School, soon to be absorbed by the University of Pennsylvania. That feud began when they both studied in Edinburgh in colonial times, and it formed the basis for an institutionally disruptive battle over military hospitals in the revolutionary period. It went on to seed squabbles that affected their fellow physicians at the Pennsylvania Hospital and the College of Philadelphia Medical School in the postrevolutionary period. It thus continued from their student years in the 1760s until Morgan's death in 1789, that is, from the colonial period to the postwar years of establishing the new nation.

Benjamin Rush may well have been the single figure most associated with feuding behavior. The most dramatic of his feuds entangled him in the Morgan-Shippen feud and led to the court-martial of Shippen in 1780. His most endemic feuds, however, both for their breadth and their length, were his ongoing quarrels with his students and fellow physicians. Rush was particularly notable for his preoccupation with establishing himself as the foremost physician of his time. He trained a larger number of students than any other physician of his generation, and he earned a super-sized reputation for his political, medical, and benevolent labors over a career that spanned from the 1760s until the second decade of the nineteenth century. Remarkably, given the extent of his labors, Rush remained isolated in the medical community. He contended that he set up his practice without the assistance of other physicians, indeed in the face of their refusal to consult with him or refer patients. Neither did he receive help from the Presbyterian religious community of which he was a part, a community he considered powerless to supply him with the numbers of patients he would need to survive. Placing his faith in the poor, befriending free blacks, creating a cadre of students beholden to him, and establishing a competing medical organization, the Academy of Medicine, to counter the College of Physicians, from which he resigned, Rush strategically crafted a circle of loyalists to bolster his ego and spread his work. Like other physicians of the period, Rush was not immune to the end result of many feuds which gravitated to duels when they became irresoluble and erupted in trials by press as well as court cases when informal mechanisms and social norms were no longer sufficient to address them.

The cases of John Morgan and William Shippen, considered in chapter 5, allow us to explore the permutations of medical feuds as they cascaded through the military hospital system of the American revolutionary army. The feud between these two men—who served in succession as Directors General of the Hospitals of the Revolutionary Army—ran from the critical issues of massive losses of life among soldiers at the hospitals and fraud and corruption in the selling of hospital stores to competition between regimental hospitals, flying camp hospitals, and the general hospital. Questions of authority over and organization of the hospitals, as well as physician disputes within the ranks, formed the basis of disputes among surgeons, physicians, officers, and politicians that risked breaking the back of the war effort. Challenges to the directorships of both Morgan and Shippen exposed weaknesses in the law of the period, including standards of evidence and witness testimony, the roles of attorneys, judges, and juries, private prosecution, and due process. Not only was the court-martial of Shippen a challenge to the developing legal order, but the trial by press waged against him by Morgan proved a test of the limits of the use of the press in medico-political debates. The satire "The High Court of Honor," by the then-recently appointed (1779) Judge of the Admiralty Francis Hopkinson,[2] effectively cut off debate in the Morgan-Shippen replay of the court martial in the press by satirizing the way feuds were publicly handled and proposing a parodic legal mechanism to punish offenders.

Medical Culture
in Revolutionary
America

1

Theory

FROM FEUDS TO LEGAL ORDER

IN THE EIGHTEENTH CENTURY INTRAPROFESSIONAL MEDICAL DISPUTES largely operated within the constraints of a nonlegal order of social norms and did not wind up as malpractice suits. The failure to go to court in the eighteenth century contrasted with nineteenth-century practice in which a large part of malpractice litigation was the result of intraprofessional disputes.[1] The difference was largely a function of the relative homogeneity of traditional communities in the eighteenth century in which the collective good was put above that of the individual. Homogeneity created the kind of stability that social order required and that private relations, more than government action, could provide.

Before the first decades of the nineteenth century, lawsuits against physicians were not a significant threat and reports on malpractice in medical publications indicated a low level of anxiety over actual lawsuits.[2] At the same time, as Kenneth De Ville suggests, a number of "social, political, legal, technological, and professional"[3] changes that would sponsor such lawsuits were already in play. One possibility is that the unofficial venues of feuds, duels, and trials by press were sufficient to address intraprofessional conflicts that were not taken to mediation and arbitration. Another possibility is that such unofficial venues were perceived as most appropriate to such conflicts and therefore were the ones most frequently accessed. At the same time, physician conflicts appear to have been tolerated to the extent that parties did not access courts to resolve conflicts. Physicians either lacked meaningful access to courts or a large number of conflicts did not rise to a level beyond the needs of lower level or socially acceptable disagreements. An alternative explanation suggests that the right conditions—legally, medically, culturally—were simply not present to develop and bring suits to a point where they could be addressed in court. Nevertheless, the extent of physician conflicts suggests that issues of the type that led to suits permeated the medical scene. Such conflicts played out publicly in newspapers, diminished the status of the profession, undermined public confidence, and inhibited the professionalization of medicine.

The old order in which the law was superfluous was one in which patients were prepared to accept "the necessity of kissing the rod, and him who hath anointed it,"[4] as a case like *Lowell v. Faxon* (1824) demonstrates. Parties were brought to believe either that their injury was God's will or that healing was the work of nature.[5] The Lowell case also made apparent that juries were reluctant to be part of a verdict that would visit the heavens too roughly upon physicians, whom they regarded as benefactors.[6] As with acts of divinely instigated plagues and pestilence, individual adversity was understood to be the result of divine providence. These were acts that had as much to do with the fortunes of a community as they had to do with those of an individual. Since victims were expected to submit to their misfortune, blaming human agents or seeking immediate causes was unlikely to address the overriding moral questions attached to such misfortunes. Attaching personal responsibility to physicians and looking for earthly causes—as opposed to second order divine natural causes—would have to wait until the dominance of individualism and faith in science in a more secular period. This is not to say that a great deal of "individualism" was not present in the late eighteenth century, given the value attached to honor, feuds, and duels over reputation. It does suggest that the kind of individual self-regard that would lead to court litigation required the convergence of several emerging cultural forces that had not yet reached critical mass.

In the old order, dominated by face-to-face relations, reputation was an important cohesive bond. Tort or contract suits, with their adversarial structure and remedial orientation,[7] might have reflected that importance, but the moral aspect of affirming reputation required a form of public judgment more responsive to community beliefs and social codes. To have disregarded both God's will and community proscriptions by suing would have meant seeking legal redress outside the confines of a stable worldview that had provided otherwise for consensus and conflict resolution. Communal enforcement had its own extralegal structures and processes based on group action, influence, and even coercion. Relationally, it rejected lawsuits as an unacceptable form of communal judgment and held human law to be superfluous.[8]

Eighteenth-century America was very much a culture of honor, both North and South. Northern cities operated like urban frontiers and required, like rural life in the South, protection of one's interests by means of retributive justice. Characterized by what Dov Cohen and Joe Vandello describe as a "herding economy," it was a culture in which cooperation was tested by predators who acted to "rustle away" one's livelihood unless one demonstrated he was not someone to be trifled with.[9] A baseline of forced gentility was necessary given the risks, but defense of reputation still required the credibility that only a threat of violence could offer.[10]

Violence was in many ways only what was to be expected, not as lawlessness but as a way of being.[11] It operated in an urban setting largely at the level of feuds and trials by press, with eruptions into dueling, riots, or court litigation associated with the most intense altercations. The value of one's honor (knowledge gained by means of reputation) operated as a noninstrumental norm that informed social practices like gossip, ostracism, or feuding, which were the functional or instrumental arms of the process. These practices resulted in either providing information about one's reputation—whether one's reputation could sustain an assault or had been legitimately enhanced, for example—or deterring future bad acts. The final part of the process included a feedback loop that reinforced conformity to the norm of honor. Deterrence proved more critical than punishing past bad acts since reputational capital was necessary to capitalize on future opportunities and the ambiguity of both offenses and resolutions in such events as feuds made punishment difficult to determine or to apply fairly.

In the development of both the medical and the legal professions as they changed over time, and given their transitional growth needs in the eighteenth century, the dynamics of feuds and duels and their resolutions became important in bridging the gap between the nonlegal and the legal orders. Moreover, dispute resolution was critical to the growth of both the medical and the legal professions. Indeed, as analysis on dueling shows the most common groups associated with an extreme version of dispute resolution like dueling were physicians, politicians, and journalists.[12] The professions, as well as their members, were caught in a crisis of reputation-building that was to determine which of its subgroups was to survive and what the relationship of the state and the professions was to be.[13]

Both medicine and law were establishing themselves in a period of economic change that included industrialization, urbanization, and the move to full-scale capitalism. It was a time in which public welfare would begin to supplant private organization in government and institutional social development. And it was a time in which the endogenous social norm of honor would give way to the predictability and reliability of exogenous interventions of the state, regularities which the nonlegal order could not provide. To grow business and to allow for the professionalization of medicine and law, such enforcement mechanisms as licensing and contracts, legal forms, doctrines, and rules would have to develop and courts would have to generate authority in dispute resolution. In a summary sense, new norms related to the legal order would have to assert themselves and replace the social norms of the nonlegal order.

But for new norms to develop, the elite privileged by old norms would either have to be displaced or give up its privileged place. Indeed, the coherence of old norms was itself dissolving as a glue holding society together.[14] Legislation, prosecution, and jury verdicts, as a result, arose to reinforce new norms even as general values of society supported their enforcement and developed credible punishments for violating them. Credibility demanded that punishment be tailored commensurate with the crime, that the trivial and the significant not be treated alike, and that nonpunishment no longer be as likely a result as punishment for an offender. Finally, the very framework for punishment would have to balance the retrospective (paying for past bad acts) and the prospective (being deterred or enjoined from future bad acts, the "incapacitation rationale") to account for legal reforms that pointed to a new century.[15]

The movement along the continuum from the nonlegal to a legal order allowed for proportional response, certainty of application, protection of rights, and equal access to equal treatment. In this analysis, under the old norms accepting a duel—given the risks to life such a duel entailed—might be taken as evidence that an accused was not the type of man to be guilty of an action challenged. Under the new norms, the accused could depend upon the support of rules of evidence, burden of proof, and presumption of innocence as guarantees of a process that was less capricious. Such a process of resolving disputes would more objectively reflect the facts of the case and be less unduly influenced by status differentials or by backroom deals outside of public view.[16]

Open access to a legal order correlated with greater distance and less equality between parties[17] which, in an earlier culture of greater homogeneity, might have opted for negotiated solutions. Where groups within the community became marginal and their issues were left unaddressed, their conflicts could rise to the level of disputes best satisfied by litigation. In such a case, the need for litigation, whether actualized or not, represented the failure of a sense of community. Grievants who sought and were denied access to the court were likely to be reduced to forms of self-help, like riots or mob actions, that would disrupt the order of the community and its relative harmony.

An alternate explanation suggests that higher status members of a community more frequently accessed the law as they belonged to the same dominant political group as those who controlled or ran the legal system,[18] making it easier to accept the authority of a third party to resolve a dispute. At the same time, breaking ranks within a community in which one was part of an elite represented a loss of confidence in the community that would argue against such recourse to the courts. Why and when different members of a community might feel cut off from the law (a containment problem) or find their ability to dispute openly curtailed (a problem of "effacement of conflict")[19] is perhaps best explained by the ideology of the community. The cultural order of the community is plotted on one end of a continuum in terms of relationships, social harmony, and divine rather than human authority. The law is plotted on the other end characterized by adversarial parties, acceptance of human authority, and a resolution based in self-interest and redress of a grievance.[20] On the cultural end, grievances were not redressed but endured. Self-interest was not expressed but reconciled with what was good for the community. On the legal end, the individual's needs trumped those of the community and conflicts were resolved.

As we shall see in this study, community-based resolutions in the social norm process[21] could play out in a number of ways. They could appear as an apology, a settlement, bluffing or bullying, withdrawal of a charge, or a legitimate or fraudulent win. Escalation of a confrontation could occur by means of publicizing it through the press, a challenge to a duel, resorting to the legal order by making formal charges, or continuing an on-going altercation as a feud, a form of bloodless duel.[22] As the focus of this study, feuds need to be put in context, both in terms of their source—reputation—and their goal—honor. Clearly, addressing an attack on one's reputation by feuding drives a negative spiral that creates reputational costs for both parties.[23] In public feuds, readers or bystanders become irritated with both the accuser and the accused leading to negative fallout for the groups of which they are members. Here the feud is blown much larger than the original offense and pulls in many ancillary parties. Once the public puts a pox on both houses, the social and professional costs become too great for the profession and the public to bear. This kind of risk is actually more difficult for high-status members to sustain, for they not only have more to lose but they have to win merely to remain status quo. Weaker parties win even by losing for, playing the role of the giant-killer, so long as they are not completely crushed they gain reputation. They have, after all, demonstrated against considerable odds that they are people of such conviction that they are willing to risk their professional lives.

The feud is, in this way, like a political campaign debate in which one must anticipate a shift in positional power once one accepts the contest. For incumbents, it is almost a no-win game. If they engage, they risk sharing the spotlight with their competitor who otherwise would have been unlikely to command so much attention. If they refuse to engage, they succumb to an accusation of cowardice, an assault on reputation that compounds the original insult to one's honor and creates an impression in the community of confirming the truth behind it. For the lower-status player, being in the game, irrespective of any material or symbolic gain, represents a way to get people to take you seriously or to "try you on."[24]

Once gained, reputation is a high-maintenance commodity that must be routinely kept up.[25] Because reputation is so fungible a public commodity, the ambiguity that arises around it makes dishonor difficult for community members to detect and honor difficult to up-keep. Feuds are a useful tool to do just that and to put a group on notice that certain issues have to be dealt with. Even fraudulent or invented feuds can be beneficial when issues around which they arise have high salience for the group. We could refer to this as the "Soprano" effect, a reference to the need among mob bosses to pick fights that can be easily won just to remind members of the boss's incontestable power. The norms reaffirmed by such tests become, however, unamenable to change and stunt the growth of the group, just as self-censorship among members as a result of feuds leads to a lack of new ideas to grow the group.

The costs that attend feuds go beyond the risk to one's positional power or to the costs of airing the group's laundry in public, thereby exposing oneself publicly. Public feuding, after all, is a high risk way of enhancing reputation attended by low precision in terms of learning information about the true character of either party. First, parties who feud find they have painted a target on their backs. Second, the allies they attract when they generate a high profile are less desirable and more needy.

Perhaps because feuds have such high costs, the mere threat of a feud can have high deterrence value, so that one might pursue a less risky alternative such as withdrawal, apology, or settlement. Similarly, the high cost of resorting to the courts, to duels, or to trial by press is more likely to lead to private feuding or settlement alternatives. Those interested in the truth value of their claims,[26] however, are sure to prefer a more expanded and less personal venue for their contests, finding in feuds and duels a lower relation between success and the truth of one's position[27] than one is likely to find in trials by press or in the courts. Absent improved efficiency in the self-imposed nonlegal order, access to such exogenous interventions as the press and the courts seems indeed to be the direction in which the social norm process in the period of this study was headed.

It would take a series of moves—social, medical, legal—before social norms and a nonlegal order would lead to a legal order. Malpractice litigation did not appear in numbers of any significance until after 1835,[28] although many of the critical factors were present in the eighteenth century: feuding and competition among physicians, problems with public confidence, and low efficacy of medical treatments. Many of the critical conditions for court-based conflict were present and professional conflicts did occur in large numbers. But the venues in the eighteenth century were different. Conflicts were addressed and resolved in their most public expression through feuding, dueling, and trials by press (with which this study deals as cultural expressions) and more privately through mediation and arbitration (which will be left to other studies to address). These public forms of conflict did not merely represent a means of expressing contentiousness or exposing medical errors. They functioned, more importantly, as forms of public judgment and extralegal litigation at a time when courts were not generally accessed to resolve medical conflicts. With the development of libel law and malpractice law in nineteenth-century American courts, increased willingness of the public to access the courts with their conflicts, and a decline in the use of the press as a surrogate form of public trial, courts would become an important source of cultural information and a place where medical conflicts could be worked out.

GAMING THE SCENE

As we consider the role of feuds and duels in the medico-legal scene of the eighteenth century, it is useful to regard two ways of theorizing the events we shall study: in terms of French game theory, with its psychological bent; and English-American socioeconomic theory, with its grounding in rational thought. Game theory posits a scene characterized by many possibilities for norms and few shared frames for understanding. As a result, there is little likelihood, as Jean François Lyotard might put it, of determinate judgment. Culture is viewed in terms of a variety of games in which players position themselves to invent moves that will disrupt the scenes to their advantage, but without clear objectives or predictable outcomes.[29] If we extend this reading, we find ourselves in a world not of our own making but one from within which we act as subjects.[30] In doing so, and following Michel De Certeau, we turn to our own use the conditions in which we find ourselves and we do so according to our own interests.[31] This construction puts everyday life in charge of inventing itself by "poaching" in many different ways on the work and holdings of others.[32] One might capture what one wants from someone else who has not made good use of it or cannot keep hold of it, calling into play the early American concept of "usufruct" which privileges those who know how to command resources and actively exploit them.[33]

As we consider game theory, several questions arise, among them whether the world we are studying is a negotiated order and whether that order is a just one. If it is just, moreover, is its justice knowable within a world that is unpredictable?[34] As an indice of order and knowability, a certain degree of regularity exists in the game world, if only by virtue of game rules. Each game has rules, norms, or behavioral regularities;[35] each rule invents new moves which allow new games to break out; each infiltrates other games; and each contests among games to dominate others. On the other side of order, however, games proliferate and members from within the games participate in multiple games, creating an exponential complexity that ultimately makes social practices, norms, games, and conventions unpredictable to the point of pathology. As part of that pathology in the game universe, the interest-based nature of behavior, together with the irrationality of such behavior, will lead to a certain amount of strategic concealment of realities or truth.[36] Moreover, the resources with which we are dealing, both economic and symbolic, all have value, so that such ineffables as handshakes, compliments, and gossip will lack clarity even as they prove meaningful.[37] Questions of justice and predictability are not, as a result, likely to be resolved successfully in the game universe.

It is, however, possible to determine how to play a game well, even under ambiguous conditions. Understanding the use of symbolic capital is one way of doing just that. Symbolic capital provides us with a way to view strategies of accumulating, defending, and attacking one's reputation for honor and prestigious status as players play the games of social norms, trial by press, and legal trials. In this study we will examine reputation-building, bullying, bluffing, and reputational fraud as a "way of seeing," with an eye to how such practices both play the game and are played by the game,[38] the stakes being very much worth a player's while since such symbolic capital as reputation readily converts into economic capital.[39] Not only does symbolic capital make good economic sense for its fungibility, but it has value as credit which, exhibited, adds interest to the principle and attracts new capital. The group to which one belongs, serving as a source of credit to measure symbolic capital, proves capable both of withdrawing that credit and of qualifying those who would draw against it.[40]

Honor as symbolic capital had particular importance in the medical and legal professions in their developmental years in the new nation, not least because one's standing in a group, relative to the group's honor, became a critical factor for individual and group status and identity. The professional group, hypersensitive to slights, devised multiple strategies to prevent or deflect offense and enforced sanctions against its members. It maintained a zero sum gain approach that held those with the most to lose to a higher standard, as if their greater wealth, reputational or material, essentially deprived others in a fixed resources system. Possession of a good reputation thereby left one vulnerable to attack by those with a need to build their own reputation. Have-nots would profit merely by the self-advertisement of taking on a well-established target. Defense of reputation was necessary not only to one's hope of a legacy but to retaining one's position at status quo, at the least, and to ensuring one's survival as a figure to be reckoned with, at the most. One had to play the game of honor or risk diminishing one's reputational capital by failing to make a show sufficient to put challengers in the position of having to withdraw, settle, or face a significant test of their claim. Indeed, it was common to overinvest to reinforce the perception of the value of one's reputation.[41] At the same time, reputation as a form of symbolic capital functions best when it is misrecognized. Most powerful when it does not have to be displayed, spent, used, circulated, or converted, it should have the veneer of permanence such that it does not have to be continually renewed.[42] Of course, in a fluid, informal order where practices are negotiated and where behavioral regularities must constantly be adjusted to the changing scene, reliance on nonrenewable reputational capital would not have proven realistic or likely.[43]

At some point, the nonlegal order created by the balance of such games exhausts itself under the weight of its subterfuges, which become counterproductive. Here the nonlegal order transmutes into a legal order that tends to greater uniformity and clarity and is able to respond with presumed objectivity and neutrality to create consensus and resolve disputes more efficiently than the proliferation of games it replaces.[44] As part of the movement from a nonlegal to a legal order, the medical profession was stimulated by the need to address anxieties about identity, both individual and social, in combination with economic change. With a changing social order, groups competing for status used their growing professionalism as leverage.[45] As Edward Gieskes constructs the changes in status, they occurred not merely as recognition of services but as a goal in themselves fought over in power struggles. Those struggles reflected complex and conflicting interactions of groups over authority and jurisdictional control in their field.[46] The process thus appears to be one of changing social conditions leading to conflict between and among individuals and groups. The conflicts themselves lead to a desire for stability from which emerges professionalism,[47] which itself contributes to the movement to a legal order.

Professionalization can be seen as a rule-based area of defined practices[48] in which struggles over legitimacy[49] revolved around the establishment of the medical profession and whether doctors could incorporate to capitalize on privileges granted to a specialized group that would be denied to the general public. An ongoing struggle over who should be excluded, who included, who should exercise power, and who claim dominion was justified by the value of regularizing professional status as a form of cultural authority based upon the profession's special and recognized knowledge.[50] Entry into a profession and its way of framing practices would depend upon one's ability to assimilate or naturalize its way of being, framing real world problems as professional ones. Pierre Bourdieu expresses the task as it relates to the legal profession, as one in which one must tacitly accept the fundamental rules and conventions of the field,[51] renounce other conventions, and retranslate events as juridical problems and only juridical problems.[52] Medicine, by comparison, could only be played as a game once one had medicalized a problem, retranslating it by including only that which could be included as a medical restatement, from a medical perspective, and within a medical frame.

In a nonlegal order, such knowledge would have been transmitted largely by apprenticeship training and without an organization of knowledge consensually agreed upon within a professional community capable of creating and preserving an official text. Since a shared frame of reference would not be possible, conflicts would prevail and change would make the field chaotic. Hierarchy and natural order would be disturbed, and anxiety would prevail. This was the condition out of which professions would emerge. Authority would need to be re-created—largely by specialized knowledge that was culturally salient—and autonomy would have to be established—largely by ownership of that knowledge and translation of real world events into the terms of the professional field.

The professional order once established becomes what Bourdieu refers to as "a kind of common familial experience"[53] characterized not only by universality but by predictability, consistency, and knowability. A vaguely perceived dispute thereby becomes explicit and convertible into that which can be expressed in a clear form with its own language, made manifest, negotiated, and attached to a solution that matches the problem that has been produced. The result is a decision granted status by the profession. It conforms to a precedent that connects the present to a past that justifies it. Selecting certain interests in or out and choosing the terms in which they will be clothed, the professional order constructs its own fiction. The construction will have transformed the prelegal or premedical interest into a professionalized case that becomes social capital in terms of the field's own logic.[54] A norm is no longer merely immanent or given; it now expresses a rationality that custom or agreement alone cannot guarantee. It is superseded by formalizing and systematizing to establish exemplary judgments that can stand as models for later decisions.[55]

Socioeconomic Frames

Taking a rational economics approach to social interactions, English and American theorists embraced a view of the rule of law as a social practice that overlaps at some points with French game theory's formulation.[56] Law, by Paul Kahn's analysis, naturalizes a set of beliefs[57] so that they can more easily be understood as part of a continuum along which we also find customs, values, and social norms related to the individual, the community, and authority.[58] Nevertheless, law is an alternative form that often suppresses custom, and it clearly organizes and resolves conflicts according to its own pathologies. In terms of its relationship to the law, nonlegal group norms can be distinguished from the legal order by the social closeness of members, the limited stakes involved, and the fact that the burden of costs is borne by the group.[59] As conditions change, relationships will no longer counterbalance within the group and begin to break down, in which case information will then become unreliable. Once outside interests are more noticeably affected by outcomes, members will gravitate to the law to resolve disputes.[60]

In a socioeconomic frame, the norms of reputation and honor emerge to guarantee group survival and its legacy, acting as a glue that holds order together.[61] In this sense, norms have utility value and must prove themselves functional. If the welfare of the group is their source, the process by means of which norms fulfill themselves is one of reducing decision costs, trading off at the same time the ability to adapt quickly to change.[62] Addressing a nonlegal order of the type we shall encounter, Robert Ellickson, with a nod to Hobbes, describes a system that expresses minimal order even under anarchic conditions, mimicking the role of law without assuming knowledge or acceptance of legal rules on the part of group members. Here, honor is highly valued and reputational capital is an essential medium of exchange in a system in which tests of reputation and information together with sanctions and punishments deter violations of honorable behavior that interfere with social order. Still, win-lose scenarios emerge out of private provocations[63] and selfish individual manipulations of the group norm[64] to disturb consensus and order. These scenarios allow for trial and error behaviors and the kind of competition that would greatly benefit some individuals with considerable costs to other individuals and to the group. Clearly they better serve an individual who is ambitious within the group or who is an outlier on its margins.

Where fixed resources are not a critical part of the equation (so that a win by one party does not necessarily entail a loss to another) low cost cooperation will, however, be supported in the group. Following tradition and sticking to the welfare of the group, group losses will be minimized,[65] including costs to detect violations of norms, to enact sanctions, and to circulate information about norms, violations, and sanctions. Costs to the individual are protected as well, for the group assumes the responsibility to protect basic rights of its members and to distribute both power and risks among them. The group's ability to control costs and deliver benefits nevertheless depends upon whether member reputation has high salience and members are convinced of the omniscience of enforcers, as well as whether the potential exists for sharing information about members' reputations.[66] Should it fail at this level of social organization, the group will lose coherence and cooperation will be impaired.

The type of norms that emerge and their forms of organization have other impacts on costs. Here, costs arise from the nature of the conduct that should be punished, the nature of punishments, the use of information, the structure of control, and the distribution of control.[67] Norms, as a result, operate most effectively when predictable sanctions are delivered to address violations of norms. Whereas systems have the choice to reward the many who conform to the norm, the lower cost of punishing the fewer number who are deviants suggests that economical systems will prefer a punishment rather than a reward regime. In a mature system, a few payoffs will nevertheless be given, including rewards for exceptional actions, bribes to discourage bad actors, and even compensation by shirkers who do not contribute work but who pay those who can perform at a cheaper cost.[68]

The overall effort is largely described as providing deterrents to penalize defectors, using sanctions that run from ostracizing, shunning, negative gossip, retaliation, and destruction or seizure of property to gift-giving, payoffs, damages, and in-kind transfers. Payment of damages is itself not always an effective deterrent, since, on the one hand, a deviant might lack sufficient assets to make payment and, on the other, someone willing to pay the price would have a free hand to commit an offense.[69] At the upper reaches of discipline, and to avoid the risk of feuds, duels, or resort to the law, such sanctions as physical punishment or incarceration are replaced by threats of violence, while destruction or seizure of property is more likely to be done under cover than publicly.

In this world of self-help enforcement, enforcers have to be wary of over-penalizing, often lacking information or a proper measure for appropriate punishment. They must, as well, appreciate that protocol requires a step-by-step, or progressive, sequence of discipline whereby lower cost sanctions have to be used before one can revert to more costly ones. Because information about reputation is a prized commodity and tests of reputation are the actual object of many disputes, negative gossip is one low-cost sanction that comes into wide use. Gossip has the advantage that it can be practiced surreptitiously and anonymously, but it is constrained by the expectation that it should be truthful. In this respect, gossip finds itself tied to ecclesiastical and natural law standards that one ought not to bear false witness, a remedial norm shared by both the legal and nonlegal orders. As a practical matter and as part of a fairness requirement, negative gossip is complemented by the obligation to circulate positive gossip once a debtor or offender has remediated his debt or offense, a widely used even-up strategy that finds its source in the natural and religious principles of reciprocity and, at the more literal biblical level, as the positive face of eye-for-an-eye retribution.[70]

As we consider how a social norms system functions in both game theory and socioeconomic terms, their relationship to nonlegal and legal orders is clarified. The nonlegal order can be seen as a background of unofficial enforcement upon which the law is imposed,[71] with legal intervention as a last resort when the inefficiencies or pathologies of the nonlegal leaves them vulnerable.[72] Given the nature of the differences between the legal and nonlegal orders, intervention may prove more or less likely under different conditions. Because norms are situation sensitive and not always clear,[73] for example, one might expect that in complex situations groups would privilege the use of the legal order. Such a situation could occur where the stakes are high, where precision is required, or where the issue overtakes the skills of the group, its members, or the norm process.[74]

This is not to say that the nonlegal order is easily or often trumped by the legal order when it does perform effectively. The nonlegal order is preferred so long as society remains relatively homogeneous and state action is not considered legitimate. Here, where the operable presumption is that outsiders control the law, insiders would then be less likely to access the law. Where the presumption is that the issue has more to do with members of the group than with strangers, it would be kept within the group.[75] For day-to-day problems under conditions where information is freely shared and peoples' reputations are known, the law is considered clumsy and costly.[76] Where simpler content and smaller stakes are involved, the relative speed, privacy, and trust expressed through the social norm process make it an attractive venue for dispute resolution. This is particularly the case when disputes related to questions of reputation and honor involve members of the group. It occurs as well when disputes arise from opportunistic behavior or involve such sanctions as stigmatizing or ostracizing the deviant. [77]

Where the nonlegal order fails to serve society's needs—that is, where the group fails to obtain surpluses for its members or squanders group resources—we find the norm process threatens to trigger feuds or harms outside groups. Here, the legal order stands poised to replace it because of its inefficiencies of scale and its inability to operate both in socially heterogeneous venues and in the midst of social imperfections. The legal order has greater certainty, predictability, anonymity, and neutrality. Society will need these qualities as it evolves toward the greater clarity and clearer rules that such an order can provide.[78]

In dealing with a world like that of the eighteenth century, the ability to conceptualize nonlegal order is critical to understanding how the professions of medicine and law functioned. Whereas the legal order, with its greater transparency, is more easily accessed, the nonlegal order depends to a greater extent upon understandings and signals that require membership in a group and intuitive responses. Informal relations respect the foundational value of customs and solidarity whereas formalized agreements are more likely to fail to address them.[79] Similarly, trust and honor codes as mechanisms for dispute resolution are highly valued in nonlegal systems. Just as public denunciations that ritualize insults and duels that act as trials of one's honor are common and effective,[80] so does the nonlegal world depend upon self-censorship as a sign of loyalty to the group. Thus we find conformity, payoffs, threats, resistance, and desertion all act as means of playing the game, incentivizing players, and enforcing rules.[81] We find gift giving and sanctioning being used to build and seal relationships or provide deterrence. Signals are thereby sent to prevent defections or to set boundaries to establish insider identity and prevent outsider invasions.

Signals prove central to communication in nonlegal systems as well as problematic as part of a larger information system. They often take on ritual or ceremonial qualities—which sometimes become empty or meaningless—and because they can be misunderstood they can lead to violence. The signals of good actors can be mimicked by bad actors, just as signals that violate norms can be purposely sent as initiation into a deviant subgroup. Like other aspects of the nonlegal order, signaling requires a certain amount of entrepreneurship as those in whose interest they are sent tailor them to particular individuals or invent them for special purposes. Indeed, norm entrepreneurship can create competition that can potentially increase one's payoffs, either through responsiveness to the signal or through compensation to stop sending it.[82]

The eighteenth century, in conclusion, is characterized by repeated dealings in a close-knit society where information is shared, past behavior known, and reputational capital valued, variables that inform the reputational games that are played and the signals that get sent. The frequency of signals sent and their reliability, as well as the fact that an authoritative sender shrinks the pool of signals, may or may not endow reputation with utility value[83] but they do build reputation as a desirable commodity or, at the very least, as an attractive feature in a cooperating partner. Since the cost of reputation is a function of the internalization of honor as a value, its stability as capital would seem to be warranted. Put together with the prospect that "successful strategies drive out less successful strategies"[84] when they are known and that herd behavior occurs in the absence of information related to reputation, it becomes clear that the purchase and advertisement of reputation is crucial to deterring attacks on it or to depleting it. When you add that the cost of not joining the herd leads to rational interest choices that themselves lead to cascading mob action, reputational capital becomes even more impressive as a form of economic exchange.[85]

It goes without saying that in such a world the need to share information and advertise reputation has its downside. Going public ups the ante when reputation has been attacked, so that merely to stay in the game one is put in the position of publicizing the attack on oneself to ostracize the offender.[86] The cost then becomes one of spreading damaging information against one's own reputation and, so far as the offender is concerned, of injunctions against future bad behaviors rather than payments for past crimes that would rehabilitate one's reputation. The community has a stake in such public humiliation and certain opportunity costs as well, for it stands to gain order within the group by shaming, scolding, harassing, shunning, or otherwise ostracizing those who deviate from its norms. But the community's efforts against the deviant can lead to minor violence against him and his family,[87] and when affairs get out of control the potential for serious feuding becomes almost unavoidable. Nevertheless, informal sanctioning was a popularly embraced mechanism for conflict resolution, since it did not rely upon a costly system of investments in courts or prisons. Already mutually engaged in business and social interactions, members can capitalize on people using their existing networks to communicate and monitor their own and others' behavior.[88]

In sum, as this study demonstrates punishment, enforcement, and deterrence unattached to legitimacy appear to be sufficient to enable the social norms model of the nonlegal order to work. To enforce sanctions and deter future deviancy, the nonlegal order need only produce dramatic, visible, and memorable punishments in some way associated with the badness of those punished. Since people will assume one is bad because one has been punished, the stigma of having been punished by itself will act as a deterrent. But some deviants might go unpunished because the costs of deviation are less than those of lost reputation. In such a case, if the times are troubled extracting high payments for relatively trivial offenses will not deter bad behaviors and innocents will suffer. When deterrence fails, groups will become more insular and self-protective and the nonlegal order's inconsistency and unpredictability will yield pathologies beyond its control. The transition to legal order at this point is imminent.[89]

2

Medical History

MADE UP OF SEVERAL ALTERNATIVE WAYS OF KNOWING—AS A SCIENCE, AS a business, and as a spiritual endeavor—medicine generated several fictions that profiled an identity and constructed an order within which it could thrive. An emerging story of science asserted itself in tension with the dominant fiction of medicine as a profession and the residual fiction of medicine as religion. These fictions constituted ways of knowing that shaped the nature of medical work and the relationship between the provider and the user of medical services. They represented constructions that sustained medicine, even as they exposed cracks that undermined their apparent seamlessness. Together, they made up an explanatory framework for life, death, and disease that was knowable as a platform for medicine, its present-day face, and its future direction. When the old story became dysfunctional, the emerging alternative story of science asserted itself with its own order and healing fiction.

The eighteenth-century medical context was one in which we find a developing confidence in medicine[1] and a separation from an ancient medical tradition that went back to the ninth century BCE. It saw the beginning of the end of fifth-century BCE Hippocratic humors theory that had divided the body into four fluids (blood, bile, black bile, and phlegm) linked to earth's elements (fire, air, water, and earth) and to the seasons, and it began to retire Galen's second century ACE notion that the good doctor was a logician and a philosopher who applied his thought to his practice.[2]

The advent of a sense of medical "profession" was to move medicine toward a more structured and constrained form of specialized knowledge that devalued traditional understandings. It formalized relations and imposed external rules replacing self-organizing modes of ordering interactions. A developing sense of profession transitioned medicine from a more highly individualized notion of work that was characterized by feuds to a more amenable construction whereby resolutions could be achieved by means of third-party authorities. As a professional fiction, it complemented the healing fiction that medicine had already exploited over time and it replaced natural and supernatural thinking and abstract theories that had conditioned earlier ways of thinking about disease.

With the Enlightenment and its interest in science and technology, medical progress took its place as part of a great vision. Science and statistics, reason and philosophical empiricism, the growth of anatomy, mechanical physics, and physiology[3] all augured well for the prospects of a new medical mission. Equally important was a developed interest in public health, sanitation, and "police."[4] The involvement of government and the passage of laws that protected the environment addressed pollution of the water supplies, the air, cities, marshes, crowded living quarters, and the healthfulness of such institutions as factories, jails, and hospitals, as well as army camps.[5] Changes would extend to reinforcing emphasis on diet and exercise and studying the conditions of life and the environment as a way to health, including reforming the health of large groups while paying specific attention to individual patients.[6]

THE RELIGIOUS STORY

No longer dominant, superstition and religion provided residual cultural explanations for disease. Before medicine became professionalized and science medicalized society, religion informed medicine both as a foundational value and in terms of the role it was to play in defining healing and forming professional identity. Patricia Watson regards the performance of physician-divines, in the words of the Puritan divine Cotton Mather, as an "angelical conjunction."[7] The premise on which they operated was the biblical one of Christ the healer and Luke the physician who served the poor by administering to their bodies as a way of administering to their souls.[8] God's testing of man through illness provided a second leg to biblical support for physician clerics. In a society in which the sick often had not the money to consult a regular physician and where there were not, in any case, many physicians, the more accessible and stable profession of pastoring served a dual role. As Watson suggests, the medical role of the divine was supported by "the widespread conviction that health and sickness were inextricably tied to sin and to the will of God."[9] If healing was a function of God's mercy, then the cleric was a natural instrument through which God might work.[10]

The fact that ministers performed as physicians early in the history of the nation reflects the lack of boundaries between the physical and the spiritual as medicine established itself. Religion was tied to disease in several ways: that God was testing man's faith in Him; that sinful man had angered God; that epidemics were God's vengeance for the sins of society; that an illness was caused by Satan; that astrological causes were the cause of an illness; or that God created an illness through nature as a second cause.[11] What was clear was that divines framed disease and narrated it to lead congregants to an understanding of their own sins as the cause of their illnesses. Performing in both roles, that of a healer of the body and that of a healer of the soul, divines covered the full range of possible interpretations so that they could shape a meaning of disease that kept the churches full and congregants dependant upon their religious leaders.[12] Visits to the sick under such conditions became an opportunity to recruit for the church and to convert to the faith.[13]

Where there was little difference between those who lived and those who died in the face of fever epidemics, having a divine at the bedside could prove to be more valuable to save one's soul than a physician might be to save one's body. Ministers called to the bedside sometimes performed bleedings and recommended other treatments as part of their ministry, whereas physicians were only called if one could afford their fee. Such conflation of the medical and religious roles in the person of the divine was based on the clergy's familiarity with home medicine, folk, and Indian remedies.[14] Similarly, a physician was likely to regard his practice of medicine as a Christian duty and to consider himself a moral agent, performing as a "missionary to the bedside."[15]

Separating themselves from the variety of people who offered care (from barber-surgeons and bone-setters to midwives and white Indians, home and faith healers), regular physicians sometimes warred with clergy at the bedside, particularly when it came to end-of-life treatment. Clergy were likely to impose their own remedies, represent the interests of a third party against the wishes of the physician, or simply undermine confidence in regular medical care. As conflicts were inevitable, one source recommended that "the conscientious physician must either yield to the importunities of a ranting priest or incur the displeasure of the pulpit & run the risque of having his skirts eternally sprinkled with blood of a lost spirit."[16] A second source of conflict was the Puritan notion that illness was a sign of sin and that it was God's will that one had been stricken. The man of faith put his confidence in nature's healing powers as revealing the hand of God in a challenge that made the physician superfluous[17] and that encouraged the development of therapeutic nihilism, whereby nature's cures were preferred to interventions of medicine.[18]

It was clear medicine and theology were not divided in the minds of most practitioners of either profession. The yellow fever epidemic was neither a strictly medical nor a strictly religious issue. Physical ills were rarely left to be solved exclusively by religious means, even if large numbers of people were convinced that the epidemic had a divine origin, nor did patients fail to seek spiritual help that would contribute to their surviving the plague. Benjamin Rush himself contributed to the debate in a letter to William Marshall in 1798, offering that "I agree with you in deriving our physical calamities from moral causes. . . . God would cease to be what He is, if he did not visit us for these things."[19]

The physician's experience of religious knowledge and construction of it for medical use is best accessed from the perspective of a practitioner at the center of events that informed medical practice and which, in turn, he informed. Here the autobiography, "commonplace" book or diary, and medical lectures of the most formidable physician of his time, Benjamin Rush, prove particularly useful. Rush might have been narcissistic, he might have been arrogant and run roughshod over his colleagues, but no one was prepared to say that he did not struggle, heroically at times, to understand and practice medicine in a way that pushed the profession in new directions. He might have set new standards in some areas (mental health in particular, as the first American physician to take an active formative role in the field as a shaper and proponent of humanized care) and taken risks in others that pushed medicine to the brink of disaster (his extreme cure for yellow fever led to medical warfare among members of the profession and undermined public confidence in its cultural authority), but before all else, Rush pictured himself as bound to serve God in his practice of the healing arts and in his shepherding of his patients.

The physician's faith was not only rooted in his belief in his religious duty as a physician but in a faith in action that resisted skepticism. The movement toward therapeutic nihilism—both in the waning influence of heroic treatments and in the growth in the number of such medical sectarians as botanics and natural healers who preached a return to nature—was met in disbelief by regulars as heretical. Nature, Rush was to advise his students, was an arbitrary and unreliable enemy: "In all violent diseases nature is like a drunken man reeling to & fro & occasionally stumbl[ing] against a door with so much violence as to break it through. . . . Always treat nature in a sick room as you would a noisy dog or cat[;] drive her out at the door & lock it upon her."[20] Nature may have been treated in sermons as a second cause—created by God who left it to act in his stead—but Rush had an almost religious distaste for trusting it with those in his care. To be a physician was to have faith in therapeutic intervention, the more aggressive the more faithful to one's charge. To subscribe to nature's cures would have been to deny his very profession as a physician and required a skepticism about drug therapy that would have amounted to apostasy.[21] Renouncing orthodox treatment betrayed a loss of faith that Rush was unable to accept on either religious or medical grounds.

Rush's rejection of God's hand through second order effects did not extend to Rush's view of divinity itself in the sick room. Dealing with the vices and virtues of physicians, he was quick to make his students understand, albeit humorously, that their role should be subordinate to that of God's: "An undue confidence in medicine, to the exclusion of a Divine and Superintending Power over the health and lives of men, is [a] vice among physicians. A Dr.——, in New York prescribed on an evening, for a sick man. The next day he called and asked him how he was: 'Much better (said he), thank God.' 'Thank God! (said the doctor) thank me, it was I who cured you.'"[22]

Rush and his medical colleagues genuinely saw their work as directly connected to their Christian principles and responsibilities, that is, medicine as a form of "natural theology."[23] Rush himself announced he would write a work that would explain "sundry passages in the old and New Testament by the principles of medicine and the laws of the animal economy."[24] Addressing the complaint that science had made physicians idolaters, Rush intended that his writing would "contain many new arguments in favor of Christianity, and will I hope render infidelity, at lest among physicians, as much a mark of ignorance as it is of impiety and immorality." Indeed, the practice of medicine appeared to Rush coterminous with the performance of one's religious duties and was infused with religious value. As a complement to obedience to the golden rule, medicine as Christian ethics represented a righteous Republican virtue. In his lectures to his students, Rush made it clear that no secular profession was afforded more assistance by Christianity than was medicine when it took the opportunity to exert moral influence at the sick bed.

> Our business leads us daily into the abodes of pain and misery. It obliges us likewise, frequently to witness the fears with which our friends leave the world, and the anguish which follows in their surviving relatives. Here the common resources of our art fail us, but the comfortable views of the divine government, and of a future state, which are laid open by Christianity, more than supply their place. A pious word, dropped from the lips of a physician in such circumstances of his patients, often does more good than a long, and perhaps an ingenious discourse from another person, inasmuch as it falls upon the heart, in the moment of its deepest depression from grief. There is no substitute for this cordial in the materia medica.[25]

Beyond the opportunity offered to perform a religious duty as part of one's daily rounds, Benjamin Rush saw the analogy between disease and the concepts of sin and evil and between the unity of creation and the unified theory of disease as foundational to his understanding of medicine. The notion of disease as a single unit rather than as many uniquely different entities was clearly linked in Rush's mind to "Unity in the works of God—as one Sin introduced all the vanity and complications of Sins, so one disease, viz. debility, produced all the vanity and complication of diseases. One negative cause in both cases produces all the positive effects that are ascribed to them. . . . Disease an unit. Many diseases, like polytheism in religion, or many evil spirits instead of one devil."[26]

Rush's personal medical theology told him that "we see parts suffer for each other separately and together in diseases, which parts did not contract these diseases. Thus the feet suffer in the gout for the intemperance of the tongue, and the whole body for the sin of one part of it in contracting the venereal disease. The whole body suffers, too, for the sin of the hands, which steal, when it is punished by whipping or hanging. To the Deity the whole human race probably appears as much a unit as a single human body appears to be a unit to the eye of man."[27]

Considering the origin of evil, Rush was clear that an analogy existed between sin and disease. Seen in the light of Rush's embrace of stimulation as the source of all disease, evil was the absence of moral good in the same way that sickness arose from the absence of certain stimuli. It therefore followed that "Sin, like disease, is weakness. It is destroyed by power, or strength, as disease is by stimuli. Nothing is annihilated therefore in the destruction of sin. Good, in the form of power and love, fills its Spirit. This Spirit expels nothing. It only restores strength to weakness and order to disorder, as stimuli cure weakness and convulsions in the human body."[28]

Evil was thus an absence of good, so that weakness must be replaced by strength. Not doing so would lead to derangement, an excess that could be described as the absence of "what is called fitness of things."[29] If Rush's beloved poor were those most afflicted by fever epidemics, he concluded, the lesson was that treating such diseases must therefore be ready at hand and inexpensive: "From the affinity established by the Creator between evil and its antidotes . . . I am disposed to believe no remedy will ever be effectual in any general disease, that is not cheap, and that cannot easily be made universal."[30] Medicine, in Rush's view, was meant to fulfill God's plan,[31] the divine promise of which was that all diseases would be conquered and "that there does not exist a disease for which the goodness of Providence has not provided a remedy."[32] Rush's work was nothing less than God's work, an apocalyptic battle, Manichean in nature, that replicated the great struggle between good and evil.[33]

If we reflect from Rush's experience of religious healing to that of eighteenth-century medicine in general, we find the physician looking to the operation of divine law made manifest in nature which, if man followed reason, would work out that law through the natural marketplace.[34] Religion in this sense was friendly to science and allowed free thought, a notion that, while it was shared by Jefferson's circle, was not adopted by those clergy who felt that man was in harmony with divine law. Medicine, like the other sciences, was caught in a battle between those who privileged reason over the church, those who felt immortality trumped mortality, and those who saw religion and science allied.[35] The prospect of theological quackery was as likely to some medical men as medical quackery was to many divines, so that the influence of both religion and medicine was bound to be in question wherever medical skill found itself at loggerheads with divine revelation.[36] Whereas doctors did not feel they were bound to preach the gospel when they practiced medicine, they were still likely to run up against one religious precept or another in their efforts to heal the sick, ensuring that the residual story of religious healing would continue to inform the practice of medicine even as it became a profession and then established itself as a science.

THE PROFESSIONAL STORY

If medicine had been read as an arm of religious duty, it was to write itself as a business and a profession before it could move on to story itself as a science. The term "profession" originally referred to a declaration of faith upon joining a religious order[37] and indicated "to profess," that is, to speak for or be called to one's vocation.[38] In the eighteenth century, the term was synonymous with "vocation" or "calling." A narrower use of the term referred to any of the three "traditionally learned professions" to which Johnson's *Dictionary* (1772) refers—religion, law, and medicine.[39] It is not clear that professions were distinguished by a status higher than other occupations at the time, certainly not until a university degree was required to practice one of the professions as a regulated field and the field was granted certain monopolistic privileges.[40]

In eighteenth-century America, European universities were preferred by those from the elite class, Edinburgh and Leyden being the most popular choices. The non-elite, by contrast, were bereft of formal training, leading John Morgan in 1765 to propose the first American medical school to attract those who could not afford to educate themselves abroad:

> Many who are not in a condition to support the expence of being educated abroad, by being instructed here in the first elements of their profession . . . have it in their power to finish their studies abroad afterwards to great advantage. This class perhaps includes the greatest part of medical students. . . . Some there are indeed, and not a few, who cannot by any means afford the crossing of the Atlantic to prosecute their studies abroad. The proposed institution will therefore prove highly beneficial to every class of students in Medicine.[41]

Medical school education in American schools in Philadelphia (founded in 1765) and in Boston (founded in 1781) thereafter accommodated many from the middling classes. Apprenticeship was, nevertheless, much more common and allowed students to link with established physicians who could mentor students and get them started in business. Apprenticing was also an economical means of managing the work force. Candidates from rural areas had to be encouraged to stay on the land or be accounted for if they were to move into other fields of employ.[42] Apprenticeship, as Rosemary O'Day describes it, was thus "a gate which could be opened, closed or left ajar to regulate recruitment."[43] Apprenticeship was useful as well in ensuring access to treatment and guaranteeing quality care. It had the additional benefit of discouraging outsiders and creating a monopoly of sorts to control competition, at least in cities where regular networks operated more effectively to establish standards of care, fee schedules, and a distribution of labor among physicians, surgeons, and apothecaries, with many practitioners mixing all three functions in their practice.

In 1602, the English cleric John Manningham noted in his diary that "The Divine, the lawyer, the physician must all have these three things: reason, experience and authority, but eache in a severall degree; the Divine must begin with the autoritie of Scripture, the lawyer must rely upon reason, and the physicion trust to experience."[44] When the three traditional professions became distinct and unique entities, distinctions began to be made among them based upon their being organized differently. Each profession could be said to exist in a social context and in relation to a certain institutional structure: the clergy in the church, the lawyer in the bar, and the physician in the hospital. Clerics were the most tightly organized as servants of the church and obedient to God. The law had to follow the prescriptions of the bar so that in response to the control exercised by the courts, the law was more carefully monitored in "recruitment, practice and membership" than medicine.[45] Medicine was the least organized, operating like the law equally in the service of man and God, although privileging man in the most practical sense. Given the lack of hospitals for training medical students and for clinical practice, the kind of prevalent institutional support that structured the law was not available to medicine until the nineteenth century.[46] The larger issues for medicine were whether it could demonstrate its legitimacy and its efficacy as a unique entity and whether medical inventions were not deceptive. The profession had to prove it had an importance that went beyond serving in times of war and epidemics and that was more extensive than dealing with amputations, broken bones, purging and bleeding, inoculations, and problem births.[47]

Because they were organized differently and had different relations with the state, differences and even feuds emerged among the professions. Indeed, clergy resented lawyers and doctors whom they considered irreligious, while the latter resented clerical poaching on their preserves and the superstitious and antiscientific bias of much religious teaching. Even so, all three professions were part of the same cloth in the eighteenth century. Their members were brought up as gentry and essentially educated in the same kind of schooling, even if their interests and roles did not always overlap. Whereas many in the professions were not university educated, educated members of the professions shared a common university culture based in the arts.[48]

The legal question for the medical profession was as much one of how the law limited the way medicine could structure itself and function as of how it could be constrained by licensing requirements sanctioned by malpractice law, or proscribed from collusion in fee setting. The only group that had been granted monopolistic privileges was the church, although the legal profession had been successful in a limited way.[49] The decline of such privileges in the church accompanied the rise of privilege in the secular professions of law and medicine.[50] Along the same lines, the medical profession could not flourish unless it had support in the law for the training of its members and competition among them: "Naturally, a profession which cannot collect fees, set its own standards, or escape standards of strict liability for its conduct is not going to flourish. Most professions require the positive support of the government and legal system in terms of approval, exemptions from external regulation, limitations of liability, and implied or express subsidies supporting the operation of the profession."[51]

As Wilfrid Prest puts it, "the social identity and the nature of the work carried out by members of the occupation or occupations in question need to be . . . related to each other."[52] Indeed, a period view of the three suggests that the cleric, the physician, and the lawyer worked together to care for the soul, the body, and property respectively.[53] Moral training, medical care-taking, and legal administration of households, estates, and businesses were not the exclusive concern of members of distinct professions. Rather, a disparate array of people performed these tasks, ranging from family members and communities, private charities and commercial specialists, to members of professional associations. This mixed picture in the fluid state of eighteenth-century law and medicine suggests that the study, interpretation, and understanding of medicine and law requires toggling among the three professions and their ways of being and meaning. People learned about the law in the process of ensuring ownership and inheritance of their properties and protecting them from claim-jumping and seizure. They discovered efficacious treatments for what ailed them in an equally hit-and-miss way, from a large number of possible sources of information and a disparate array of providers. Narrowing to a fine point of medicine was going to require trust in shared values and norms along a continuum of shifting options and changing circumstances as well as consensus on agreed-upon penalties and rewards, none of which was necessarily available without considerable invention and persuasion, often without even a small degree of confidence in its probable efficacy.

Medicine as a Business

If medicine was to put flesh on its bones as a professional story, it would have to "rise to the concrete," as Marx held in another context.[54] In this regard, Rush's lectures to his medical students made clear he was not a man who saw medicine simply as an abstract process detached from the embodied experience of actually being a physician. Rather, he appreciated fully the compromises and constraints made necessary by operating medicine as a business, which he took up in at least four lectures.[55] Business for Rush depended at least as much on the nature and character of the practitioner as it did on business acumen or professional qualifications. Manners and proper protocol counted for Rush, even if his own practice covered large numbers of the poor, who were unlikely to appreciate such niceties. On the other hand, they were certain to benefit from his charitable convictions and his impeccable devotion to their welfare.

In lecture ten on acquiring a business, for example, Rush maintained that character strongly informed one's success, to which he attributed three possible causes: the honorable, the "artificial and accidental," and the dishonorable.[56] Honorable attributes included study, punctuality and faithfulness to one's patients and engagements, acceptable manners, sympathy with the sick, attending the poor, decent dress, respect for religion, curing difficult diseases, and practicing surgery.[57] Writing and publishing were important (except for poetry or other nonmedical subjects, for a doctor was not supposed, as a tradesman, to know of such things),[58] and "A Diploma honourably acquired by previous study and an examination in all the branches of medicine"[59] were critical. By contrast, dishonorable ways of acquiring success were related to actions that suggested a lack of virtue, poor manners, and values that failed in their respect for hard work and religion. A man of rough, if honest tendencies, Rush had no time for "Splendid, or popular acts of friendship or humanity"[60] and was largely unimpressed by those who spoke many languages (including Latin and Greek), affected a singular manner of dress, conversation, or behavior, or expressed eccentricities of manner and conduct. He warned his students away from physicians whose bold vices, like cursing and drunkenness, introduced them to business and from those ignorant of principles of reason who thereby deceived their patients and other physicians.[61]

Rush paid special attention to practical aspects of the therapeutic manner of the physician. Thus he advised that riding about without object in bad weather was hardly appropriate for a physician and advised against "Speaking in all companies of the number or rank of patients, or ordering a servant to remain with a carriage before the doors of persons of distinction who are not sick."[62] Rush presented the practice of the disreputable physician as the antithesis of his own practice: "Great minuteness in inquiring into the symptoms of diseases. The inspection of the lips and teeth by a magnifying glass, the tasting of the urine and sweats, the smelling of the feces, and even getting into bed with sick people in order to discover the quality of their perspiration, have all been practiced with success as the means of acquiring reputation and business in medicine."[63]

The pseudo-refinement practiced by some physicians, including "Trifling and absurd refinements in the prescriptions of medicine as to dose, manner of preparation, and exhibition, and attaching important consequences to the neglect of them,"[64] was associated with affectation, reliance on intuition, and a neglect of reading. Among such practices, Rush included barely inspecting one's patient, which had become a fashion of sorts for some physicians.

> There was many years ago a physician in this city . . . [who] hated the sight of a sick room; and as he seldom went into one without being under a previous convivial engagement he hastened out of it as speedily as possible. . . . The supposed quickness of his intellectual operations justified his careless manner, and converted his weaknesses into fame. A lady, whom this physician frequently attended, was once heard to say, she would rather receive a visit from him, if he only opened the curtain of her bed and looked at her, than be attended by all the physicians in Philadelphia.[65]

At the same time, Rush himself was an experienced physician who had lost income and patients because of his politics and medical theories. A man who welcomed new ideas, he recognized that early endorsement of such ideas could spell trouble for the physician. New principles led to justifiable fears of malpractice, either because one applied them and the patient failed or because one did not apply them and the patient failed. Being the author of new ideas had its own special problems.

> where discoveries disorganize old habits of thinking and practice, they excite envy and opposition against the authors of them by contemporary physicians. To prove this remark, I need only mention that Dr. Harvey lost all his business after he published his account of the circulation of the blood; and that Dr. Sydenham was thrown into the back ground of his profession, after he introduced depleting medicine and cool air in the cure of inflammatory fevers. The former revolutionized anatomy and physiology; and the discoveries of the latter tended to rob the physicians of London of half their opinions, and perhaps of a great proportion of the emoluments of their practice.[66]

Without attribution, Rush noted his own "discovery"—"The early declaration of the existence of pestilential diseases in a city or country, and of their originating in domestic causes"[67]—as another idea for which a physician would pay dearly. Expressing his own experience with a heroic cure for yellow fever, Rush found that patients were reluctant to give credit for dramatic therapies.[68]

> There is a cause of the loss of the business of families and individuals . . . which it is difficult to account for; and that is unexpected cures of desperate diseases, performed by uncommon exertions of skill and humanity, and sometimes by the temporary loss of reputation, from the novelty or boldness or the remedies employed for that purpose. Is it because the persons, who are the subjects of these cures, feel gratitude for their deliverance from a premature grave, to be a debt too great to be paid, and wholly incompatible with their independence? . . . many people forgive an injury much sooner than an obligation.[69]

From Rush's perspective, patients carried a lot of the responsibility for their cure,[70] especially when they neglected to follow the physician's treatment plan or improperly attributed failed treatments to physician error. Patients often attributed cures to their own constitution or objected to being presented with a bill. At a time when professional services were rewarded by gratuities and only the mercenary sued for fees, physicians risked offending patients and making it easier for other doctors to raid their practices when they tried to bill their patients. Of equal concern were instances where a patient's newly elevated financial status and consequent change of social connections led to a change in one's physician.

As a matter of course, Rush advised his students that doctors must expect to be called from their bed and to hear complaints about the operation of medicines and tiresome recitations of patients' histories. They could expect to be applied to for advice at all times, without thanks or compensation, and be subjected to rude conduct from visitors to the sick room. Equally, they could anticipate hurtful consultations with other physicians, and "the ingratitude, the duplicity, the treachery, and the rancor of their brethren."[71] With all that physicians must endure from each other, they should not expect gratitude from the public,[72] advice that Rush was quick to share with his students as it related to the yellow fever epidemics in Philadelphia.

> In the month of December, 1793, the citizens of Philadelphia assembled at the statehouse, and voted their thanks to the committee who had superintended the city, during the prevalence of the fever of that year. A motion was afterwards made to thank the physicians of the city for their services. This motion was not seconded. The services and sacrifices of those physicians may easily be estimated, when I add, that their patients were chiefly poor people; and that out of thirty five physicians who remained in the city, eight died; and of the survivors, but three escaped an attack of the fever.[73]

The Patient's Perspective

The physician's perspective that Rush provides was not the only way of understanding the medical relationship. Patients made choices for treatments and providers (including self-medicating) and storied their illnesses to give them meaning (the narrative or "spiritual autobiography" they assigned themselves to interpret God's plan for them). Such choices occurred with both vernacular and regular medicine, which in many cases were not that far apart in terms of both practice and beliefs.[74] Rural and urban, commercial and home remedies, popular and professional medicine, and the wide variety of types of providers shared many common assumptions and practices and were often mixed and matched by patients.[75]

If we consider eighteenth-century medicine from the perspective of the poor as patients, as Mary Fissell does, their utilization and interpretation of the medical system can be seen as a question of religion and politics.[76] Eighteenth-century vernacular medicine has, in fact, been linked to religious dissent.[77] From the Anglican perspective, dissent presented the potential for civil unrest and was linked to Catholicism, which also relied upon "superstitious divinations and prophesies."[78] Read in this way by establishment religion, the body lent itself to sedition, which was itself manifested in popular riots and social instability, so that "popular theodicy" provided underlying popular and religious interpretive practices that were destabilizing.[79] The notion that signs on the outside of the body reflected the condition of one's interior (the soul) was very much a part of enthusiastic (read here dissenting or evangelical) religion, which included Methodists, Baptists, and the Quakers and was reflected in lay healing. The sacred relied upon signs, and possession was part of the expression of inner light. Bodily manifestations interpreted that inner light, which was a sign of divine portents,[80] as popular religion connected signs of sin with visible signs on the body. The natural philosophy of wonders, tied to direct religious experience, became, according to Fissell, uncontrolled and was ultimately to be constrained by rationality. Discrediting spectacle and appearance thus undermined the "hermeneutics of lay healing" in the pursuit of the new interpretative control offered by experimental science.[81] The poor might have remained associated with popular healing to retain their own medical voice, but illness-interpretation[82] was to take a new, professional turn by the end of the eighteenth century.

From the political point of view, the relationship of patient and provider when it had to do with the poor required dependency on their part and upon their accepting the elite's definition of their worthiness to receive care by being chosen as deserving poor. The poor were subsequently denied their ability to narrate their own illnesses, and truth was considered to reside within the body. The trained physician, the one privileged to see into the body, effectively expressed ownership over it. That ownership was experienced through the choice of poor bodies for autopsy and dissection and the use of the bodies of the poor in hospitals, dispensaries, and workhouses for experimentation.

Considering the widespread endorsement of the patient's narrative,[83] the science of physical signs under the authority of the physician found itself undermined. Regular physicians demonstrated that what they needed from their patients was their interpretive autonomy, which would come to represent the physician's own cultural authority. Medicalization of the body denied not only the patient's perspective but the connection to religious interpretations that gave meaning to the patient experience. Physical signs offered a presumed objectivity that the subjective narrative could not. They thus came to speak in the patient's place.[84] They did not do so, however, in readily accessible terms. Rather, signs were expressed in Latin to place them beyond the grasp of the patient and to demonstrate they were clearly owned by the trained physician. At the same time, labeled signs emphasizing symptoms were expressed in a nosological system that ordered particulars to create general rules without considering causation or underlying principles. The system held that each disease—made up of a set of symptoms—was a specific entity or species.[85] Gradually, nosology gave way to pathologies that arose from understandings generated through autopsies and dissections, which provided a "process-oriented disease description."[86] Patients became "teaching aids rather than consumers of medicine" as their bodies became commodified.[87]

THE STORY OF SCIENCE

Medical Knowledge

Ultimately, the discovery and application of knowledge would frame the way of being in medicine, its identity, and its emerging story of science. Rush himself readily admitted to an unevenness in his theory and practice of medicine, with little in the way of hypothesis testing or experimentation to clinch clinical observations. From the time he came back from Europe to practice medicine in 1769 to the time he took over for Dr. John Morgan as professor of theory and practice of physic at the Medical School of the College of Philadelphia in 1789,[88] he made clear just how he proceeded. To begin, he brought to private practice the knowledge he acquired in medical school at Edinburgh and then in military hospitals during the Revolutionary War. But it was a combination conflating politics and medicine that, admittedly, was to disorient his thinking: "in Edinburgh . . . the adoption of republican principles, had acted like a ferment in my mind, and had led me to try the foundations of my opinions upon many other subjects as well as that of government. To the activity induced in my faculties by the evolution of my republican principles by the part I took in the American Revolution, I ascribe in a great measure the disorganization of my old principles in medicine."[89]

In private practice, Rush gradually became disenchanted with the prevailing medical theory, that of Dr. Cullen (who proselytized a grand nosological system and placed balancing the excitement and relief of the nervous system at the center of medical treatment),[90] and determined to find his own way: "In some diseases my practice was regulated by theory, but in others it was altogether empirical. I read, I thought, and I observed upon the phenomena of diseases, but for a while without discovering any thing that satisfied me. . . . At length a few rays of light broke in upon my mind upon several diseases. These were communicated first to my pupils, in my lectures, and afterwards to the public, in a volume of observations and inquiries in the year 1786."[91]

Rush's happy ideas came upon him as if received from some innate understanding, deep thought, or some higher light, but certainly not as the result of any rigorous science on his part. Assuming the leadership role that had been vacated by Morgan at the medical school, he showed little change in his approach.

> It now became my duty to deliver a System of principles in medicine. After much study and inquietude both by day and night, I was gradually led to adopt those which I have since taught, from my professor's chair and the press. The leading principle of my System was obtruded upon me suddenly while I was walking the floor of my study. It was like a ferment introduced into my mind. It produced in it a constant endless succession of decompositions and new arrangements of facts and ideas upon medical subjects. I was much assisted in the application of the principles that had occurred to me, by conversing with my pupils. Their questions and objections suggested many hints to me which enabled me to fortify my principles where they were weak and to extend them to new diseases. Dr. Brown's System of medicine,[92] which was published about this time, assisted me likewise a good deal in my inquiries.[93]

Privileging new ideas above all else, novelty rather than truth, accuracy, or a tested idea, Rush jumped from idea to idea anxious to make his own discoveries and inventions and put his own stamp on medicine as an innovator:

> Many new ideas occurred to me when riding, walking, or between the times of my waking and leaving my bed in the morning. I made it a practice to commit them to paper with a pencil when absent from home. In

sickness, and in the convalescence from fever, many new ideas were likewise obtruded upon my mind. In writing it was likewise invigorated, so
much so that I have more than once relinquished an opinion I sat down
to defend, and embraced the one I was opposed to. Conversation often
suggested new views of subjects, even with persons who knew less of them
than myself. But teaching was the principal means of increasing new
combinations in my mind. They frequently occurred in my Chair, and
were delivered extempore to my pupils. The nature of my profession
prevented my trying the effects of Solitude upon my intellectual faculties, but the few fortuitous experiments that I made, gave me no reason
to expect any thing from it, for I do not recollect ever acquiring a single
new idea by sitting still and doing nothing in my study.[94]

He relied a great deal upon conversations with fabulous strangers
and anecdotes he heard from travelers. People in all capacities held
equal fascination as subjects for his copy books, including literary
men, a balloonist, politicians, quacks, and divines.[95] Rush regarded
properly conducted conversation as "intellectual commerce," an
exchange of ideas that would "multiply associations more rapidly
than solitary meditation."[96] Capable of rendering ideas "more dura-
ble in our own minds," conversation combined one's own reading
and observations with the reflections of others to create more knowledge and to provoke what Rush regarded as "spontaneous controversies." Reminiscent of the medical feuds and the doctors' wars in
which Rush was to find himself embroiled throughout his career,
even his way of knowing was characterized in its highest emanation
as a controversy, albeit one "to which both [parties] frequently lead,
and which in private circles have for their objects, truth, and not
victory."[97]

Given the opportunity through the Pennsylvania Hospital
(founded as the earliest hospital in America in 1751) for greater
contact with actual cases and having "neglected no part of my former studies so much as Physiology,"[98] Rush failed to see the merit
of sacrificing his time and reputation to gather such material for
clinical lectures. Upon this base rested his certainty in his own discoveries and his desire to share them with the public by publishing
them abroad. Discouraged by "marks of ignorance of the most common and obvious facts and principles in Epidemicks," Rush pushed
forward to oppose the "errors and prejudices" and "the most criminal ignorance" of his fellow physicians and the greed of apothecaries who would have "derived large sums of money from the sale" of
his remedies. Fully certain of the rightness of his cures, Rush "en-

deavoured to teach the people to cure themselves by my publications in the newspapers, after they were deserted by their family physicians."[99] Divinely appointed, Rush's revelations, as he told the story, were attended by success, proof of his claim that "it pleased God to make me the instrument of introducing into general practice" the treatment that was to conquer yellow fever. Once he was stigmatized for the same "discovery," Rush would regard himself as martyred at the hands of "all who had been either publickly or privately my enemies."[100]

Rush's medical lectures to his students expanded more fully on his approach to medical knowledge, beginning with the seven modes of acquiring knowledge which he outlined as observation, reading, thinking, experimenting, recording, conversing, and composing. Placing "observation" first, Rush meant to alert his students to be alive to all that surrounded them, "having all the senses of the body constantly excited to receive impressions from every quarter."[101] The value Rush placed on such knowledge was very high, for he considered it "more correct than that which is obtained from any other source; inasmuch as it is subjected to the examination of the senses, as well as to reason, before it is treasured up in the mind." Books, by contrast, were regarded as a means of expanding one's sensory observations beyond that which one could in a limited life independently observe. Books were still, however, essentially ways of multiplying oneself to have access to the "observations of thousands." Where Rush appreciated the progress of knowledge in the sciences, he nevertheless regarded more modern books as "formed chiefly from the decayed materials of old ones"[102] and thereby as different ways of combining old materials. Moreover, his preference was to read a few valuable books often rather than a great number on the same subject, largely to control an intemperance in reading that he considered a form of gluttony: "It bloats the mind, and renders it weak and sickly. It moreover tends to destroy its active powers."[103] Ever one to prize his own opinions over that of others, Rush reminds us here that reading, rather than opening him up to new ideas, was just as likely to get in the way of the power of his own inventions.

Rush's final comments on books opened on a somewhat different way of viewing them, for he was careful to remind his students that whereas reading was closer to observation, which exercised the mind, it should be restricted to history and travels; he regarded the study of books in the sciences as labor from which one subsequently must seek repose. A man of active habits, Rush preferred books by men engaged in active employment to those written by men closeted in a library. He spoke of the "spontaneous exercises of the faculties of the mind"[104] and the mind "invigorated by solitary walking and riding," for "It is by means of reflection and contemplation, that we combine facts and deduce principles from them."[105] Knowledge, in sum, was identified with active thought, so that Rush's most admired colleague, Dr. Sydenham, was cited as never without a "book," "but it was the book of nature, from which, by the aid of his thinking powers, he obtained so exact a copy that it has been esteemed . . . to be equal, in every respect, to the fair original."[106] Rush proved less enthused when he spoke of experimentation as a source of knowledge. Here, he referred to torturing "Earth, air, water, fire, animals, vegetables, and fossils" to reveal their secrets. Although experiments should be conducted, he lamented that "this source of knowledge is less productive than might have been expected, from experiments being often made to establish preconceived theories; and hence we so frequently hear of opposite results from the same experiments."[107]

Recording and composing knowledge, the last two of Rush's recommended ways of knowing, were intended to multiply, fix, and regulate such ideas as were accumulated in the minds of his students. Composing was the way to "learn to reason correctly. By placing facts upon paper, we take into our view a large number of them at a time; and the eye dwells longer upon each of them, by which means we are enabled more easily to examine their relations to each other, and to draw just inferences from them. But we not only add to our conviction of the truth of particular opinions by writing in defence of them; but we often, by the same means, convince ourselves of their error."[108]

For Rush this self-referential exercise represented the preferred way of engaging the mind to "acquire order, perspicuity, and correctness, in speaking."[109] Again he removed to the world of oral discourse, to the realm of walking and riding, of conversing and observing, of positing and contesting rather than of experimenting and testing. For Rush, composing was, moreover, conducted characteristically through a diary, a medium he held in the highest regard. He advised his students that it was "the means of strengthening the mind and acquiring knowledge."[110] Knowing oneself became the primary object, so that assiduous attention to the merits of diary-keeping would itself reveal the mind's true propensities. Treating diary entries like a psychological autopsy, Rush suggested reading what is recorded for what it professed about oneself, that is, that to which one was naturally devoted. The student who recorded eloquent speeches was meant for the pulpit or the bar; he who recorded facts connected with philosophy was meant for medicine.

To prevent his students from confusing his way of knowing with a proliferation of meaningless and contradictory bits and pieces, Rush advised them in his lectures that standards of truth and utility led to principles that could be deduced from the facts collected.[111] Knowledge collected must be culled and that which "is not in unison with truth and utility"[112] should be refused admission: "As a virtue out of its place is a vice, and as a talent out of its place is a weakness, so knowledge out of its proper place is ignorance."[113] For Rush, principles arose from reason, which preexisted facts bound by principles. If man's highest power was reason, then reason must direct above all else. It was reason that should dictate principle which should then guide one's use and understanding of facts: "The learned pigs which are exhibited as shows in our country, 'observe' and 'think'; but they cannot reason. This protracted operation of the mind can be performed only by man. Should we build facts upon facts, until our pile reached the heavens, they would soon tumble to pieces, unless they were cemented by principles."[114] For Rush, medicine was beholden to principles, for without them it was but "an humble art, and a degrading occupation. It reduces a physician to a level with the cook and the nurse, who administer to the appetites and weakness of sick people. But directed by principles, it imparts the highest elevation to the intellectual and moral character of man."[115]

As a man of his age, Rush could have been expected to fall into the cast of a rationalist. But Rush was uncomfortable with that label and was willing to consider empiricism and the related practice of quackery, practices that other physicians found less amenable as sources of knowledge. Indeed, in his very first lecture to his students—upon the occasion of the merger of the University of Pennsylvania with the Medical School of the College of Philadelphia—Rush warned his students of too quick a distinction between rationalists and empiricists. He reminded them that "exclusive reliance upon each of them" is prone to certain evils: "Physicians have been divided into empirics and dogmatists. The former pretend to be guided by experience, and the latter by reasoning alone in their prescriptions. I object to both when separately employed. They lead alike to error and danger in the practice of physic."[116] Rush held that human memory was incapable of retaining the diffuse knowledge empiricism required—"a correct and perfect knowledge of all the diseases of the human body, however varied they may be"[117]—so that it was a fruitless pursuit. Considering each physician's mind an individual memory bank, he denied that one physician's experience could be complemented by the experience of others, for few men experienced events in the same way, so that they recorded and interpreted them differently: "An hundred circumstances, from the difference of treatment, produce a difference in the symptoms and issue of similar diseases, and in the operation of the same medicines. The efforts of nature, are, moreover, often mistaken for the effects of a favourite prescription; and in some instances, the crisis of a disease has been ascribed to medicines which have been thrown out of a window or emptied behind a fire."[118]

Rush's first lecture to his students provides us with a variant of an eighteenth-century understanding that would condition the thinking of physicians well into the nineteenth century. He identified, for example, as the greatest evil "a disposition to reason upon all medical subjects." The mind, he contended, would not be suspended from acting and would insist on "drawing inferences from facts. To observe, is to think, and to think, is to reason in medicine." Thus even those who argued against speculation in medicine would find themselves theorizing their practice. Rush's conclusion that "no empiric ever gave a medicine without cherishing a theoretical indication of cure in his mind"[119] critiqued the empiric's pretense of operating without a theory. He contended that they practiced without having recognized the theory by means of which they operated.

Similarly, Rush critiqued rationalism's exclusive reliance upon theory as based upon "imperfect knowledge," the "limited extent of human understanding," "the influence of imagination and passions, upon the understanding in its researches after truth."[120] Having refused to side with either dogmatists or empirics, Rush came down on the side of principles. Where he lacked a principle to guide students in his lectures, he relied upon facts. Ultimately, Rush would not decide between dogmatists and empirics, and he decried the mischief that had been done by both. Neither had occasion to exultation, both "have more reason to lament the immense additions they have made to pestilence and the sword in their ravages upon the human race."[121] Principles and facts must therefore be united; theory must accumulate facts and observation must be tethered to the power of theory to arrange all the parts and produce ideas: "with just principles, it is no more necessary for a young physician to see all the diseases of the human body before he prescribes for them, than it is for a mariner, who knows the principles of navigation, to visit all the ports in the world, in order to conduct his vessel in safety to them."[122]

Science

The new construction of medicine would mean a rejection of what was called "rationalism," a dependence upon abstract concep-tualizing that had little in common with scientific medicine or true medical reasoning.[120] Wars and epidemics had allowed for hands-on, large-scale medical experimentation and inventions for such dis-eases as typhus and camp and jail fever (sanitation) and smallpox (vaccination and inoculation) and for such conditions as battle in-juries (bonesetting and amputation). In addition, treatments in the birthing room led to improvements in problem deliveries through the use of forceps, induction of labor, and caesarians. Nevertheless, technology needed to be developed and sustained to move beyond the merely promising. Importantly, scientific instruments of greater precision were yet to be effectively used as a norm of practice.[124] The microscope, invented in the late sixteenth century, while widely used in the seventeenth century was reduced to a gentleman's toy in the eighteenth century.[125] Thermometers, developed in the early seventeenth century, needed to be calibrated to become a useful way of gauging body heat that could replace urine-casting.[126] The stetho-scope was not developed until 1819, although comparable tech-niques were used from the mid-eighteenth century. Alternatives such as tapping the chest (percussion) and listening to the chest with the ear (auscultation) were from ancient times commonly used to locate water or pus in the chest.[127]

Experiments on animals had to become systematic and objective and to move away from crude science. Typical experiments had in-cluded blowing air into the lungs of dogs with bellows to test theo-ries of the mixture of air and blood in the lungs; measuring the force of blood in horses by inserting metal tubes in the jugular vein and carotid artery; pricking the skin of decapitated frogs to test their reflexes; exploring gastric acids by training kites (birds of prey) to ingest and regurgitate tubes of food; and electrifying guinea pigs.[128] Given such practices, Samuel Johnson among others objected to experimentation "published every day with ostentation" and intended to "extend the arts of torture."[129]

Therapeutics were intermittent and varying in their development. Surgeons treated syphilis, wounds, and amputations for the most part, as well as stomachaches, headaches and diarrhea. They had used boiling oil or a red hot iron to cauterize gunshot wounds or to treat gangrene. Rhinoplasty (rebuilding the nose) was possible, as was the removal of bladder stones; removals of diseased eyes or cancerous breasts were attempted.[130] Operations existed to replace protruding intestines and to cure anal fistulas, but major invasions of the body cavity were not possible until anesthetics and antiseptics became available in 1846 and 1867, respectively.[131] In the absence of anesthesia, patients were forcibly held down, stunned by a blow to the head, or had their senses dulled with copious alcohol or opium. Specializing surgeons developed the means to extract the lens of the eye to treat cataracts and to ligate blood vessels to treat aneurysms. The sixteenth century had contributed iatrochemistry or chemical remedies to supplement herbal medicine,[132] although iatrochemical practitioners were often regarded as quacks who lacked specific disease knowledge, tended to have a limited number of drugs, and applied them indiscriminately.[133] With the same drugs used to treat a wide variety of conditions and with purges and emetics the preferred therapeutic, the most commonly used drugs included mercury, quinine (known as Peruvian bark), belladonna, and opium. This is not to say that there was not an extensive pharmacopia (materia medica) of drugs, botanics, and exotic remedies available, or that polypharmacy (the mixture of proprietary compounds, often very complex) was not practiced,[134] but merely that the efficacy of available remedies was hit-or-miss.

In terms of medical reasoning, eighteenth-century medicine had not developed a systematic scientific approach capable of confirming hunches or expanding limited observations. Hypotheses were formulated but not confirmed, studies with control populations were not conducted, and statistics were not yet effectively collected or used, in spite of the fact that statistics began to be gathered and analyzed by the mid seventeenth century.[135] Clinical experiences were largely used as the primary means of verifying one's therapeutic practice, so that the ability to confirm specific disease entities, which physicians were not really looking for, was not present. Pathology was developing along with anatomy so that animal dissection and human autopsy became means of confirming disease causes, understanding the effects of disease on the body, and locating specific possible cures. Laboratory science and medical experimentation practiced on the poor and the mad in public hospitals, jails, or almshouses would, in combination with pathology, yield more accurate disease etiologies and diagnoses.

From the late eighteenth century movement was away from abstract theorizing, or speculative medicine, through transitional modalities like nosology, empiricism, and disease specificity to "strategies grounded in experimental science that objectified disease while minimizing differences among patients."[136] This meant heroic treatments like bloodletting and other aggressive depleting therapies (such as purging and puking cathartics) would fall into disuse, however endemic their practice had become and however gradual their decline might be. Alternative treatments, French skeptical empiricism, and sectarian medicine together with a continuing and strengthening belief in the healing power of nature were given new impetus because of the failures of both regulars and quacks. What resulted was a balance of rational and empirical medical knowledge. Reason served as the foundation for a system, while observation and experience, short of actual experimenting, provided a scientific method.[137]

The most widely spread medical advances resulted from the work of the sanitarian movement, which focused on creating a sewer system and establishing laws for the placement and depth of outhouses, setting standards for digging wells and, ultimately, creating citywide water supplies, including pipes and a pumping source.[138] Keeping the city swept, licensing cartmen or scavengers for citywide pick up of garbage and emptying of privies, assigning certain industries (like slaughterhouses, leather tanning, candle-making, and gunpowder factories) to sites outside the city limits, and draining marshes would prove critical to removing sources of infestation and keeping the air clear of noxious odors and pollution.[139] Theories of "miasma," that is, disease as a function of foul air, would only fall by the wayside when germ theory made inroads on the medical scene.

If we are to look to additional strategies that defined the eighteenth century, we would have to look to inoculation, quarantine, and "pest" (or infectious disease) hospitals as the major responses to which communities resorted. Workhouses and almshouses came into being through private subscriptions as ways of dealing with vulnerable unemployed populations most at risk for overcrowded, poorly ventilated, and unhealthful living quarters. Cities took more seriously the threat of fires, organizing private fire companies by subscription and passing laws that restricted wooden structures to prevent destruction of available housing and the loss of whole city districts. Governmental agency to protect the public welfare was introduced in the second half of the eighteenth century through the concept of medical police. Defined as "the care of the state for the health of its citizens . . . preventative and curative,"[140] state restoration of the public health would eventually ensure the growth of population needed to found the new nation,[141] guarantee a sufficient source of properly trained physicians, and pass laws to protect public safety.[142] Such a role for government would extend to a preemptive responsibility among physicians, who would in the future have to focus on planning for epidemics, controlling communicable diseases, organizing and operating hospitals, and supervising health in newly developing forms of institutional care like orphanages, workhouses, and prisons. Their role would extend to providing environmental sanitation through public health boards and education in hygiene and procreation for occupational and social groups.[143]

In sum, a comparison of the residual religious and the emerging scientific stories of medicine demonstrates how great a span of thinking characterized the eighteenth century. It was a liminal time in which the tectonic plates of early American medicine were shifting and movement among the three stories—religious, professional, and scientific—was irresistible. If we were to speak of the three stories in terms of nonlegal and legal order, it would become apparent that the conditions were overripe for the demise of the former and not yet ripe for the dominance of the latter. The eighteenth century would find itself a laboratory of instability and change whose study would be rewarded by a greater understanding not of directions and goals, but of flux and ambiguity. It is this flux that chapter 3 takes up to figure the context, conditions, and influences out of which medical feuds would emerge as the form of relationships and interactions that would characterize physician practices and medical institutions of the period.

3

Quacks and Corpses

QUACKERY—THE STATE OF MEDICINE AS IT MOVED INTO THE EIGHTEENTH century—and dissection—the state toward which medicine was moving as it headed into the nineteenth century—offer a reading of medicine that pins it to something of a fixed point in the tale of eighteenth-century medicine. At the same time, these twin poles offer a sense of movement or flux that suggests something of the variegation within the medical discourse that makes it difficult to locate in a definitive way. Quackery was heterodox within itself and overflowed into the world of regular medicine in a way that was shapeless and uncontainable. Dissection revealed implications for politics, social theory, and law that made it impossible to be viewed in medical isolation, that is, as a discrete medical phenomenon. Both quackery and dissection, each in its own way, provide a narrative telling of medicine that implies self-organizing forces operating within and through history and in relation to a set of fields— religious, legal, medical, social, and literary. Their interactivity is not only necessary to an appreciation of how medicine was understood but it constitutes through its synergy a higher level tale untethered to any discipline but linked to many. Quackery and dissection can be viewed through the prism of patterns of order discovered within disorder as well as crucibles that tried the mettle of medicine. They were open to complex informing practices in a world of raw experience and were themselves experiences much like trial by ordeal or trial by press. Both were informing practices without which medicine could not have happened as it happened in the eighteenth century.

THE QUACK EXPERIENCE

The history of medicine from the seventeenth through the nineteenth centuries appears to pit regular physicians against quacks in an oppositional, opportunistic struggle in which regulars offered themselves as the force behind medical specialization and professionalism—including the development and growth of licensing, medical regulation, medical colleges, and societies. At the same time, regular medicine was characterized by an uneven and unproven record of healing, an inability and disinterest in treating chronic and mental illness, a failure to lead forcefully in the sanitarian public health areas of clean air and water, garbage disposal, sewers, and food spoilage. Its lack of success extended to failure to understand the causality of or effective treatments for prevailing epidemic and endemic diseases.

Meanwhile, quackery was used as a leveling term that could bring regulars in line with prevailing social attitudes. Where regulars showed too great a concern for the poor, they were called quacks. Where theories of local pollution called for cleaning the environment to control disease, they were considered quackish because they offended local commercial interests. Where popular medical manuals were published to allow for home care and self-treatment, they were considered self-promotional, on the one hand, and guilty of marginalizing the system of regular medical care, on the other. Regular doctors who put out puff pieces, who published advice during epidemics, or who defended their reputations and practices in the press were attacked as quacks.

Examining the life of a singular quack of some notoriety, Henry Tufts of New England who practiced from 1775 to 1831, Daniel Williams describes the quack as one who was convincing in many roles, but particularly in that of the doctor. This quack had been convincing as "a burglar, a horse thief, a counterfeiter, a jailbreaker, a Revolutionary soldier, a deserter, a farmer, a trapper, a trader, a traveling showman, a speculator, a gentleman, a devil, a fortune teller, a wizard, and even as a preacher."[1] Based on such a description, it became clear that vilification of the quack would lead to public scrutiny of the regular as well, just as the regular was straining to maintain his professional credibility by asking the public to act as judge and jury.[2] The English physician Thomas Beddoes argued that doctors needed to heal themselves as he defended his own right to publish cures and to self-advertise. So long as regulars published pamphlets that were like quack bills and advertised themselves by entertaining well-to-do patients, how different, he asked, were they from their "blasted brethren." "So long," he claimed, "as regulars and apothecaries colluded in loading the public with unnecessary visits and gallons of superfluous medicines to cure often semificti-tious diseases, quackery would thrive."[3] Hugely popular self-help manuals, like those by physicians John Gunn and William Buchan,[4] left regulars in a poor position to attack quacks for their populariz-ing of medicine. They actually benefited the quack, for they brought the regular to the level of the quack and undermined the public's confidence in regulars, even as they gave the quack free publicity.

Given the conflation of the regular and the quack among eigh-teenth-century practitioners, a different model of quackery might prove useful, one that removes eclectic and inventive, unortho-dox—or, rather, heterodox—healers from the margins and regards them as part of medical change that was to prove necessary to the survival of the profession. Quacks had the effect of reinforcing an emphasis on the experience of the body and put pressure on elite medicine to open its membership to include alternative healers, ex-perimental medicine, and new practices. Quacks put more choice in the hands of the consumer, who thereby had greater power. The public marketplace made possible by quacks offered anonymity to those with confidential complaints and needs—veneral complaints or access to abortifacients, for example. The marketplace spread in-formation, educated the public, defused ignorance, and weaned the public from dependence on orthodox sources of advice or treat-ment. It focused attention on positive medicine and on healthful-ness with its general tonics, nostrums, and potions, even as it sponsored more responsibility for one's own care, greater self-help, and more attention to pain management and relief for chronic dis-eases, an area in which regular practitioners had showed little in-terest.

With all this, the medical marketplace was to prove capable of en-forcing a new tyranny: hypochondria. Medicine became so available as to prove addictive, so that a cycle of new products produced new cravings and a morbid fascination with self-medication. Capitalism, commodities, and consumption converged to produce a rich variety of medical goods at rock bottom prices that exploited the public's suggestibility. Panaceas were offered, strength and health were pro-moted, and relief rather than outright cures was stressed. A system was created in which the public felt it got a lot for its money and was released from the regular care and daily dosing of a physician. Quacks patched patients up and kept them working, having gradua-ted, like their clients, from the school of practical experience. Their relative lack of training and mercilessly commercial pursuit of business, as a result, left quacks in a position of providing much bad medicine and outright fraudulent treatments.

To offset criticism and in their effort to maintain an open marketplace in which they could freely compete, quacks attacked restricted medical societies and degrees that they considered "yet another form of professional mysticism."[5] According to the pamphlet *The Imposter Detected* (1776), the quack's merit "depends upon the knowledge of nature, and of things, and not of words; . . . To think otherwise, is to suppose that every physician must be a magician; seeing medicines are incapable of healing, unless accompanied with the knowledge of the import of certain sounds, or the signification of words of certain languages, to which they have no relation, but what is given them by the arbitrary appointment of man."[6]

For fear of abandoning the public to quacks and feeling "obliged to stand up against vile commercialism,"[7] regulars themselves tested the public market.[8] The question was raised, if preachers publish their sermons why not physicians their nostrums so that others might learn from them. Benjamin Rush carried the argument further to advise regulars of their potential debt to quacks, from whom, he felt, they had much to learn. He hinted to the medical student John Foulke that, in addition to attending "celebrated hospitals" and "cultivating intimacy with a few eminent physicians and surgeons," he should "Converse freely with quacks of every class and sex, such as oculists, aurists, dentists, corn cutters, cancer doctors, etc. etc. You cannot conceive how much a physician with a liberal mind may profit from a few casual and secret visits to these people."[9] Rush gave freely of his medical advice not only in his lectures to his students but in training poor African Americans to bleed his patients and in publishing advice to the public so that people might treat themselves in the absence of physicians during the yellow fever. As a physician who maintained a large practice among the poor, Rush was not, however, sanguine about the public's knowledge of medical matters, which he attributed to general ignorance.[10]

> They not only confide their health and lives to quacks; but they often place the most implicit reliance upon what are called spells and charms to cure their diseases. A piece of stolen butcher's meat, rubbed upon warts, and afterwards buried in the earth, has long been a popular remedy for those excrescences upon the hands. The prescription of a woman who has not changed her name in marriage, is considered as a cure for the hooping cough; and a seventh son is supposed to possess, by a kind of birthright, a supernatural power over all diseases.[11]

THE VALUE OF LIFE AND DEATH

It was not enough that patients in the eighteenth century had to navigate their way through a plethora of competing medical providers and treatments with few guarantees offered by medical degrees or licensing and with limited institutional support from hospitals, dispensaries, or clinics, but they had as well to deal with end-of-life threats to the welfare of their souls, given the potential uses to which their bodies might be put with the development of anatomy, dissection, resurrection (a term used to describe grave-robbing), and autopsy. The eighteenth-century debate over medicine had, after all, much to do with the value placed on death.

In the death culture of the eighteenth century, the public and private spheres had been regarded as coterminous and mourning was seen as a social and collective experience. Social identity and public virtue had described the value of the death experience, and the religious experience expressed concern for salvation and one's relationship with a supreme being. The death experience at the end of the century, however, was separating into a private ritual located in the family and celebrating the individual, incorporating a moral sense rooted in sentimentalism that linked the physical body's life and death to one's mortality.[12] The ceiling for treatment of the dead body was indicated in the development in the late eighteenth century of funerary rites that accompanied the growth of sensibility, a middle-class value that created fashionable tastes in mourning clothes, funeral art, deathbed vigils, costly coffins, personal cemetery plots, and even funeral souvenirs for mourners.[13] The graveyard itself reflected changed tastes and the increased social value of the corpse. Simple temporary crosses and marker stones were common in colonial times in a churchyard with a communal charnel house to which disinterred bones would subsequently be assigned. Their replacement by permanent monuments and independent cemeteries led in the nineteenth century to burial grounds established outside of towns as memory gardens that would control fears of contagion from gases that exuded from graves and provide homes for the dead that could bring pleasure to visitors. Individual spaces for burial supplanted reusable plots and coffins to create permanent resting places, and dark, small churchyards in which bodies were buried in layers for lack of space were replaced by separate cemeteries each with its own unique identity.[14]

The idea of a beautiful death grew up to sanctify death as a special event that should be memorialized and set off with a sacred boundary between it and life.[15] To maintain the fiction of the beautiful death, death was narrated to give the deceased a social identity and the death itself a dramatic form that could be encapsulated in the funeral ritual. Customs that violated the dignity of the event were excised, including practices that focused on demons, ghosts, or sorcery. In the sentimentalized view of death, the body itself was to be honored to capitalize on its value to the living as a sign of how they would be similarly valued and memorialized upon death. The body had value and power in terms of the symbolic good will a good death brought to a family, even as it was vulnerable and dependant upon the good will of the living to ensure it a good death.

At the same time, popular theology continued to give the dead body considerable importance. That theology depended upon a belief in the continued connection between body and soul for a period of time beyond death, certainly until the soul's status was resolved as it related to final judgment. The dead body was thus to be protected to ensure the soul would proceed to its fate at final judgment and be reunited with the body.[16] The winding sheet in which the corpse was wrapped was referred to as "swaddling clothes" and served as a reminder of Christ's own burial. Not only were shrouds, which developed into an ultimate form of night clothes, sometimes part of one's trousseau upon marriage, but they became a repository of small, personal gifts to the dead, which were buried with the corpse.[17] Funeral cakes, drinking, and sin eating (paying a stranger to assume, or "eat," the sins of the dead) at funerals were all intended to lighten the soul's burden of sin as it passed into another world.[18] Ringing bells and opening doors and windows to let evil spirits out of the room at a wake were part of funerals as was the covering of mirrors to ensure that painful truths were not reflected and that the vanity of life was noted. The stopping of clocks was designed to ensure that the time of death was marked.

"Waking," or watching the dead until burial, had become a practice much honored in its observance, to the point that those who left bodies unattended were fined and professional mourners were paid to attend to the dead. The term "waking" was itself a carry-over from periods of the plague when bodies in a coma were sometimes taken for dead. The wake protected against hasty burials to remove the contaminated and allowed for remarkable recoveries.[19] Not only were corpses to be viewed, but until family privacy became a prevailing standard, they were available to be seen by the public. Corpse watching was designed to protect the dead from pollution of the devil and to ensure resurrection. Plugging up the holes of the body was designed to keep the devil from entering the body as well as a prophylactic against bodily fluids escaping during funerals. Because an unquiet soul was likely to haunt the living who denied it respect, its uncleanness was addressed by ritual corpse-washing. The washing was like a baptism of the dead for its next life.[20] In spite of possible contagion, corpses were often touched to relieve grief, bring good luck, accept the finality of death, or to deal with the fear of death. For some, touching demonstrated a final forgiveness or a desire to take on the dead's prior strength. The belief that the dead were still attuned to the living was a sentiment taken as court evidence in a case in 1629 where a corpse was supposed to have bled when touched by its murderer.[21]

The poor, who were unlikely to afford the elaborate funeral practices of the better-off, had at least to maintain a proper wake and to accompany the corpse to its final resting place and promise it a safe rest. But they were no more able to guarantee their kin a respectful death than they were to assure them respect in life. Not only was the negative model for treatment of the poor body in death largely associated with the way the poor were treated in life, but "Incarceration in the almshouse and burial in potter's field already signified social death."[22] Experimented upon in life as a trade-off for being admitted to hospitals and poor houses, their dead bodies could legally be assigned to dissection to recoup the costs of pauper burials and the care of the poor in almshouses. Trafficking in the bodies of the poor was thereby relegated to the same category as such "skin trades" as slavery and prostitution.[23] Adding to the equation that dissection was an added penalty under the law for certain capital crimes that largely affected poor defendants only ensured that the poor would resist having their own assigned to autopsies, condemned to dissection, or robbed from their graves. Resurrectionists, as a result, represented a far greater threat to the poor and their values than the economic status of the poor and the willingness of some to sell remains of family members to anatomists might indicate.

DISSECTION AND ANATOMY

Until states passed their own laws, largely throughout the nineteenth century, American courts were influenced by British common law that held corpse-robbing was no felony because the body was not property[24] and that allowed the bodies of criminals condemned to execution to be used for dissection. In 1733, for example, students of "Physick, Surgery, etc" made a request for the body of an executed Indian. In the same city in the very next year, a newspaper notice appeared of the dissection of an executed burglar.[25] A 1784 Act in Massachusetts attached dissection as a penalty, along with denial of a Christian burial, for participants who killed or were killed in duels. Among the condemned, it appeared that a sentence of dissection was as much to be feared as execution, so that we hear of applications, like that by Whitling Sweeting in New York in 1792, for clemency on that part of the sentence.[26]

Ruth Richardson describes dissection as the most exemplary of punishments, the intention of which "was to deny the wrongdoer a grave."[27] Restricted as a penalty to murder, it was withheld as a punishment from such other death penalty crimes as property crimes. Dissection was meant to signal something much greater than merely the loss of life. It was considered, as one commentator put it, the "*ne plus ultra of punishment.*"[28] The fact that it was also the penalty paid by those poor patients who, having succumbed to their illnesses in hospitals or workhouses, were unable to pay for their own funerals,[29] suggests that the innocent poor were to be grouped with the vilest criminals of their times, who were themselves members of the poorest class.[30] To diffuse such a notion, the Anatomy Bill, which became law in England in 1832,[31] contained a provision that all bodies were subject to anatomization unless an objection was raised, but failed to provide that no bodies could be dissected without consent.[32] The Anatomy Bill was silent on punishment for grave robbery, suggesting a lack of serious protection for those most afflicted with such treatment, again the poor.[33] Although provisions were required to be made for burial of the remains of those assigned to dissection, they went largely disregarded and sponsored great resentment among the poor.[34] Some took the act to mean that the rich, too, were liable to having their bodies dissected, although it was always clear that the rich would never respond to appeals to "dedicate their bodies after death to promote the advancement of science."[35] Nor would surgeons who benefited from dissection, those who voted for the Anatomy Bill, or pensioners who received money from the public be likely to donate their bodies to science. Dissection was thus indelibly inscribed as a form of punishment and was largely applied to the poor, whether the crime was murder or merely the crime of being poor.

Whereas medical colleges did not begin rapidly expanding in America until the nineteenth century[36] and the most developed discussion of dissection only occurred between the late eighteenth century and the period of the Civil War, there was considerable interest in the use of corpses in early and mid-eighteenth century. The need to train medical students created a commercial opportunity for the supply of corpses. So long as students had few human cadavers, they had to rely on dissecting animals.[37] In the late 1760s, students at Harvard formed a society known as the "Spunkers" in which they clandestinely "owned a skeleton, discussed anatomical, physiological, and other medical questions, and dissected animals, chiefly horses, swine, dogs, and cats."[38] At the Pennsylvania Hospital, Dr. Thomas Bond defended the need to support clinical work for students using cadavers and requested the opportunity to display bodies to his students for instructional purposes when patients died of unusual causes.[39] Describing rounds at the hospital in 1766, he argued that books alone could not supply an adequate sense of a disease and that diagnosis could only be confirmed by autopsy.

> [the doctor] pronounces what the Disease is, whether it is curable or Incurable, in what manner it ought to be treated, and gives his reasons from Authority or Experience for all he says on the occasion; and if the Disease baffles the power of Art, and the Patient falls a sacrifice to it, he then brings his knowledge to the Test, and fixes Honour or discredit on his Reputation by exposing all the Morbid parts to view, and Demonstrates by what means it produced Death; and if perchance he finds something unexpected, which betrays an Error in Judgment, he, like a great and good Man, immediately acknowledges the mistake, and for the benefit of survivors points out other methods by which it might have been more happily Treated.[40]

The value of dissections was defended again in 1793 by the French doctor Jean Deveze in relation to his work operating the yellow fever hospital at Bush Hill in Philadelphia. Deveze demonstrated, on the basis of his dissections, that yellow fever was in fact not contagious and that local origins were responsible for the crisis in the city. This position put him significantly at odds with prevailing contagion theory which, suggesting the disease was imported, thereby had the advantage of not offending local leaders. Accused of making Philadelphia itself appear an unhealthful city (an honor he earned

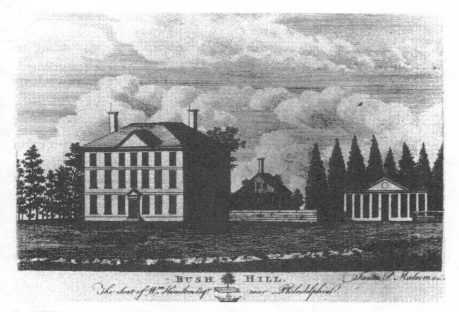

Bush Hill, the seat of William Hamilton, Esq., near Philadelphia, used as a fever hospital in 1793 during the yellow fever epidemic. Engraving by James Peller Malcolm, Dec., 1787. *Universal Magazine*. In Martin P. Snyder, *City of Independence: Views of Philadelphia Before 1800* (New York: Henry Holt & Co.).

earlier than Benjamin Rush, who jumped on the noncontagionist bandwagon later in the epidemic) and of denying thereby the possibility of the fever having been transported from the French colonies in the West Indies, Deveze defended himself by citing his work in autopsying yellow fever victims:

I opened a great number of bodies, and consequently was under the necessity of dipping my hands in the black and corrupted blood that proceeded from their mortified entrails, and breathed the infected vapours that exhaled from them. I was, it must be acknowledged, one of the most exposed to the disease; had it been contagious without doubt it must have easily shewn itself in me, for, independent of the danger to which my duty exposed me, I was in a state of indisposition that made me likely to receive the action of the deleterious miasmata and to facilitate the operation: nevertheless I was exempted.[41]

In the yellow fever epidemic of 1798, physicians Isaac Rand and John Warren of Boston testified as well to the medical felicity of dissection as a tool in diagnosing and prescribing for the disease. Prefacing the report of their dissections, they endorsed its usefulness to serve both purposes: "The following cases of dissection may throw some light on the nature of the disease, as it prevails in this town, and may, we hope be of some use, in investigating the treatment best adapted to the purpose of checking or suppressing its destructive ravages."[42]

Whereas the value of dissection might have been apparent, the source of and traffic in cadavers was very much in contention. Students in Edinburgh had to pay for the corpses they would dissect or for the body parts they could buy from the surgeons under whom they studied. Others willed their own corpses to dissection in exchange for their tuition.[43] Alternative sources of corpses included the bodies of suicides, sailors who died on ship, corpses imported from abroad, open pit burials, unclaimed bodies, and donation.[44] Whereas providers in New York packed the dead bodies of negroes and sent them to the South in barrels of salt and brine,[45] winter proved the most profitable season as corpses could be transported great distances without spoiling. Philadelphia became particularly renowned as a site able to supply New York and Boston's medical needs as well as its own.[46] Competition for corpses proved intense as schools had to go farther and farther afield to serve their growing needs. Bodies were harvested at the rate of some four hundred fifty a school year in New York, where the mayor himself resolved disputes over contested corpses when schools differed over which should receive more.[47] In Philadelphia, a secret treaty was signed to ensure a division of bodies that was fair, "to sustain the medical interests of Philadelphia, and to prevent the public scandal and excitement incident to the cultivation of anatomy."[48]

RESURRECTION RIOTS

The first public notice of a "resurrection" or dissection riot occurred in Philadelphia in 1765 and involved an attack on the carriage and house of Dr. William Shippen by a mob of citizens.[49] Shippen had opened a private school in his home to train medical students in the winter of 1762, preceding by three years the founding of the medical school in Philadelphia. Offering private lectures and the examination of cadavers, the school was advertised "for the Advantage of the young Gentlemen . . . who Circumstances and

Connections will not admit of their going abroad for Improvement to the Anatomical Schools in Europe; and also for the Entertainment of any Gentlemen, who may have the Curiosity to understand the ANATOMY of the HUMAN FRAME."[50] Shippen announced lectures in anatomy to be illustrated surgically on the body.

In these Lectures the Situation, Figure and Structure of all the Parts of the HUMAN BODY will be demonstrated, their respective Uses explained, and, as far as a Course of Anatomy will permit, their Diseases, with all the Indications and Method of Cure, briefly treated of; all the necessary Operations in SURGERY will be performed, a Course of BANDAGES exhibited, and the whole conclude with an Explanation of some of the curious Phaenomena that arise from an examination of the GRAVID UTERUS, and a few plain general Directions in the Study and Practice of MIDWIFERY.

Shippen charged for tickets to the lectures and offered an open invitation to an elite group of public observers. Advertising publicly the use of cadavers together with a course on obstetrics suggested that Shippen was willing to brave the ire of a public that was not only insecure about desecration of human remains but uncomfortable and unfamiliar with men attending to women's bodies, however medical the purpose.[51] Shippen appeared to have considered open dissections a public good that could educate and engender the support of those who would attend.

On September 26, 1765, when Shippen advertised a set of similar lectures and demonstrations set to begin on November 18, this time associated with the new Medical School of the College of Philadelphia and advertised together with a course of lectures by Dr. John Morgan, he took care to announce his use of cadavers in a way that might inoculate him against attack.

It has given Dr. Shippen much Pain to hear, that notwithstanding all the Caution and Care he has taken, to preserve the utmost Decency in opening and dissecting dead Bodies, which he had persevered in, chiefly from the Motive of being useful to Mankind, some evil minded Persons, whither wantonly or maliciously, have reported to his Disadvantage, that he has taken up some Persons who were buried in the Church Burying Ground, which has distressed the Minds of some of his worthy Fellow Citizens.———The Doctor, with much Pleasure, improves this Opportunity to declare, that the Report is absolutely false; and to assure them, that the Bodies he dissected, were either of Persons who had willfully murdered themselves, or were publickly executed, except now and then one from the Potters Field, whose Death was owing to some particular Disease; and that he never had one Body from the Church, or any other private Burial Place.[52]

Taking up corpses of criminals, suicides, and the poor buried at public expense in a public burial ground rather than the dead from church or private burial grounds was designed to appeal to working class and middle class citizens.[53] These groups were particularly concerned with the sanctity of their own dead at the hands of opportunistic grave robbers known to sell bodies to physicians who taught hands-on knowledge of the diseased body. Members of a sailor's mob, nevertheless, apparently believed that Shippen's cadavers had been uprooted from a church burial ground. They were angry that the bodies of their mates were not given the same consideration as citizens in the town who had family to bury them privately.[54] The mob attacked Shippen's home. He was forced to escape through an alley and the carriage "supposed to contain him received along with a shower of other missiles a musket ball through the center of it."[55]

The grave robbing the mob feared did occur with some frequency and largely among those with lesser social standing. The burial of bodies within the confines of a church or churchyard depended upon one's wealth and relative social standing.[56] Those inside the church, buried in the floor or in the walls, were wealthier, as were those buried close to the outside walls or on the sunny side of the churchyard.[57] Immigrants and blacks, the poor and unattached strangers, buried on the outskirts of the churchyard or outside the church burial grounds altogether in a potter's field, were left to the mercy of those who plundered graves. Petitions from the free black community in New York, where a segregated Negroes Burying Ground was part of potter's field near the almshouse, were ignored in 1787 and 1788 when the city council declined to take seriously complaints that "under cover of night . . . [medical students] dig up the bodies of the deceased, friends and relatives of the petitioners, carry them away without respect to age or sex, mangle their flesh out of wanton curiosity and then expose it to beasts and birds." The second petition referred to the fact that "few blacks are buried whose bodies are permitted to remain in the grave,"[58] indicating once again that the economically defenseless were particular targets of resurrectionists and raising an issue of the relative value of bodies. Those in almshouses whose lives had proved costly to society as a

William Shippen's house on Fourth and Prune Street (between Spruce and Walnut), on land purchased in 1744. This was the site of Shippen's anatomy school and of a resurrection riot in 1765. Photo courtesy of Kostas Myrsiades.

"drain on the public purse"[59] were considered legitimate candidates to prove themselves useful to the living as objects of medical dissection. One way or another, the poor were condemned to serve the medical machine,[60] either as experimental subjects for physicians in public hospitals or as corpses for dissection. These uses of the bodies of the poor ensured that the stigmatization previously associated with Indians, slaves, immigrants, criminals, and prostitutes would extend to them as an economic class and thereby spread to all those at the margins of social acceptability.

The bodies of the trade and merchant classes were implicated as well, if the botanic Samuel Thomson is to be believed. Thomson accused regular physicians of using dissections to mask their mistakes when their cures killed their patients. As Thomson wrote in 1843, "This scene too often occurs amongst the poison practitioners [referring to the use of iatrochemistry, chemical compounds]. If the medicine kills, they open the body to make the friends think it was the disease, instead of the bleading and medicine that killed. They bleed when the blood is thick and glutinous, all that will run out— the remainder ceases to circulate, and the patient pants and dies— they hold a post-mortem examination, to deceive the friends, and the experimenter goes unpunished."[61]

Working class objections to dissection and the raiding of private burial grounds nevertheless accounted for most of the riots. On April 13, 1788, for example, a New York mob of some three hundred to four hundred men forced its way into City Hospital and confiscated several dissected bodies, sacking the hospital in the process and leading to the arrest of several medical students. By the time the crowd marched on the city jail, it had swelled to 5,000 and a militia of 50 to 150 men had to be called up, leading to the deaths of three rioters and three militiamen.[62] This event led to the passage in New York of a statute in 1789, called an "Act to Prevent the Odious Practice of Digging up and Removing for the Purpose of Dissection, Dead Bodies Interred in Cemeteries or Burial Places."[63] The act outlawed body-snatching, but it also provided for legal appropriation of cadavers necessary to medical study. Convicted criminals could be assigned for dissection so long as a surgeon was in attendance at the execution to take possession of the body.

In their proper context, dissection riots were not quite the mob actions they seemed. Rather, they shared a great deal of the popular sentiment of a time when legal enforcement was weak or unavailable. Mobs tended, in fact, to be socially accepted when they were focused, when they did not lead to great injury or death,[64] and so long as they acted to extend law that was slow or technically inapplicable. In many ways, mobs "lay behind many laws and civil procedures that were framed during the 1780's and 1790's."[65] The kinds of events they became exercised over were a good reflection of their status as a "extralegal arm of the community's interest"[66] at a time when rebellion was still respected as an expression of popular discontent. Food shortages, epidemics, customs seizures, and impressment of sailors constituted some of the bases for mob actions that reflected community welfare rather than special interests.[67] Indeed, those who made up mobs were hardly to be "confined to the seamen, servants, Negroes, and boys generally described as the staple components of the colonial mob."[68] Rather, many were members of the upper classes, including property holders as well as professionals who represented the community.

One description of eighteenth-century mobs puts them down as a bloodless alternative to an abusive situation.[69] Prior to mid nineteenth-century development of institutionalized policing, the community itself was relied upon in a "hue and cry" form of assembly, like calling out a posse to apprehend a felon. A semilegal unofficial institution, the mob represented a self-organizing community callout in defense of public order.[70] Even when, in the strictest sense, it engaged in marginally legal activities, the mob had "popular legitimacy."[71] In postrevolutionary times, the mob continued an active popular role as a free people producing government in exceptional circumstances. Mob action, like feuds and duels, was a common and accepted extralegal remedy, a form of public judgment not unlike trial by press, if substantially more aggressive and spontaneously organized. The limit to such action was the same limit as that set for a nonlegal order: once the law provided a developed, legitimate system of order, it would prove both unwieldy and unnecessary to rely upon social norms and popular action to resolve disputes.[72] The decline of such community actions, either because of the absence of conditions that made them necessary or because controls became more onerous, made the use of courts more likely.

As our sketches of quackery and dissection have indicated, the eighteenth-century medical world was characterized by a proliferation of medical providers and treatment practices and by popular dissension and riotous reactions to demands of the growing profession that flew in the face of popular values related to death and the death experience. Chapter 1 proposed that such characterizations would be consistent with the kind of nonlegal order that has been theorized for medicine in this period, whereas chapter 2 clarified how a practitioner like Benjamin Rush was likely to have perceived life under such conditions. The stories of medicine that we have thus far encountered suggest that medicine was in a state of change whereby old constructions were rapidly being challenged, alternate stories were being posited, and emerging stories were beginning to take on new value and support. It remains for us to consider actual behaviors of physicians during the eighteenth century. If, as we have proposed in chapter 1, the nonlegal order was typified by feudlike interactions preoccupied with questions of reputation and honor, with self-regulating rules and self-actualizing norms, we should be able to trace such an order in the relations of physicians of the period. Not only should we find such relations in their interpersonal affairs, but we should see them reflected on a larger scale in institutional interactions. It is just this effort that shall take up the remainder of the study in chapters 4 and 5.

4

Medical Feuds in Philadelphia

THE EIGHTEENTH CENTURY WAS A TIME OF RABID MEDICAL FEUDS, OFTEN resulting in duels, but even more often playing out on the pages of newspapers. Feuds provided a picture of medical competition, medical therapeutics, institutional conflicts, development of a science and a profession, tensions between the economics and science of medicine, and relationships of physician to physician as well as physician to patient. They involved credit for innovations in medicine, medical theorizing and politics, public health considerations, organization of the delivery of medicine, and the training of medical students.[1] In sum, feuds touched on almost every aspect of eighteenth-century medicine so that they stand a good chance of shedding new light on the profession from its problem symptoms to diagnosis, therapeutics, and prognosis.

Feuds represented a nonlegal form of order at the other end of the spectrum from legal order and operated based upon the social norms that underlay such a nonlegal order. When feuds began to dissipate as a form of social order, patients and physicians learned to access the law not only to resolve conflicts, affirm honor, and rehabilitate reputation but to codify through the law what medicine must and should be able to do in terms of its public contribution as a necessary means of establishing the nation's health, at both an individual and a collective level. Not only were feuds within the medical profession important in terms of their dynamics and ends, as well as their effect on the development of the medical profession in the nineteenth century, but they had implications for the nation building that was going on in America in the post revolutionary years of the republic.

The eighteenth-century social scene operated like a force field into which a player insinuated himself and asserted agency, but it was also a field that acted to diffuse its power through players, as a carceral force. Here, dispositions induced agents to act within a

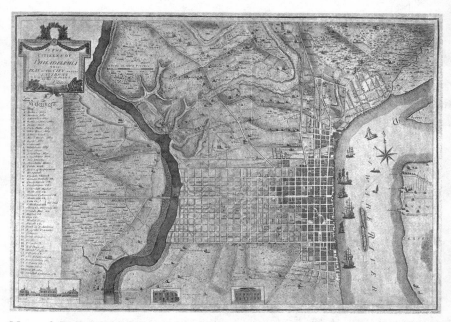

Map of Philadelphia. Engraving by Robert Scot, c. 1796. Peter C. Varle,
Geographer and Engineer, DE. Scott Dunlap, Philadelphia. In Martin P. Snyder,
City of Independence: Views of Philadelphia Before 1800 (New York: Henry Holt & Co.).

common way of being, a form of society written into the body as an
orchestration of the commonsense world, a collective experience
without rules so much as practices. Within a model based on social
norms, social practices provided information about reputation that
reinforced the norm of honor. Knowledge about reputation represented knowledge about the value of honor, which provided a socially viable noninstrumental norm. Honor, working backwards,
expressed power that maintained the system. The power that honor
produced yielded deterrence through punishments that led back to
conformity to the norm of honor. By contrast, at the level of social
practices—such as gossip, ostracism, feuds duels, and litigation—
ambiguity made punishment difficult to determine or to apply fairly.

Honor was like economic interest, as it was accumulated, defended, desired, had value, and could be used as capital. It was, as a
result, self-interested and reputation-building. It created interest itself to add to the principle, even as it attracted credit and new capital and was convertible into other forms of capital. Reputation in its
turn produced social practices to aggregate greater reputation.

Those practices reproduced behavioral regularities that acted to stabilize a scene. Reputation operated by means of its own code, creating a sense of its permanence even as it adjusted to the constraints of the social scene in which it operated. Reputational capital often had to be risked merely to retain the status quo. At the same time, preserved and made to appear permanent, reputation could be left as a legacy.

Turning to one's own use the conditions in which one found oneself, and doing so based on one's self-interest, appeared in many ways to be the hallmark of the world according to medical feuds. Poaching on each others' work as a way of inventing oneself, separating oneself from the background in which one found oneself, and making the most of one's holdings represented the strategies of those in the competitive, self-organizing world of social norms. The struggle was one of constant adaptation in a domain of limited resources and resources jealously commanded and held. Justice had not been clearly defined, indeed had yet to be socially determined for a republic still making itself, and was therefore hard to appeal to. Feuds occurred in a landscape that was indeterminative and directionless. Moves developed, broke out, and collided within and among groups in random ways, so that the shape of events appeared to be patternless and uncontrolled. Moreover, actions escalated according to a cascade of events that was only vaguely understood and largely unpredictable. Under such conditions, the balance of action and reaction was tenuous and events were loosely ordered. Resolutions were unlikely to have the resilience to act as precedents or predictors for the future.

There was thus little in the way of a disposition to encourage behaviors that were regular or rule-bound. Disinterestedness was only a glimmer in the eye and utility value the be-all and end-all for agents. All this took place under the aegis of presumed forms of control like moral order, natural law, or codes like the dueling code. What prevailed was the priority of such readily exchangeable symbolic capital as reputation, which—accumulated, defended, and spent—provided status. On the basis of the capital that status represented, that is to say honor, groups like the medical profession sanctioned or rewarded their members as well as enforced means of control. The balance that was struck was enough to keep the nonlegal order alive, but not enough for it to survive the needs of an emerging professionalism and the move from a proto-capitalist economy to full-blown competition and monopolistic efforts in a large-scale arena of interfacing supply and demand in both the legal and medical spheres.

WILLIAM SHIPPEN AND JOHN MORGAN

With pressure on physicians to identify themselves with new discoveries, to create cadres of loyal pupils, and to compete for a limited number of medical professorships, the opportunities for feuds were manifold. William Shippen and John Morgan were in the field early in an explosive contest associated with the Philadelphia Medical College that became the longest running medical feud in early America, lasting a quarter of a century from 1765 to Morgan's death in 1789. Morgan and Shippen feuded famously over who first proposed the founding of a medical college, the first in America, with Morgan getting most of the credit as an originary force. This early feud festered to the point that feuds were referred to as a Philadelphia tradition[2] and even led to a national crisis over management of the revolutionary continental army hospitals that resulted in the replacement of Morgan as director general and the subsequent unsuccessful court martial of his successor in that role, Shippen.

Benjamin Rush, who got caught up in the Morgan-Shippen feud on Morgan's behalf during the Revolutionary War, reported that Morgan had a sad and poor death attributed by some to never having gotten over the shock of his dismissal from the Continental Army's medical directorship, an event he considered to have been instigated by Shippen. Rush wrote in his *Commonplace Book,* "This afternoon I was called to visit Dr. Morgan, found him dead in a small hovel, surrounded with books and papers, and on a light dirty bed. He was attended only by a washerwoman, one of his tenants. . . . What a change from his former rank and prospects in Life! The man who once filled the world with his name, had now scarcely friends enough left to bury him."[3]

Nineteen years later, sent for by the dying Shippen to attend him, Rush described that death scene as well in his *Commonplace Book.*

This day at 6 o'clock in the evening died at his Seat near Germantown, aged 72, Dr. Wm. Shippen. . . . He had talents, but which from disuse became weak and contemptible. He was too indolent to write, to read, and even to think, but with the stock of knowledge he acquired when young he maintained some rank in his profession, especially as a teacher of anatomy, in which he was eloquent, luminous, and pleasing. . . . he died a believer in the Gospel, and that all his hopes of happiness were founded on the merits of Jesus Christ. Over his faults, &c. let charity cast a veil. He was my enemy from the time of my settlement in Philadelphia in 1769 to the last year of his life. He sent for me to attend him notwithstanding, in his last illness, which I did with a sincere desire to prolong his life. Peace and joy to his soul for ever and for ever.[4]

The feud between Morgan and Shippen began in 1765 in a contest over the Medical School of the College of Philadelphia, later the Medical College of Philadelphia.[5] In 1766, Shippen and his physician father William Sr. refused to join the Medical Society that Morgan founded and headed.[6] In 1769, the feud extended to a controversy over the priority of names in Rush's dedication of his Edinburgh dissertation, in which he acknowledged both men.[7] Morgan and Rush opposed the appointment in 1770 of Shippen's brother John to the faculty of the medical school,[8] and in 1771 Shippen interfered with the attendance of students at Rush's classes at the medical school.[9] A decade later, Rush and Morgan threatened to resign their appointments if Shippen was also appointed to the University of Pennsylvania when it absorbed the medical college in 1781.[10]

The height of the controversy, however, occurred during the period of the Revolutionary War in conflicts over the directorship and organization of the hospitals of the Continental Army from 1775 to 1781. This dispute involved several altercations, including Morgan's removal as director in favor of Shippen in 1777 and Rush's precipitate resignation from the medical unit in 1778; the 1780 court-martial of Shippen in which Morgan and Rush acted as assistants to and witnesses for the prosecution; and the trial by press in 1780, following Shippen's acquittal, in which Morgan and Rush continued to make accusations and publish court testimony.[11] Leaving aside for the time being the events that transpired during the Revolutionary War, which we shall take up in detail in the next chapter, we shall focus here on the founding of the Medical School.

Upon his arrival in Philadelphia from London in 1762, Shippen had presented to the Pennsylvania Hospital a gift from the English doctor John Fothergill of seven cases of medical exhibits and anatomical drawings.[12] Along with the gift, Fothergill included a letter that recommended Dr. Shippen for a course of lectures at the hospital and cited Dr. Morgan as "an able Assistant, both of whom," he

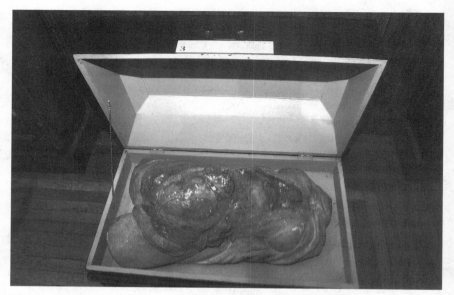

Display case of a fetus *in utero*. **Donated by John Fothergill and delivered by William Shippen to Pennsylvania Hospital in 1762. Courtesy of the Pennsylvania Hospital Historic Collection, Philadelphia.**

suggested, "will be able to erect a School for Physick among you."[13] The hospital failed to act on Fothergill's recommendation even as it received his gift and accepted Shippen to lecture on anatomy using the new materials as illustrations.[14] Within the year, Shippen had set up his own private anatomy school at Shippen House on Prune Street, much as William Hunter had done in London.[15] Morgan had remained in Europe to become a fellow at the Royal Academy of Paris and the Royal Colleges of Physicians at both London and Edinburgh. When he arrived in Philadelphia in 1765, he came as a recipient of those medical honors along with a developed proposal for a medical school.[16]

The two men appeared to be following parallel, that is to say non-converging paths to the same goal, each convinced he had the more appropriate experience for such an undertaking. Shippen initially preferred a freestanding institution, while Morgan, more astutely, preferred affiliation with the established College of Philadelphia. Indeed, he had already raised money for the college, his alma mater, while in Edinburgh in 1762.[17] On May 9, 1765, the *Pennsylvania Gazette* announced Morgan's appointment as "Professor of Theory and

Practice of Medicine in the College of Philadelphia," citing his foreign medical honors and an address he would deliver, "(which will
be soon afterwards published) in order to shew the Expediency of
instituting Medical Schools in this Seminary, and containing the
Plan proposed for the same; in which there will be room for receiving Professors duly qualified to read Lectures in the other Branches
of Medicine, who may be desirous of uniting to carry this laudable
Design into Execution. Dr. Morgan's Plan has been warmly recommended to the Trustees, by Persons of Eminence in England, and
his known abilities, and great Industry, give the utmost Reason to
hope it will be successful, and tend much to the public Utility."[18]

Morgan sealed his appointment with his address in which he dismissed Shippen's competing plan by noting, "It is with the highest
satisfaction I am informed from Dr. Shippen, junior, that in an address to the public as introductory to his first anatomical course, he
proposed some hints of a plan for giving medical lectures amongst
us. But I do not learn that he recommended at all a collegiate undertaking of this kind."[19] Morgan offhandedly recommended Shippen
should the college choose to establish a professorship of anatomy,
reducing Shippen's founding of a private school of anatomy to his
"having been concerned already in teaching that branch of medical
science."[20] Indeed he cited as a rationale for his own plan not only
that it should serve "as a tribute of gratitude to my alma mater" but
that "private schemes of propagating knowledge are instable in
their nature."[21] Associating himself with the college's mission, and
thereby recalling his fund-raising for the institution, he distinguished Shippen's work as an inferior course of action.

Having delayed publication of his "Discourse" and taken the time
to gauge reactions to his speech, Morgan offered in print "to eluci-
date a few passages, which have been thought exceptional in the discourse by particular persons."[22] He did not directly address Shippen
or his supporters but did advert to an issue they might have raised.
As Morgan expressed it, some members of the profession objected
to his being "particular" in having "spoken expressly of the practitioners of this town."[23] Not only had he meticulously avoided doing
so, he claimed, but where it was unavoidable, as with the hospital
physicians, he did so "in terms of the highest respect":[24] "But I have
no where intentionally aimed the shaft of censure at any one, or attempted the character of a particular man; much less have I dared
to attack indiscriminately a whole body of men. As far as I have engaged in painting the errors or faults of any, I have endeavoured to

represent general actions of men, such as they are, and not the picture of individuals."[25] Indeed, according to Morgan, his only fault was his honesty in diagnosing the state of medicine rather than "having justly reflected upon, or censured the conduct of others,"[26] largely those without qualifications to practice medicine, those who practiced relying on abstract knowledge rather than science, and those whose practice combined the roles of doctor, physician, and apothecary rather than focusing on a single role as a medical provider.

It is worth noting that Shippen was the only American physician Morgan mentioned by name in his speech, although he referred generally to six doctors of unquestioned skill and integrity[27] at the hospital in Philadelphia. Not only did he recommend Shippen specifically for a position at the proposed medical school, but he noted indirectly the gift Shippen delivered of medical materials from Fothergill, indicating that these two men had "esteemed the improvement of such knowledge amongst us worthy of notice, and the institution of lectures in every branch of Medicine as deserving the patronage of all who wish well to arts and sciences. It would therefore argue great inattention in us to neglect the first opportunity that offers, of giving effect and stability to the design."[28] Morgan astutely sidestepped any imputation of ingratitude for Shippen's earlier suggestion of a school without actually crediting him and used the Fothergill reference to launch his own design for the school.

Shippen was left little recourse but to apply to the trustees of the college for an appointment and, in the process, to remind them of both his own seminal role in planning a medical school in America and Morgan's end run around a presumed mutual understanding to do so: "I should long since have sought the Patronage of the Trustees of the College," he claimed, "but waited to be joined by Dr. Morgan, to whom I first communicated my plan in England, & who promised to unite with me in every Scheme we might think necessary of so important a Point."[29] In his third-person announcement of his first lecture at the college, Shippen felt once again compelled to assert his priority as an originator of the idea for a medical school, presumably through the founding of his private academy.

The Doctor takes this opportunity to inform the public, that his first course was read in the year 1762, and was premised by an oration, delivered in the State house, before many of the principal inhabitants of this city; wherein he proposed a plan for the institution of a medical school

Pennsylvania Hospital Operating Theater, built in 1804. Courtesy of the
Pennsylvania Hospital Historic Collection, Philadelphia.

Pennsylvania Hospital. Engraving by John Steeper and Henry Dawkins, 1761, before the operating theater was added to the top center building of the structure. The hospital itself was founded in 1751. Montgomery and Winter, DE. Printed and sold by Robt. Kennedy, Philadelphia. In Martin P. Snyder, *City of Independence: Views of Philadelphia Before 1800* **(New York: Henry Holt & Co.).**

in Philadelphia, to which he then declared that course of anatomy was introductory.

The use of such a Institution, and the practicability and propriety of it at that time, were expressed in these words: "All these (meaning the disadvantages that attended the study of physic, etc.) may, and I hope will soon be remedied, by a medical school in America; and what place in America so fit for such a school as Philadelphia, that bids so fair, by its rapid growth, to be soon the metropolis of all the continent? Such a school is properly begun by an anatomical class. . . .

Doctor Shippen thinks it necessary, for some reasons, to publish this extract from his oration, to acquaint those who were not present when it was delivered, that he proposed, and began to execute, a plan for the institution of a medical school in this city four years ago; which, he has the pleasure to inform the public, is now improved, by being connected with the college of Philadelphia, and has succeeded beyond his highest expectations.[30]

Despite their continuing differences, Morgan and Shippen, very likely at the insistence of the college trustees, each added his name

A contemporary photograph of Pennsylvania Hospital. Photo courtesy of Kostas Myrsiades.

to an announcement that medical lectures at the college had opened. In the announcement, the two men were referred to as professor and neither was given the added title of founder of the medical school.[31] Indeed, their courses were announced as courses and not as a program of study. Nor were the courses associated with a medical school. The courses continued to be ascribed to the college itself throughout subsequent announcements made in the *Gazette*.[32]

When the feud blossomed to include Rush, it involved the three most distinguished medical figures in early America: Morgan, the founder of the first American medical school; Shippen, the originator of medical obstetrics and anatomy in America; and Rush, the most prestigious practicing physician in the eighteenth century, a prodigious publisher of papers, and preceptor of more future physicians than any other medical educator of his period. In the amplified feud, a variety of disputes appeared, ranging from the informal to the formal, from the use of social sanctions to public ostracism, shunning, and even slander to court trial and trial by press. In 1771, when Rush, teaching alongside Shippen at the medical school, discovered that his colleague had dissuaded students from attending his lectures, he noted to his brother Jacob, "Better, infinitely better, is it to be at eternal variance with a man of his cool malice and treachery, than to have any connections with him."[33] Rush's description of Shippen suggested what was in fact the case, that Shippen had been shunned by the Rush-Morgan faction which gained credentials within its own subgroup by ostracizing him. Within the larger group of the medical profession as whole—certainly within the medical school—all three men fell into disrepute and the profession found itself under a public microscope in a way that undermined its cultural authority. Morgan allowed his professional resentment to so overwhelm him that in 1781 when the University of Pennsylvania absorbed the Medical School of the College of Philadelphia, he refused to teach at the university if Shippen was appointed there as well. Shippen had just resigned as the director of the Continental Army Hospitals, and Morgan and Rush had gone public in the press to challenge his performance in that role. Rush in particular took the low road by countering a letter from Commanding General George Washington that Shippen produced commending him for his service. Rush suggested that Shippen's presentation to the public of a letter from the general about his service could be compared to Benedict Arnold asking the public to excuse his treason.[34] Rush eventually saw the writing on the wall, where Morgan could not, and rescinded his own threatened resignation from the university. Morgan, by contrast, lost the professorship he had held since 1765. His medical practice dried up, and he died isolated and in penury.

From trivial insults to career assaults, the Shippen-Morgan feud as it was played out in the College of Philadelphia Medical School and the Pennsylvania Hospital established a model for physician relations that threatened the professional status of medicine. Given Philadelphia's standing as the leading medical center of America—home of the first hospital and the first medical school in the country—and the standing that Shippen and Morgan themselves attained as European-trained innovators with American roots, their feud set a tone and established a pattern that was to be replicated recursively throughout the regular medical establishment. Interfering with the staffing of the very institutions that had become essential to the future growth of the field made Morgan both a force to be reckoned with and an enforcer of an idiosyncratic view of how reputation and honor should work. Overinvesting in building his own reputation by pursuing medical honors in Europe, Morgan had brought home a disproportionate share of reputational power that his colleagues either suffered under or sought to rebalance. Withholding an appointment for Shippen's brother to the medical college and resigning when Shippen himself was appointed to the University of Pennsylvania Medical School was Morgan's way of wielding reputation as a form of power, in the latter case risking it to retain his personal stake in the status quo. Keeping his silence about Shippen's contribution to founding a medical school denied his competitor a share of the reputational gain that would ensue from such a major undertaking and aggregated reputation once again to Morgan's account. But Morgan's play would later yield unanticipated consequences in his struggle to retain his directorship of the military hospitals in the continental army. It was a reaction he might have forestalled had he considered the high-risk, hard bargaining losses characteristic of win-lose, zero-sum gain bargaining that such feuds earn.

Shippen played his own hand a bit more deferentially, moving from aggression to self-defense to preserve his gains when he added his signature to Morgan's in the announcement of the College of Philadelphia Medical School and when he accepted a position at the Medical College. Shippen was not, however, a pushover. He used Fothergill's exhibits and anatomy illustrations astutely to capitalize on the clientelism of the Englishman and to buy himself favor with the Americans. It was clear, nevertheless, that he had misgauged Fothergill's support for him as well as Fothergill's influence among the Americans. Fothergill was careful to navigate an evenhanded position to avoid becoming embroiled in the Morgan-Shippen feud.

Both Morgan and Shippen were aware of the value of networking to accrue power. Morgan did so by raising money for Philadelphia College in Edinburgh before he proposed the Medical School and in the Caribbean after the school was founded. He continued his effort by publicizing his plan for establishing a medical school within the college, rather than as an independent entity, in a public address designed to attract supporters and funding. Shippen tried to link support for his private anatomy school to support for his proposal for a medical college, but was outflanked by Morgan's association with Philadelphia College. Shippen's later solicitation of a letter of support for his war-time service from George Washington was designed to associate him with Washington's faction. Rush's insulting remark linking the letter to a Benedict Arnold defense was itself intended to strengthen Rush's ties to a faction that challenged Washington's leadership during the war.

BENJAMIN RUSH

Benjamin Rush was at the center of medical feuding from at least the 1760s until 1800. Throughout his life he kept a running tab on the physicians who were his enemies and those who were his allies. His pupils, Doctors Nathaniel Chapman and Charles Caldwell, provided ample evidence of the former as did his most prominent enemies, Doctors Adam Kuhn, William Currie, Caspar Wistar, and William Shippen.[35]

Rush's autobiography spoke of the difficulties in establishing a medical practice in the face of differences among physicians. In his first seven years, for example, some physicians refused to refer patients to him because of his early association with the theories of Dr. William Cullen, who created an "elaborate nosology" that was considered both an influential and a controversial taxonomy for diseases:[36] "The system of Dr. Cullen was calumniated and even ridiculed in the newspapers with my name connected with it. Perhaps my manner of recommending it provoked this opposition, for I know by experience as well as observation that an indiscreet zeal for truth, justice, or humanity has cost more to the persons who have exercised it, than the total want of zeal for any thing good, or even zeal in false and unjust pursuits."[37] Precluded from consultations, Rush assailed in a lecture to his students those "negative qualities in a physician as render him the favorite of all his brother physicians." Physicians who excite no envy, he contended, "unite readily with every mode of practice, and thus become a kind of consultation hacks."[38]

Rush considered that not only his medical but his political positions did him little good. Rush was a physician both of his times and in contention with his times. Linked to his teacher William Cullen, his peer, and fellow student, John Brown, and the theory of excitement and relief of tension,[39] he carried theory to excess in his own purging and bleeding regimens. Thomas Jefferson in a letter to Philadelphia physician Casper Wistar could easily have included Rush in his indictment of period practitioners, although he did not do so, presumably for reasons of friendship.

He establishes for his guide some fanciful theory . . . of mechanical powers, of chemical agency, of stimuli, or irritability . . . or some other ingenious dream, which lets him into all nature's secrets at short hand. On the principle which he thus assumes, he forms his table of nosology . . .

and extends his curative treatment. . . . I have lived myself to see the disciples of Hoffman, Boerhaave, Stahl, Cullen, and Brown succeed one another like the shifting figures of a magic lantern. . . . The patient, treated on the fashionable theory, sometimes gets well in spite of the medicine.[40]

Rush clearly belonged in the register that Jefferson labeled the "adventurous physician."[41]

As for his politics, Rush referred specifically to his declared republicanism, in particular the role he played in the American Revolution, both as an army physician and as a signer of the Declaration of Independence.[42] The enmity against Rush extended to the position he took against "the iniquity of the slave trade."[43] His politics proved particularly offensive when he compared American slaveholders and British oppressors, asking, "What is the difference between the British Senator who attempts to enslave his fellow subjects in American, by imposing Taxes upon them contrary to Law and Justice; and the American patriot who reduces his African brethren to Slavery, contrary to Justice and Humanity?"[44] Rush's antislavery politics created resentment in Philadelphia not only among those who were slaveholders but among those who felt such work distracted from his medical practice. Rush admitted he had offended those he would most need to build a thriving practice. Wealthy Philadelphians, after all, tended to be federalists and slaveholders and included many who had sat out the war and were uneasy with his republicanism, "for a great majority of them had been loyalists in principle of conduct. It was said, my meddling with politicks was their reason for not confiding their health or lives to my care."[45]

Rush's correspondence, his autobiography, and his commonplace book demonstrated his preoccupation with his medical relationships, which he reflected upon at length. In a letter to John Adams, he examined the source of his soured relations within the medical community as well as more generally.

I have sometimes amused myself by enumerating the different kinds of hatred that operate in the world. They are the "odium theologicum," the "odium politicum," the "odium philologium," and the "odium medicum." It has been my lot—I will not call it my misfortune—to be exposed to them all. The divines hate me for holding tenets that they say lead to materialism and that are opposed to the rigid doctrines of Calvin. The politicians hate me for being neither a democrat nor a monarchist, neither a Frenchman nor an Englishman. The philologists hate me for writing against the dead languages; and the physicians for teaching a system of medicine that has robbed them by its simplicity of cargoes of technical lumber by which they imposed upon the credulity of the world. The last I believe is the most deadly hatred of them all.[46]

Rush had a great deal of difficulty establishing himself as a doctor. He had no family connections to help him set up in business and failed to make a good fit with any of the religious societies in Philadelphia, a potential source of patients.[47] Not predisposed to join another society, Rush found the Presbyterian society of which he was a member too small to sustain a practice and the object of either jealousy or dislike among the more numerous Quakers and Episcopalians, which left him scrambling for patients: "The Quakers had long been in the habit of confining their business chiefly to persons who belonged to their Society, or who favoured their views in politicks. . . . I mention it as a reason why I had recourse to the only mode of succeeding in business which was left for me, and that was by attending the poor. My conduct during my apprenticeship moreover paved the way for my success in adopting it, for I had made myself acceptable at that time to the poor by my services to them."[48]

Rush was thus dependant for a large part of his career to treatment of the poor, for whom he felt a particular affinity as a charitable and Christian duty.

> I led a life of constant labor and self-denial. My shop was crowded with the poor in the morning and at meal times, and nearly every street and alley in the city was visited by me every day. There are few old huts now standing in the ancient parts of the city in which I have not attended sick people. Often have I ascended the upper story of these huts by a ladder, and many hundred times have been obliged to rest my weary limbs upon the bedside of the sick (from the want of chairs) where I was sure I risqued not only taking their disease but being infected by vermin. More than once did I suffer from the latter. Nor did I hasten from these abodes of poverty and misery. Where no other help was attainable, I have often remained in them long eno' to administer my prescriptions, particularly bleeding and glysters, with my own hands. I review these scenes with heartfelt pleasure.[49]

Rush's practice among the poor—like his service in the revolutionary army hospitals and later on the streets of Philadelphia during the yellow fever epidemic—was to prove a living laboratory for learning his medicine. As he writes in his *Autobiography*, he owed whatever he contributed as medical fact or principle related to epidemics to his "familiarity with diseases among the poor" and to his "unfettered prescriptions in their diseases."[50]

Nevertheless, Rush found, even among the poor, that the "tide of public clamour that was excited against my practice" led to his being deserted by his patients and sponsored the careers of other physicians whose "false tales" of Rush recommended them to public favor.[51] Rush felt that a strong pull of gratitude should have obligated his patients and colleagues to him and did not appear ever to have reconciled himself to their disloyalty. On purely medical grounds, putting aside other objections, he attributed the antipathy of his patients to "the novelty of my opinions and practice."[52] Among the other medical differences that separated him from his colleagues, he cited the uniqueness of views that demystified the elite nature of the profession:[53] "I had declared medicine to be a science so simple that two years study, instead of five or more, were sufficient to understand all that was true and practical in it. I had rejected a great number of medicines as useless, and had limited the materia medica to 15 or 20 articles, and in order to strip medicine still further of its imposture I had borne testimony against enveloping it in mystery or secrecy by Latin prescriptions, and by publishing inaugural dissertations in the Latin language in the medical school of Philadelphia."[54]

But even where Rush's treatments were admired or adopted by some physicians, as occurred in the midst of the controversies over the yellow fever epidemic of 1793, he still took issue with his colleagues. Here, he felt he had not been given his due for re-introducing and popularizing an aggressive mercury purging treatment used more than a dozen years earlier by an army doctor. In a letter to Dr. Caspar Wistar acknowledging that he was "but a humble copiest in the use of Calomel & Jalap in bilious fevers. I learned that form of giving mercury from a Senior Surgeon in the military hospitals of the United States in the year 1777,"[55] Rush nevertheless protested the slight to his role in promulgating the use of the treatment, turning it into a question of disrespect and even abuse.

There are few men in Philad. whose word I would have treated with so little respect as you have done mine in your publication. I had not merited such treatment from you. . . . In having wished for your support, while I was contending against the ignorance and slanders of so many of our Physicians, I did not expect to derive the least credit from it to *myself*.

. . . My opinion of the motive of your conduct in your publication, and of its influence upon the practice of some of our Physicians is as fixed & immutable as truth itself, and should the above comments upon your letter . . . be as generally known, as your friends have circulated their abuse of me, longer dashes, and other invectives would be connected with your name, than any that have come from Yours &c Benj. Rush.

Doctors Isaac Rand and John Warren of Boston were more circum- spect than Wistar, making certain to put Rush's name above that of Dr. James Clarke of the "island of Dominica" even though they gave greater credit to the latter for having "more explicitly and highly recommended" heroic mercury purging.[56]

Rush's feuds were initially related to the difficulties of setting up a medical practice, a linkage that was widely shared with other doctors both in America and in England.[57] Not only did established competi- tors marginalize newcomers by refusing to consult with them or allow them privileges at the hospital, but they rejected theories that were new or theories with a decidedly European bent, just the kind of theo- ries that new physicians were likely to introduce. They clearly had lit- tle interest in crediting Rush with the reintroduction of a treatment in which they had no stake, which was controversial, and which had been unevenly adopted. Their social practices—gossip, shunning, and poaching—were responsible for Rush's slow start in inserting himself in Philadelphia's medical scene and contributed to Rush's life-long hostility, a hostility that verged on paranoia. This response was to undermine the prospect of lasting resolutions to his feuds and to normalize the use of feuds as a social practice in which Rush would become expert.

Rush had the added difficulty of being associated with physicians who were not only not in fashion but who were European. He be- longed as well to a small religious group with little influence, which inhibited his ability to network for patients. Associating himself with the poor was a status-deflating move that further marginalized him from mainstream practitioners and placed him decidedly on one side of a yawning political divide, a side that was revolutionary (pro- French), republican (states' rights), and anti-slavery (against estab- lished slave owners). Rush thus faced a gossip campaign against him that further shrunk his practice, so that patient loyalty was tested and a number of patients deserted him.

JEAN DEVEZE

The issue of credit, once raised, was often a question of turf as much as respect, but also, significantly, one of reputation for medical contributions. An illuminating event in this regard, and one that affected the progress of medical treatment, was a little known feud during the 1793 yellow fever epidemic between the medical establishment of the city and Jean Deveze, the French physician who took over Bush Hill, the yellow fever hospital in Philadelphia. Perhaps the least documented feud of all, this feud was conducted largely through silence and disregard and was only truly revealed a decade after Rush's death and several decades after the events themselves.[58] We get the whole story when Deveze returned to France and decided to publish his version in French journals.

The larger questions of the feud turned on three issues: whether yellow fever should be considered contagious (Rush changed his mind from contagion to non-contagion and Deveze weighed in earlier than was propitious with his view that it was not contagious);[59] whether the treatment should be mild or extreme (Rush and Deveze went head to head on this one, with the French experience weighting the balance in favor of conservative treatment); and whether physicians with experience in the local conditions in Philadelphia and with the work of the fever hospital (Doctors Physick, Cathral, Annan, and Leib) should be preferred at the hospital to a French doctor with experience in the West Indies from which the fever was presumed to have emanated.[60] Upon Deveze's offer to join the American physicians at Bush Hill in September 1793, the committee to oversee the hospital assigned Deveze a room to see patients, under the direction of the four American doctors. Three of the four physicians, however, refused this arrangement as well as two other proposals made by the committee whereby the hospital would be divided into separate units, each with its own appointments.[61] According to the Minutes of the Committee, the American physicians advised the committee "that they need not expect the attendance of the Physicians this day; and to desire them to proceed to the care of the sick and to endeavour to obtain the necessary medical aid which their situation may require."[62]

Deveze described his reception as one in which the physicians initially "refused to allow me to assist in their work." When the hospital was divided, "they let me make my rounds but refused to make theirs and resigned the next day. So I found myself in charge of the entire service."[63] Their incomprehensible desertion of their posts in a period of such peril stunned Deveze who, mindful of both the responsibility and danger that had descended upon him, felt bound to remain: "The desertion of the local physicians in time of danger affected the Committee painfully. . . . the Committee asked me to renew my assurance that I would not abandon them. I had given my word, which made this new request seem to me unnecessary. But I would not have done it even had I been certain of meeting death in accepting the tasks they gave me. The desire of being useful and of proving my gratitude to the people of Philadelphia would have prevented me from recoiling from this terrible task."[64]

Deveze was not to be afforded the credit he deserved for his service in the epidemic. Determined to rely on the evidence at hand rather than the speculative theories of rational medicine, he autopsied yellow fever victims at Bush Hill and kept case notes to guide treatment that led to therapies more appropriate to the nature of the disease than those relied upon by local physicians. Although Deveze treated the largest number of patients during the epidemic and had the greatest success in terms of successful management of those cases that arrived at the hospital in a treatable condition, he was barely mentioned in the writings of other doctors of the period. Rush, for example, reluctantly addressed "the comparative success of the French practice" and referred to "The reputation of this hospital, and of the French physician" early in the epidemic. He identified "a French physician, who was assisted by one of the physicians of the city" at Bush Hill, but he found that the number of deaths reported there (448 of the 807 cases) "is truly melancholy!"[65] That Rush's treatments were not adopted at the hospital was foremost in his account, for, as he reports, calomel (a form of mercury) and jalap were not used and preference was given to "moderate bleeding and purging with Glauber salts." As Rush praised by name others of whom he approved, including women and priests, he appeared determined to leave Deveze unnamed. Indeed, when Rush noted that only three physicians remained abroad in the city, he again neglected to mention Deveze who worked continuously throughout the epidemic.[66]

Unlike his contemporaries, Deveze refused to engage in contentious exchanges or self-advertisement. Publishing his observations in 1794, he wrote "I now, once for all, declare that I renounce all controversy."[67] In his later commentary, the French physician gave his own account of the behavior of his fellow physicians in denying him his due.

> One may think it extraordinary that . . . neither my work nor my name should have been mentioned in [Rush's] publication. That was for two reasons; the first is the custom American writers have inherited from their ancestors, the English, of never quoting foreign authors; they would feel dishonored if they acknowledged owing anything to a foreign nation. The other reason as personal to myself. As soon as the letter which I have reprinted in my preface was known to the public, the physicians of Philadelphia assembled to deliberate on what they should do. At first they wished to reply to me, but having learned that I wished to propose experiments to decide the discussion which would be caused by their reply, they changed their minds, well convinced of the disgraceful position they would be in if, after their clamors and their intrigues it should be plainly proved to them that they were wrong. Consequently they decided to keep silent; and as they knew I had decided not to remain in Philadelphia, they mutually agreed never to quote me on any subject and thus to bury in oblivion the fact that a foreigner had lavished his care on their fellow countrymen, and had enlightened them on the principal characteristics of the disease which afflicted them, though most of them had fled at the moment of danger.[68]

As for Rush, his isolation in the medical community was deepened by attacks on his behavior in 1793 when he made publicly available his treatment plan for yellow fever in the *Federal Gazette*.[69] Not only did the notice offer a remedy with which many of his medical colleagues disagreed, but it smacked of "quackery" by offering medical treatment in the public marketplace. Rush refused to fault himself, feeling justified by the crisis itself as well as what he called the "criminal ignorance" of others and his duty to preserve the city. In self-defense, he remained independent of his colleagues, turning his back on them, as they had in earlier times turned theirs on him, by refusing to consult with them.

> The most offensive thing I did to my brethren was refusing to consult with them. This was an effect of a painful sense of duty to the sick, who are always the sufferers or sacrifices by consultations between physicians of opposite principles and practice. I had often before the year 1793 seen and deplored their consequences, without daring to object to them. At this time I was impressed with a more affecting sense of their folly and wickedness, and to my independence in refusing any longer to

submit to them, I owe the rapidity with which I ripened and established my mode of practice.[70]

Rush would, of course, pay heavily for such independence. In the face of attacks like that made in a proposal by a company of citizens to "drum me out of the city,"[71] he would feel himself forced to resign from the College of Physicians and to establish a competing Academy of Medicine.[72] Other physicians took advantage of his vulnerability to separate him from his patients.

> Many dishonorable arts were employed to shake the confidence of my patients in my remedies by emissaries from the idolaters of bark and wine [an alternative treatment for yellow fever]. One while they were told that I bled people to death, then that I was a horse doctor, and where both their charges failed of their intention, the old slander of *madness* was slyly insinuated against me. In my publication next spring, I hope to divert you with some anecdotes of our citizens and of our physicians that will show their folly, ignorance, and craft in a light that will expose them to the contempt of all wise and good men.[73]

The charge of madness[74] became more than an insinuation by the time of the yellow fever epidemic of 1797, as Samuel Hodgdon makes clear.

> Rush behaves like a Man escaped from Bedlam, he has told two Gentlemen of my acquaintance within two days past, to *fly*, for Contagion was every where, and that respiration could not be performed without the utmost hazard. One of the persons laughed at him, the other whose nerves were not so strong was very much affected. If I should hear such language from him I shall advise him to have his head shaved and take his seat in the Hospital. I am not disposed to be severe upon him, but such speeches coming from *him* will do our City more injury than a thousand such Men and such talents as he has credit for could ever with the best disposition do it good. . . . Good God can the people be any longer deceived by a Mountebank and resign all their comforts into the bloody hand of experiments and inconsistency.[75]

Jean Deveze represented a foreign input into the medical scene in Philadelphia that was resisted much as physicians who had not graduated from Cambridge or Oxford—doctors from universities in Leyden or Edinburgh—were rejected in London. Because Deveze came to Philadelphia from the French Caribbean, he was regarded not only as an extrinsic source, but as a foreign one, in particular a

French one, and, moreover, as a competitor with a view of medical treatment in the Philadelphia epidemic that was contrary to the then-prevailing notion of the city's medical practice. What Deveze brought to the table was his unwillingness to engage in feuding behavior in response to assaults on his attempts to practice medicine, including his continued silence that lasted until he reestablished himself in France. The American doctors who refused to practice with him at the fever hospital conspired by essentially writing him out of the history of the epidemic, using a silent treatment that consigned him to oblivion. Deveze faced off against American doctors in three critical areas—embracing contamination over contagion, clinical autopsies over rational theory, and conservative over heroic therapy—going so far as to propose a contest of experiments to demonstrate his case. Deveze, in sum, refused to play the honor game, and kept his responses within the frame of scientific discourse. His approach threw off American physicians for whom reputation underscored their social practices. Unlike Rush, for whom attacks on his sanity and attempts to drum him out of town constituted not refutable assertions but challengeable offenses, Deveze never considered acting out any more than he would have considered engaging in a "mad" act as a show of power.

CHARLES CALDWELL

Rush was hardly an innocent in his medical interactions, as his relations with his pupils demonstrated. Demanding absolute loyalty, he routinely described newly-rising physicians as adherents to either side of a contest, which led him to write of a newly appointed professor, Dr. Barton, "I consider him as a recruit to the enemies of the new system of medicine, and that he will be supported in proportion as he barks at me."[76] In an interesting side note, Rush acknowledged his oppositional view of events in his private manuscript, which included a cover sheet referring to events that took place in August 1797: "Correspondence relative to some of the tricks and lies of Physicians in which a certain Hugh Hodge appears like a coarse and vulgar Doctor—a certain Revd. A. [?] like, a Jesuit, who'd do anything sooner than justice.—whilst Dr. Wistar appears like a Gentleman."[77]

Among those with whom Rush quarreled, Charles Caldwell, a student of Rush's, found his teacher particularly contentious. He admitted he could have avoided much difficulty and profited greatly had he merely gone along with Rush: "Had I kept in favor with Dr. Rush, by adopting and defending all his opinions, I should have been adopted by him as his successor (for such was his power), and would have inherited, in appearance and public opinion, his reveries and opinions as well as his chair. But I chose to forego the latter rather than bury my reputation under the errors of the former."[78]

Caldwell's initial dispute arose when he accused Rush of having laid claim to a discovery of Caldwell's, a cure for fever based upon getting "thoroughly drenched in a shower of rain . . . the result of an accidental experiment on my own person."[79] At Caldwell's dissertation defense, Rush raged at his pupil over the issue, while a second examiner, Dr. Wistar, who had objected to some points in the dissertation, remained calm and respectful. Caldwell described Rush's behavior from the outset as an attack "rather than a fair and dignified statement of objections made by a professor to the production of a pupil."[80] Caldwell rose to the challenge and Rush, Caldwell reported, was "almost hysterical with rage."[81]

> "Sir, do you know either who *I* am, or who *you* are yourself, when you presume thus arrogantly to address me?"
> "Know you, sir?" I calmly, but contemptuously replied. "O! no; that is impossible. But as respects myself, I was, this morning Charles Caldwell; but indignant, as I now am, at *your injustice,* call me, if you please, *Julius Caesar, or one of his descendants!'*[82]

Rush was the only one of Caldwell's professors who refused to sign the student's diploma. He made it clear, according to Caldwell, that "except on certain conditions performed on my part, the doors of the school would be certainly closed against me."[83]

Caldwell pursued his charges against Rush irrespective of the risk. As a student, he read a paper at the medical society, where Rush's "theory guard,"[84] Caldwell's derisive term for Rush's student posse, was in attendance. When the other students argued with him from the floor, Caldwell responded, "I feel always justified in stating the truth, whatever of suspicion or even of blame it may throw on the character of either a professor or of a professor's prompt, but unnecessary defender."[85] He followed up by calling upon Rush to give a fair interpretation to the matter and admit his debt to his pupil.

Even after Caldwell became a professor himself, he continued his attacks on Rush. He provoked him by announcing a public lecture in which he would openly combat Rush on the latter's view of the "Brunonian hypothesis of life,"[86] a unitary theory that proposed all disease was a variation of a single disease.[87] A few days later, attending a lecture by a colleague, Dr. Coxe, Caldwell found himself once again the object of taunts from Rush's "theory guard." The event as he described it is worth quoting at length.

no sooner was his lecture concluded than there arose a loud but not a general hiss. . . . At first, I believed that the mark of disrespect was designed for Dr. Coxe. And so indeed did the professor himself, and was momentarily much disconcerted and agitated by it; and the class itself became highly excited. At length a voice exclaimed: "Caldwell—it is Caldwell that is hissed—not Dr. Coxe." I then advanced into a more conspicuous part of the room and with a menacing action of my arms toward the place from which the sound had reached me, exclaimed in a calm and contemptuous voice: "I know of but three sorts of vermin that vent their spleen by hissing; an enraged cat, a viper, and a goose; and I knew not till now, that either of them infested this room." On this, from the same quarter came the cry: "Turn him out! turn him out!" And there was immediately around me a party of my own pupils, chiefly from the States of Georgia and Kentucky, to whom I was communicating instruction by lectures and examinations; and who, apprehensive that I might be assaulted, requested me to accompany them out of the room, and they would protect me. My immediate reply, calm and courteous, but as positive as words and manner could make it, was: "I thank you, gentlemen, for your proffered kindness; but I do not need it. I can protect myself." Raising then my voice, so as to be heard throughout the room, I added: "From this spot I will not move, until those insolent fellows shall have left the room, unless they remain in it (looking at my watch) until twelve o"clock, at which time I must leave it myself to make good an engagement. And should any one of them have the audacity to approach me as an assailant, he shall have abundant cause to remember his impudence and deplore his rashness until the end of his life, which may perhaps be nearer at hand than he is prepared to imagine; for I will precipitate him to the bottom of this pit, and determine by experiment which is the thicker and harder, his brain-pan or that brick floor."

Thus terminated in peace the petty affair that had commenced in hostility. No one, my own pupils excepted, approached me. The defeated gang of insulters left the room, and in a few minutes afterward I followed them, accompanied by my manly and faithful adherents.[88]

A series of notes from students appeared in Rush's manuscripts related to the disputed discovery that had caused Caldwell such grief. One by one, Rush's pupils—including John B. Otto, W. Allstory, and Sam Cooper,[89] among others—wrote to support Rush. In one case, a student expressed appreciation for a recommendation letter Rush had written. Certifying the priority of their mentor's claim, either because he had published or lectured on the matter before Caldwell made his claim, the notes appeared to have been solicited by Rush.

Rush's sensitivity on the issue of the loyalty of his students left him vulnerable to their being seduced away by other faculty, as he suggested in his autobiography. Citing the "secret hostility to me in many of my brethren," he noted that "One of my brethren discovered his enmity to me in constant efforts to dissuade the students of medicine from attending my lectures."[90] In his later years, Rush was to look back at the squabble over bragging rights to the presumed discovery, among other events involving Caldwell, with a perspective that demonstrated how deeply he was invested in the support of his pupils. He wrote to his youngest son James, himself a physician, that "Dr. Caldwell's opposition and hostility to me have met with a severe check. In consequence of his saying the students would attend his lectures, were they not afraid of old Rush blackballing them when they were examined for degrees, the whole class met and expressed their indignation against him and at the same time passed a very flattering vote in favor of your father. The next day afterwards (for his impudence is equal to his vices) he was refused admittance into the lecturing room by the janitor of the University."[91]

Caldwell himself went on to become a lifetime master of the medical feud. He claimed victory, for example, over Rush's beloved Brunonianism, asserting that it "finally expired on the death of Dr. Rush, and was inhumed in the grave of its illustrious defender."[92] Caldwell took even greater pleasure in the thought that he had precipitated the death of President Smith of Princeton merely by the use of his pen, the ultimate use of the power of rhetoric.[93] The origin of his contentious nature, interestingly, was not much different from Rush's, as Caldwell confessed in his autobiography. Arguing much like a conspiracy theorist, Caldwell painted himself as a figure envied by his competitors, connived against, and ultimately forced to respond to unprovoked calumny.

> My associations in the army had been with some of the ablest and most distinguished men of the country and the age. . . . No wonder, therefore, that I felt, or conceived I felt, a decided superiority to most medical pupils, as well as the ordinary cast of young physicians. . . . On account of

it, feelings of hostility against me were engendered, petty combinations formed, and corresponding schemes devised and concocted, to thwart me in designs I was believed to be meditating. And some . . . ripened at length into malicious conspiracies, which seriously impeded me in my career of ambition. But for their influence, it is highly probable that I should never have migrated from Philadelphia to the West. . . . by that confederacy of the high and low, the richly gifted and the deeply unprincipled, my schemes of ambition in Philadelphia were defeated.[94]

As Caldwell's autobiography makes clear, his feuds were planned and executed with care to identify both opposition and support for his position. In the lecture on Brunonianism, for example, he was well aware that he faced the resentment of the Rush claque, but was encouraged by those who applauded the lecture: "By some of my friends this unequivocal throw of the gauntlet was regretted and condemned, as an act uncalled for and injudicious, which would necessarily augment toward me the resentment of Dr. Rush and his friends. By others it was applauded as a manly and independent measure, which would enable me to display to the best advantage whatever of resources and power I might possess.[95]

In an earlier foray to snag a professorship to succeed Rush at the University of Pennsylvania, a position ultimately awarded to Nathaniel Chapman, Caldwell was more nuanced in his approach, conceding his chances once he weighed his possible support: "The number that *proffered* me their aid was far too large to be all accepted: but the number well qualified to give aid worth acceptance, was too small for my purpose."[96]

Like many of their altercations with other colleagues, the dispute between Rush and Caldwell ebbed and flowed with a considerable period of intervening peace. The peace was unfortunately breached by the interference of a rumor circulated against Caldwell to which Caldwell strenuously objected. Physician factions appear to have played a role in renewing the dissension between the two men, to which Caldwell adverted in a letter: "Much to my injury, yet more to my surprise, a report I am told, was yesterday propagated through the medical class, that I had offered to you a personal insult in a note written to you in relation to my lecture on the physiology of the spleen."[97] Caldwell appealed to Rush's "candour and magnanimity," for, as he wrote, "you well know that no note of any description has ever passed from me to you on the subject of any lecture I have yet delivered or mean to deliver." Caldwell made clear that he attributed the rumor to an enemy, once his friend, and that it was advanced without his knowledge; he advised the gentlemen who attended his lecture not to report the rumor further. Caldwell closed by putting himself on the side of the angels in the hope of repairing the breach in civility: "notwithstanding what has occurred between us to interrupt our intercourse of civilities which had continued for years, and which I am so unconscious of having been the first to sever, I take pleasure in subscribing myself your obedient and very humble servant."

Charles Caldwell exposed a view of feuding behaviors in which an uneven power balance led to bullying and appropriating the work of the less powerful, together with an expectation of concessions and deference. Benjamin Rush's students were in a position in which they had to curry favor, join in his "theory guard" posse, and feed his ego or risk being denied the support they needed—a signature on their degree or a letter of recommendation—to complete their training and move forward with job prospects. Rush went so far as to ambush Caldwell at his dissertation defense to punish his student's failure to fall in line. Rush expanded feuds by means of a body of inferior henchmen who joined him in carping at and drowning out resisters to his authority. Professors themselves competed for student loyalists, influencing students to avoid attending other professors' lectures and to ostracize other professors. Feuds became so endemic that even fledgling professors like Caldwell became expert at them, to the point of taking pleasure in destroying careers by means of a poisonous pen. Self-justifying belief in conspiracies enabled feuders to maintain their self-regard as so superior that others' jealousy led to attacks. Feuds thus became an ongoing defense system. They led to counting heads to calculate whether a critical mass of supporters provided a more favorable cost-benefit ratio or whether a strategic concession might be more in order under less than optimal conditions. Tactical decisions ensued that assured successful execution of feuds, putting oneself on the innocent side of breaches of the peace and guaranteeing deniability when rumors got out of control.

NATHANIEL CHAPMAN

Nathaniel Chapman, the physician who filled Rush's professorship when he left the University of Pennsylvania, had also been

Rush's pupil. In his dissertation, he had defended Rush and, as Rush acknowledged, Chapman suffered for that association with his professor: "I told you that I *suspected* your having been my pupil was a disadvantage to you. I was led to assay this opinion in cognesence of your telling me soon after you [returned?] from Engd that Dr. Wistar had never spoken to you since you had lived with me."[98] According to Rush, as Chapman went into practice he began to understand, as Caldwell had, that being affiliated with Rush would prove a problem.

> After failing to get into business and suspecting that his former connection with me was a bar to his success with that class of people in our city who possess patronage in everything but power, he began to calumniate me. For this, he has been cherished by all our physicians who are opposed to my system of medicine, for "parties," as General Gates used to say, "like armies, receive all able-bodied men." He has publicly renounced my medical principles and said all that I have ever written "is fit only to rot upon a dunghill." I am not moved by this instance of ingratitude, for I am accustomed to much greater.[99]

As for Chapman, he contended that Rush had offended in several particulars, but the most egregious was Rush's interference in an appointment to a professorship, to Chapman's detriment. Rush advised his former pupil to abandon his application in favor of a candidate, Dr. Dewees, to whom Rush felt obligated.[100] According to Chapman's biographer, Rush essentially denied Chapman's charges while Chapman failed to provide evidence that would support his complaint.[101] But no apology was forthcoming on either side, and since Rush demanded either withdrawal of the complaint or an apology, the relationship remained a wounded one. Rush was reputed by Chapman to be unwilling to serve at Pennsylvania Hospital should Chapman be appointed there as a physician. Once again, Rush threatened to resign if an appointment was made to which he objected.[102] Chapman, by contrast, was in the untenable position of having to produce positive proof of his charges. He could, he claimed, provide proof, but preferred not to. His presumed excuse, according to Rush's son James, was on the order of gossip and innuendo: "A few days after, Dr. R. heard accidentally in the city that Dr. C. has *put it about* that he had proofs but that his authority was a lady!! And she refused to be brought forward in the affaire and thus much for the *charges, arguments,* and *proofs* of this Knight of the Lying Trumpet."[103]

"Cudgeling as by Late Act of Congress, U.S.A. or————. Etching by C. P. Eldwood,
1798. Essex Institute, Salem, MA. In Martin P. Snyder, *City of Independence: Views of
Philadelphia Before 1800* (New York: Henry Holt & Co.).

Chapman was no innocent in the field of feuds, having had five
running feuds over time with physicians and duels with two of them.
Capable of being quite provocative, Chapman made "scandalous
and unfounded reports" about a doctor, Granville Sharp Pattison,
with whom he maintained a long-running feud. That feud not only
wound up in print but resulted in a challenge to a duel. Chapman
declined to accept, citing a thirteen-year disparity in their ages to
Patisson's disadvantage, which resulted in his being posted in a bill
to the public. The bill read, "Whereas when properly applied to,
[Nathaniel Chapman M.D] has refused to give any explanation of
his conduct, or the satisfaction which every gentleman has a right to
demand, and which no one having any claim to that character, can
refuse, I am therefore compelled to the only step left me, and Post
the said Dr. Nathaniel Chapman, as a Liar, a Coward and a Scoundrel."[104]

The threat of being challenged to a duel, of having to fight one
or be posted, was more than an outside chance for those involved in
feuds, which meant that parties prepared to go to the wall had an

advantage over others with more to lose. Given Rush's volatility and his reputation for a kind of professional suicide, his pupils, the faculty at the medical school, and practicing physicians who ran afoul of him had to have recognized that they were on thin ice with Rush, especially where his reputation was concerned. His pupils in particular were sensitive to the need to remain on Rush's good side and to retain his good will.[105] The risk of failing to stay in favor was reflected in correspondence where Rush, feeling himself unsatisfied, made veiled threats that suggested the imminent prospect of further action. In one matter that amounted to a charge of malpractice, Rush, for example, threatened legal action: "Having been informed that you have reported that I bled young [?] to death, and that I had mistaken the gout for a yellow fever in [?], I take this method of informing you, that you must immediately prove or deny those aspersions as I shall avail myself of the protection which the laws of the state afford for reputation by suing you for defam[ation]."[106]

In a draft letter, Rush outlined the tactics he planned to use. He referred to a published report propagated by the author of the remark and revealed his intent to publish a certificate of testimony contradicting the report. The reader was offered the opportunity to show the as yet unpublished certificate to the gentleman to whom he had related the story, in which case Rush would erase the reader's name from the certificate. The accusation was withdrawn within a day by its author.[107] With the dispute settled on his terms, Rush proved generous: "I am perfectly satisfied with your conduct. The certificate shall not be published in any form. I lament with you the occasion of a dispute with a neighbour, and join you in its being so happily settled and beg you to believe that I am with usual respect your friend and well wisher."[108] As he often did, Rush expressed his concern as not for himself but for his patients who relied upon his "opinions and prescriptions. I have for *their sakes* determined to investigate and expose every falsehood that is propagated against me and when it is actionable, to prosecute the author of them."[109] Positioning himself strategically in line with the presumed welfare of his patients, Rush sought thereby to avoid an accusation by appealing to the collective welfare of them all.

The actions Rush threatened against his accusers, as we have seen, could be formal or informal, including going public in the press, filing charges for slander, or challenging them to a duel. Rush was not alone in becoming involved in threats of physical violence. We find physician duels and canings alluded to or explicitly referenced related not only to Rush but to doctors Charles Caldwell, Nathaniel Chapman, and Andrew Ross, as well as Rush's sons John and Richard and the journalist William Cobbett, among others with whom Rush came into contact. In his affair with Chapman, for example, Doctor Pattison referred to his nemesis not only as someone whom he had challenged to a duel but as one who had himself challenged another doctor, Doctor Dewees. In spite of Chapman's reluctance to accept his challenge, Pattison noted that Chapman "had always been an advocate for dueling and had about three weeks before I wrote him, declared on the steps of his own door, to several students, and one medical gentleman, that if I did not keep quiet at Baltimore he would call me out and blow out my brains. . . . He astonished every one with the history of his prowess, and spoke much of ten paces."[110]

In sum, Nathaniel Chapman's feuding raised the question of strategizing, factions, and successful coalitioning. Having found that his association with Rush made him the enemy of Rush's enemies, Chapman felt he had a greater likelihood of success in publicly accusing Rush and thereby gaining the good will of those whom Rush had offended. Chapman's feuds revealed as well the hidden nature of behaviors that worked out of sight to manipulate and control others. Asserting his power to procure a professorship for another candidate, Rush tried to pressure Chapman to stand down. Chapman's refusal to accede or to remain silent drove the event until it became a fully fledged public feud which neither party would resolve by apologizing. Chapman used gossip as his weapon, refusing to provide evidence of his accusation against Rush and claiming the honor of a woman as his excuse. The wound remained open and, as he had done with Shippen's application for an appointment to the Philadelphia medical college, Rush threatened resignation if Chapman was given privileges at Pennsylvania Hospital.

Quid pro quo operated as a balancing mechanism in many of the social practices that informed Rush's feuds. His threat of further action if accusations were not withdrawn matched to a promised generosity in victory were often more than enough to ensure Rush an infusion of reputational capital to keep his feud machinery well oiled. As a fall-back position, the ever-resilient Rush could repair to a standard defense of his patients whose welfare and continued trust in him as a physician required that he investigate and engage all assaults upon his reputation.

Like Caldwell, Chapman soon learned that gaining a reputation for successful feuding was essential to keeping up his honor. As a result, he became adept at challenging duels, which left him at risk of having his bluff called. Those with exceptional resources or nothing to lose had an advantage when faced with such challenges. This left Chapman in at least one case on the distaff side of a feud, posted publicly in print as a coward.

RUSH'S SONS

As instructive as feuds and duels involving Rush's pupils and his colleagues, those involving Rush's sons demonstrated the ways in which feuds metastasize to catch up a variety of adjunct parties and to create a network of feuders. The caning of Dr. Andrew Ross by Rush's elder son John in a case of mistaken identity provided a case in point. Ross was presumed to be the author of a published piece titled "Respecting Dr. Rush's Conduct and Transactions During the Prevalence of the Malignant Fever of 1793," the source of which was actually Dr. William Currie.[111] Although Ross twice denied being the author of the piece, John Rush still penned a note challenging Ross to a duel that extended the feud from one in defense of his father's name to one that now implicated his own reputation and honor: "The impolite manner in which you treated my note of this morning, and the epithet of an *impertinent puppy* which you have applied to me, demand satisfaction. If you refuse to give it to me, I shall consider you as a scoundrel, and treat you accordingly."[112] Accompanied by what William Cobbett called "one of Rush's young doctors," John Rush delivered the note in person and set upon Ross first with his fists and then with a cane. Concluding that the assault was at the instigation of the father, Dr. Ross felt provoked to request a meeting with the elder Rush: "Doctor Ross requests Doctor Rush to meet him to-morrow morning in the Jersies with a friend. Mr. Walker will let him know time and place."[113] The exchanges that followed were reported by Cobbett as follows.

Rush.—"Doctor Rush wishes to know for *what purpose* he is to meet Doctor Ross to-morrow morning in the Jersies."
Ross.—"Doctor Ross will let Doctor Rush know when they meet."
Rush.—"Doctor Rush's time being much engaged at present, he cannot consent to leave town, without knowing *the business* he is to go upon."
Ross.—"The sole purpose of the meeting is to have *personal satisfaction*

of Doctor Rush for the ruffian assault of his son this morning, of which he considers the Doctor as the sole instigator."[114]

Led like a fly into Rush's spider's web, Ross unwittingly provided him with the unequivocal language he would need to prosecute. Rush responded, "Sir, I do not fear death, but I dare not offend God, by exposing myself, or a *fellow-creature,* to the chance of committing murder; I have not injured you, and I freely forgive you all the injuries you have attempted to do me. The treatment you received this morning from my son was not instigated directly or indirectly by me; *it was occasioned by your calling him an impertinent puppy.* Your note, without that insulting language, would have satisfied him."[115] In these words, Rush declined the challenge and the very next morning opened criminal prosecution against Ross. A warrant was sworn and Rush had Ross seized, although Ross's friends immediately provided bail.[116] The proliferation of charges and counter-charges and the swelling of the ranks of those involved typified the way in which feuds worked and how easily they got out of hand.

A second incident in which John Rush came to his father's defense concerned William Cobbett. A friend of the family, Brockholst Livingston, was dispatched by Benjamin Rush to prevent an anticipated attack by his son John against Cobbett, a case in which his father depicted John lying in wait "in a sailor's *undress* near Cobbett's door."[117] According to Cobbett, John Rush delivered a challenge which the former, who appeared brandishing a poker, refused to accept, leading his attacker to withdraw from the scene. Benjamin Rush considered that a second libel suit against Cobbett (a first, having succeeded handsomely in December 1799)[118] would be necessary to put an end to Cobbett's newspaper campaign against him. More importantly, it would ensure the well-being of his impetuous sons. He penned a letter to this effect to his friend and agent Livingston.

To prevent the repetition and continuance of his abuse, Mr. [ ] and Mrs. [ ] advise a suit (criminal or civil as you may think proper) immediately to be instituted against him for his later publications, and if he publishes after the suit is commenced, to have him confined and fined for a contempt of court. Surely your judges and citizens will not be tame or indifferent spectators of the outrages offered by (*him*) an alien to the laws and courts of a sister state—much less can they hear without sympathy and honor of the risk (*I run every hour*) a grayheaded and inoffensive citizen runs every hour of his life of hearing of murder being connected in one way or other with the names of his sons.

I leave this business wholly to your judgment and friendship. Let nothing be done in it unless you are sure the force of law can be effectively employed to silence him [Cobbett], and thereby to restore my sons to calmness and safety. You are a father. *Feel* and *act* as you would wish me to do for your children in a similar situation. If assistance be necessary in conducting this business, call upon Colonel Burr or any other of your eminent lawyers. Your services shall be liberally compensated.[119]

The Rush sons, particularly John, were hardly novices in such affairs. Rush in his autobiography referred to John as "in a state of deep melancholy brought on by killing a brother officer in the Navy, who was his intimate friend, in a Duel."[120] His middle son Richard assaulted Dr. Glentworth for a comment attributed to him in a piece published by Cobbett.[121] In yet another instance, Richard crossed the Delaware River to fight a duel, only to shoot into the air rather than at his opponent.[122]

Feuds risked being transformed into duels just as one duel fought raised the likelihood of additional challenges to a duel. Those who had yet to generate a reputation found they could do so on the cheap by challenging someone who had himself already earned a reputation. By contrast, those who fought many duels felt driven to proffer challenges to up-keep their honor and reinforce the seriousness of engaging with them in feuds. On another level, duels were often useful not in themselves but as a referent, as the end point of a continuum. Thus, written challenges, caning, posting, mediation, and concessions at the behest of a second all became stations visited as one bore the cross of dueling to its ultimate destination. A party could get off the path at any of its stops. As Rush's sons indicated, the momentum toward a duel could be interrupted in many ways. As Rush himself demonstrated, it could be diverted into litigation if a party managed things just right. That feuds led as often as they did to duels was an indication of the failure of feuds to have a desired effect without paying the high cost of one's life. Indeed, many duels were fought over accusations that were lower-level insults than those which were the subject of most feuds.

CONCLUSION

In sum, medical feuds in Philadelphia occurred, among other things, over competition for appointments to teach at a medical school, whether one had to be a physician to become a member of a medical faculty, who could vote on a candidate for a medical degree, the granting of honorary degrees to non-physicians so they could teach medicine, the appointment of foreign doctors to teach medicine, and attributions of discoveries as well as attempts by doctors to smear other doctors by circulating rumors.[123] Disruptive feuds of the sort we have examined would continue until medicine was stabilized as a profession by licensing and training requirements, delineation of privileges, protection of trade secrets, standards for accountability and liability, as well as assurances over fee setting and collection. The factionalism among physicians within the field of medicine along with the patronage that existed both there and in relations between physicians and patients were among the leading factors responsible for feuds. Doctors were already wary of accusations that aggressive or heroic therapy had given their sectarian and quack competitors an excuse to accuse them of risking their patients by means of extreme measures and of "blind allegiance to theory and rationalism."[124] Doctors remained open targets as long as contention reigned in their ranks, so that irregular practitioners could capitalize on the disunity of regular physicians and their subversive attacks on one another's therapies.

So long as feuding was a dominant way of addressing conflict, doctors would find that they would be denied the public support they needed to establish medicine as a profession and that their professional solidarity would be undermined. Improvements in the medical field would be blocked by doctors who felt that experimental treatments would open a free field for new attacks against them and that attempts to treat those cases most in need of treatment would leave them liable.[125] In a treatise on yellow fever addressed to Philadelphians in 1803, the same combination of envy, contention, and self-interest was attacked for keeping doctors from organizing in the interest of the profession and for keeping medical science from developing new therapies. The anonymous author, Plain Truth, directed his remarks to the public, intent that they would grasp the truth of "plain language" and common sense, which medical men appeared to have lost.[126]

When an author makes a discovery of any kind, who are his enemies?
1. Those he contradicts.
2. They who envy his reputation.
3. Those whose interests are opposite to that of the public.

The advocate for the public felicity is the Martyr of the truths he reveals. What is the cause of this? The too great influence of some members of society. . . . if the cry of envy, Ignorance, and Interest are raised against the author of the truth, and he be not protected either by law, or people in power, he is lost. A man therefore purchases his future retribution by present misfortune.

. . . . He who speaks the truth, doubtless exposes himself to persecution, and is imprudent. Imprudent men, are therefore the most useful sort of men. . . .

The greatest impediment to the progression of truth, is the warp of authority. The signature of great men, suspends our close enquiry, and thereby the detection of oppressive errors, is too long delayed. Let us believe that great men are liable to serious errors, within the reach of inferior minds.[127]

Once the public latched onto a view of medicine as a profession rooted in science with a mission of public service, the order of social norms with its feuds and duels and its nonlegal order based on common experience began coming to a close. Moving a short step closer to legal order, professionalism made issues more explicit and negotiable. It undermined ambiguity and was solution oriented, so that the hidden nature of feuds began to be closed off and long-term resolutions became more likely. Precedents were set so that conflicts could check with the past; the present, no longer a stand-alone event, was thereby less likely to be repeatable.

Framing issues as "professional" allowed the profession to inform social practices. Medical profession, that is, scientific, framing medicalized a problem, stating it within a medical frame, from a medical perspective, using medical rules and conventions and privileging a professional way of being. Unlike feuding, professionally framed practices did not create reputation or support a norm of honor linked to a disorderly form of order. For a profession to grow and stabilize, old norms would have to be superseded, and a tight pattern match developed so that professional knowledge and relations would have greater regularity, precision, and predictability. The value ascribed to profession was, like the value of honor, a form of capital, and, like legal order, a form of order. Nevertheless, it did not rise to the level of honor as a totalizing social code, nor was it on the same order as law as an ultimate form of order.

As we have seen, social norms in the world of feuds reinforced only retributive justice, not corrective or distributive, so that for many they were neither efficient nor fair, nor were they deterrents for the most part. Insofar as they allowed for forceful private resolutions, they disturbed public order. As a form of self-help, they were thus problematic for the group as a whole and would be resisted both for the reputation of the group and for their acceptance by group members. If feuds were welfare-maximizing for more than the party that prevailed in the feud, perhaps they would have reaffirmed social norms as a model, but based as they were on a win/lose model, they had not this benefit either.

Feuds were high stakes gambles insofar as they entailed risks of being blown into larger altercations and going public, both of which led to losing control of the feud event. A form of disorderly order rather than lawlessness, feuds acted as a code, a way of being, and were characterized by high ambiguity in terms of the truth value of claims made, their indeterminate resolutions, and the conditions of informational deprivation under which they were conducted. Tending to lose/lose opportunities at worst and win/lose resolutions at best, feuds led to minimal order (synchronically, within a slice of time) and were continually unraveling (diachronically, across time). As negative disagreement spirals, they had high reputational costs for both parties, conducing to "cat and mouse" games over small stakes and games of "chicken" over larger ones. Not only did feuds carry high costs, but they had low deterrence value for future altercations, were amenable to mistakes, and encouraged cheating. In terms of acquiring or revealing information, they had flat learning curves, poor efficiency, and poor adaptability, requiring constant reassessment of agreement or consensus, which was always temporary and contingent.

Losses to the group constituted risks as well as costs, just as if the group had been a party to a feud without the prospect of reaping any reputational gains. Groups thereby became involuntary monitors of individual feuds which entailed unreimbursable expenses as well as undesired responsibilities as enforcers. Clientelism that had begun as a reward for group membership—delivering services and creating networks—became part of a punishment regime, a source of sanctions. Because change was thereby stultified, growth occurred in the direction of breaches in the collective order, largely the result of self-interested individual violations.

As long as physicians remained integrated within a community and could appeal to religious sentiment and the physician's beneficent communal role, feuds were tolerated as they did not assault community harmony or its cultural order. Here, reputation acted as a social glue and maintained a moral component that reinforced a stable world view based on community consensus, a view that made legal order superfluous. Groups were socially homogeneous and conflicts largely remained at a low level or did not rise beyond a socially acceptable disagreement. Conflicts did, however, marginalize outside groups, which led to mob actions, like the resurrection riots, that would ultimately require access to the courts.

Refusing a challenge to a duel was a sign of movement toward legal order, just as the rejection of capricious conflict-resolution that led to taking a case to court was a sign of transfer to a new order that gave priority to logic and support of evidence, evenhanded treatment, and due process. Taking issues to court inscribed a controversy as juridical, marking rules and conventions in terms of legal relevance. Universal and autonomous, the law institutionalized norms that then became naturalized. Once people felt the law was made for them and that it served them better than social norms, the presumed neutrality and anonymity of legal order would emerge and self-censorship—both individual and collective—would be relaxed. The new order would pose its own opportunities and risks, which competition and entrepreneurship would soon reveal without many of the constraints reputation and honor entailed but with many of their traditions still intact. The dramatic and memorable punishments of the world of feuds and duels might be missing, but stability was waiting in the wings to take their place.

5

Medical Feuds in the Revolutionary Army

MEDICAL FEUDS PROVIDE INSIGHTS INTO THE WAYS MEDICINE OPERATED at ground level in the eighteenth century. Personal feuds related to status ranged from other physicians poaching one's patients and medical students to competition over professional appointments and claims to innovations. They soon cascaded into such larger-scale medical issues as feuds over the founding of the first medical school in the nation, the organization of military medicine, and the management of epidemics. Feuding thus disturbed an already fragile balance in the profession, allowing us to interrogate practices and put forward some hypotheses to explain the workings of medicine at both the individual and the institutional levels. We have viewed how feuds operating within a nonlegal order erupted into violent acts ranging from beatings to duels. We have watched how unregulated competition divided the profession and how unresolved social conflicts led to mob actions and riots. It remains to examine an area in which we find feuds emerging from the realm of social norms and transitioning from a nonlegal order to a legal order in a trial, in this case a court-martial.

Where social organization is made up of small cohesive groups, law is an unwieldy alternative, largely because of freely shared information and the fact that people know the value of each other's reputations. Based upon trust, custom, and status, a community develops solidarity and operates through self-censorship to reinforce insider identification with the group, which prevents defections and keeps outsiders from infiltrating. Conformity to accepted norms operates as a control mechanism that can invoke resistance, sponsor threats, or provide for payoffs. As part of the social norm system that guides conformity, a certain amount of entrepreneurship exists that is competitive and can increase one's payoffs or that can lead to feuding. In either case, interactions occur through signals that are sent and responded to. Some signals are individually tailored to advantage a member of the group and some are sent merely so that one will be compensated not to send them. However they are used, signals are central to nonlegal order as gatekeepers and opportunity creators.

The nonlegal order is strategic in that whoever controls information or demonstrates he has and is capable of using his reputational status can drive out less successful strategies. What is critical here is the willingness and ability to advertise one's reputation in order to preserve it and to preempt attacks upon it. When reputation has been attacked, going public has the advantage of making the stakes higher for one's adversary, but risks at the same time spreading damaging information about oneself. Such public humiliation has opportunity costs, increasing the shame associated with belonging to a feuding group but also reinforcing order within the group. The larger community, having a stake in such feuds, will itself exert pressure against those who express deviant influences, especially in a public venue, for fear that a loss of control will incur more serious feuding. The process here, so long as groups do not become too large or a dispute does not become too widely spread, can be relatively simple. Informal sanctions are not costly and group members have sunk costs in terms of social and business relations. Thus the nonlegal order only needs to deliver a clear, visible sanction to one party or reward to another to have a powerful effect on the parties as well as the public. All this is without resort to courts or jails and occurs where there is limited government.

Nevertheless, there comes a time when the perception of an unjust result, that is, the unpredictability or inequity of a result, will create a pathology in the nonlegal order that makes groups feel less connected to their community or unrepresented in it. Here, the nonlegal order ceases to be efficient and a legal order becomes imminent. If the state is as yet insufficiently developed, a liminal period will intervene where the benefits of neither the nonlegal nor the legal order are apparent. This situation could easily last until the replacement of one form of order by the other becomes possible or necessary, rather than seeing a gradual transition take place. Certainly where circumstances have outrun a group's skill set or where the stakes are high and a situation complex, the likelihood that a system based entirely upon social norms could survive is small. Here, the legal order would impose itself, with its characteristic virtues of greater neutrality and clarity, with its more transparent set of knowable rules, and with its ability to act predictably in terms of precedents. The situation we face in the dispute between John Morgan and William Shippen is one in which self-organizing rules had not yet been fully replaced by a formal legal order that can be assumed or taken for granted, but where we can view the process of transitioning to it.

We will focus in this final chapter on two cases that shed light on the instability of the law in America of the war years, reflected in changes ranging from the relative power and responsibilities of government officials and judges to rules of witness testimony, standards of evidence, the rule of law, and legal representation. The first case involves the management of hospitals in the revolutionary army under John Morgan, which resulted in his dismissal. The second treats the replacement of Morgan with William Shippen, which resulted in a court-martial. Extensive material offers us an exemplary opportunity not only to hear from the participants themselves but to generate a sense of how they storied the narrative constructions of the events in which they were featured.

John Morgan

Military Hospitals and Medical Organization

John Morgan, the second director general of the Continental Army Hospitals,[1] saw his job as exposing "the waste and depredation of men whose schemes tended to the subversion of the General Hospital, in which they laboured to raise themselves into an importance, which neither the General [Washington] nor Congress ever intended, and from whence have shooted those clamours, against me, which have been so carefully cultivated, with a design to injure my character with the publick, under a pretence of interesting them in the sufferings of the sick, to which the imprudences of others have given rise; and to shift the blame on me."[2]

Morgan framed the events that transpired from his assumption of the role of director general in October 1775 to his dismissal in January 1777. He cited his own "vigilance, care and activity," the plans he devised and the advice he communicated, the evils he foretold and the remedies he proposed. In concert with these, he dramatized himself in terms of "the toils and dangers to which I have continually exposed myself in discharge of my trust, [which] I concluded would always be a sufficient shield to protect me from every affair, till I could have notice of the designs and movements of my ene-

mies, been prepared for my defence, and have had time to have re-
pelled them. Those instances of zeal, diligence and uprightness of
conduct, I hoped, were such, as neither malice could scandalize, nor
envy misinterpret."[3]

Within this oppositional construction, Morgan couched his near-
heroic struggles over the critical months from March to September
1776 to bring Congress and General Washington, the commander
in chief, to recognize and amend festering problems within the
medical division by adopting his plans and endorsing the orders he
devised to exert control over what had become chaotic conditions.
He told the story of a downfall engineered by "a mean and invidious
set of men [who] looked upon my elevation to the rank of Director
General and Physician in Chief with an evil eye."[4] Their chief rationale, and "the root of enmity," Morgan contended, was to oppose
his reforms of abuses with an eye to retaining their right to dissipate
the hospital stores over which Morgan had responsibility.

Having inherited a diffused structure of local regimental hospitals
from a previous organization of the army, Morgan had embraced a
British-style reform of the hospitals.[5] The reform featured a central
general hospital structure that incorporated two strategic flaws.
First, it exacerbated the power struggle between the central hospital,
governed by a newly created appointment by Congress, and existing
established regimental hospitals, governed by surgeons traditionally
appointed by regional commanders.[6] Second, it allowed Morgan's
opponents to accuse him of affection for and complicity with the
British. Morgan's colonial experience left him possessed of "a strict
discipline, to which he had been accustomed the whole of the last
successful war,"[7] which predisposed him to British-style organization. After his dismissal from the army and while he was accusing
Shippen of undermining the medical department,[8] he became
much too familiar with the British occupiers of Philadelphia, which
led to suspicions about his own loyalties.

Morgan's career trajectory was structured by several internal splits
during his tenure as director general that undermined the authority
he brought to his struggle to gain control over the army hospitals.
The most critical initial event was the split between his central organization and the Northern medical department headed by Dr. Samuel Stringer. In August 1776, Congress intervened by congressional
order to resolve Stringer's refusal to accept Morgan's authority over
the former's medical department and Stringer's demand for medical stores controlled by Morgan.[9] The division of responsibilities de-

vised by Congress left Morgan vulnerable to conflicts with the directors of other medical units, significantly William Shippen appointed by Congress as director of a hastily convened Flying Camp designed to meet the immediate needs of a British attack on New York.[10] It was Shippen rather than Stringer who would lead Congress to split the army hospital in October into east and west sides of the Hudson (Morgan to the east in New York and Shippen to the west in New Jersey).[11] It was this move that would upend Morgan's authority and install Shippen as director general. Shippen capitalized on themes already in play when he came on board: power struggles over authority of the regimental hospitals; divisional splits between departments; desire for control over hospital stores Morgan had collected for the general hospital; and suspicion of Morgan's British-style reorganization of the army.

What is not clear is the balance of events, how they played out, and which aspect of Morgan's situation was the most critical in sabotaging his efforts as director general. The framework that rises most immediately to hand is Shippen's conspiratorial efforts to avenge himself against Morgan for his role in founding the Medical School of the College of Philadelphia and Morgan's lack of organizational skill and his personal difficulties in sharing authority and in interpersonal relations. This reading is sufficient only if one accepts as determinant the power of an individual to fix the course of history. Once we step back to examine other forces operating in the mix, it becomes apparent that the endemic influence of the regional hospitals, however limited their size or impact individually, offers a story of a disruptive interference in army discipline capable of disabling the ability of an overriding authority to gain and hold control from the center. In addition, the question of order within the continental army itself was a significant factor contributing to Morgan's performance as director general. Morgan's own *Vindication* in defense of his performance as director general revealed a paralyzing obsession with being authorized from without for every significant move he made. Finally, the role played by George Washington as a countervailing force was to leave Morgan dependant upon what some called a moderating and others a vacillating authority.[12] Washington's input was unlikely either to rescue him from above or to allow him sufficient power on paper to exert his own rescue. Washington's diplomatic style led him to avoid issues he could not resolve. Morgan, by contrast, played a confrontational role in which he insisted upon receiving his full complement of rights as a legal subject. This posture vindicated him, even as it savaged Shippen, but not without first costing him whatever remaining good will he might have commanded within the medical unit and within the general command.

To grasp the kind of administration that constrained him, it is worth considering the controls to which Morgan was subject. To begin, Morgan's original job description was vague enough. Congress authorized the director general by means of its Resolve of July 17, 1775, in the following terms: "Director and Chief Physician to furnish medicines, bedding and all other necessaries; to pay for the same; superintend the whole; and to make his report to, and receive orders from the Commander in Chief."[13] As relates to his staff, Congress's "Minutes" further resolved "That the appointment of the four Surgeons, and the Apothecary be left to the Director General and Chief Physician."[14] Within three months of his appointment, Morgan appealed to General Washington to clarify the charge. On these terms, he claimed, he was not instructed to furnish every regiment from hospital stores "as though it was a store house, or magazine for the whole army" rather than for the sick and wounded.[15] What Morgan considered even more unaccountable was that regimental surgeons never "thought it their duty to make any report to me of the state of their sick, to leave me room to judge of the propriety of issuing or of refusing to issue out whatever stores they are pleased to call for."[16] In an attempt to support Morgan's position of director general, Major General Nathanael Greene provided him with a letter that did, indeed, try to navigate the stormy waters Morgan's authorization had left him in.

> You may remember I called upon you while I had the command on Long Island for the plan of the General Hospital. This I did as well to satisfy myself of your proper line of duty, as to convince the Commanding Officers of Regiments that you had not such extensive powers as they seemed to conceive of.
>
> It was from reading the Hospital establishment and finding you limited in your powers and seeing the distressed of the Regimental sick, without the possibility of a remedy, that I was induced to write to the General of the absolute necessity of some further provision being made for the Regimental Surgeons and the Hospitals under their care. . . .
>
> It was about this time that I wrote to Congress from Fort Lee urging them, the necessity of enlarging your powers, as well as to give you an opportunity to silence the clamour against you, as to do justice to the service.[17]

Honest to a fault, Morgan was willing to accept blame, but only to a point: "As to that part of the charge which relates to my withholding the hospital stores from the regimental Surgeons, in order to oblige them to send their sick to the General Hospital, I acknowledge the fact, but deny the reason which malicious Surgeons and some other officers have assigned to it, that of stopping their rations to put in my own pocket."[18] To that end, Morgan even provided a testimonial from Joseph Trumbull, commissary general of the American army, who informed the *Pennsylvania Gazette* readers that he had examined his own books and clerks and that neither Morgan nor "any General Hospital Physician or Surgeon whatever" had been paid a "SINGLE PENNY," whereas numerous regimental surgeons had in fact been paid "LARGE SUMS."[19]

The issue of hospital stores was to morph well beyond Morgan's control. The regimental hospitals justified demands made on the stores by contrasting the steady state of hospital stores with their own devastatingly depleted resources.[20] Dr. Stringer, jealous of Morgan's hoard,[21] made demands on behalf of the Northern Department. The Medical Committee of Congress itself, Morgan's supervisory superiors, coopted stores from Morgan's sources in Philadelphia. Frustrated by complaints from the army, the committee set up its own treatment facility in that city without advising Morgan.[22] Shippen, as director of the Hospital of the Flying Camp, accused Morgan of hoarding supplies that went unused for a period of three months, to the overall detriment of the army.[23]

In his defense, Morgan told a tale of corruption and profiteering without accountability on the part of regiments and without supervision by the director general, a greater crime which he was obliged to oversee and reform. Having stabilized the General Hospital, he expressed a proprietary interest in maintaining his creation in a healthy state as a legacy of his contribution to the war effort. As General Greene testified in the letter Morgan had solicited, "I do not recollect . . . that there were any complaints of the sick suffering much in the General Hospitals. The complaints and sufferings of the sick were principally among the Regimental Hospitals for want of medicine and other necessities."[24] Regiments were issued restricted stores for which they had to produce an order balancing their needs and hospital resources. As Morgan structured the process, they were to order "in such quantities, as their present occasions may require, but so as not to unfurnish the hospital, or exhaust the stock, faster than I can get a fresh supply."[25] Nothing if not a faithful bureaucrat, Morgan was determined to put a stop to officers supplying their own tables from the veal or mutton of hospital stores.[26]

> Cordials and refreshments were drawn by others, from the stores of the General hospital, which by the parts some of the officers took in supporting the demands of those men, gave room for many to believe they shared in the plunder themselves.
>
> Is it any wonder, on being repeatedly informed of these particulars, that I put a total stop to the unauthorized practice of the regimental Surgeons drawing stores from the General hospital, without obliging them to be accountable for the same?[27]

Were he to gratify, Morgan claimed, all the requests addressed to him as director general by officers, regimental surgeons, and even doctors in the provinces who served officers in a private capacity, he "would exceed all the expences of the whole army besides."[28] For Morgan, the question was clearly one of refusing to supply "whatever their unbounded appetites and fancies craved from the General hospital." He refused to subvent charges of five pounds a day for "attendance on common soldiers, who ailed but little" or to turn a blind eye to regimental surgeons who sold soldiers places on the sick list.[29]

Morgan's tale of the limits of his authority constituted his best defense. His commission, he asserted, "only extends to the care of the HOSPITAL itself; and yet every regimental Surgeon, apparently, expects me to supply him with whatever he wants, and to prepare every thing to his hand, or to lay the odium of his deficiency at my door."[30] Fully cognizant that his denials would be widely decried, Morgan pushed forward to establish clear lines of command and the legitimacy of Congress's resolves. A literal reader of those resolves, he was unwilling to legislate on his own beyond them.

> the cry of the regimental Surgeons is, there is no provision made for us. "My answer is, nor have I any orders to provide for any but what are under my own direction in the General hospital. They ask where they are to get instruments and dressings, and what use are they, if left unprovided. I refer them to their commanding officers, and to make representations of their situation to them, to apply to Congress to establish means of furnishing what they want; whatever orders are given me, they shall be obeyed, but I cannot go beyond my instructions."[31]

For Morgan, orders represented a higher reality that conferred legitimacy beyond mere facts on the ground or high principles. As a matter of first priority, written orders constituted justification, recommendation, and interpretation all in one, beyond their usefulness in establishing a record with utility value for personal purposes.

> Where there was an appearance of danger of any misunderstanding or interference with other public designs, my business was transacted by writing to, and by conferring with, some of the then sitting members of Committee, whose approbation I obtained for all I had done. An inventory of those stores which I sent away from hence, for the use of the hospital and army, was left with the Committee, that in case the former owners should return to this city, and by their future conduct be entitled to claim a restitution of their effects, the value might be duly ascertained; and a particular and faithful account of every thing I had done in this affair, was transmitted by letter to the Adjutant General, now Major General Gates, to be laid before the Commander in Chief, and I received his acknowledgments in return, and his approbation not only of the services I had rendered the army, but of the officer-like manner of performing it.[32]

Reliance upon orders was never a mere stratagem with Morgan; it was, rather, a narrative that served as an article of faith. Where other departments maneuvered to avoid obeying orders or feigned acquiescence,[33] Morgan covered himself by traveling to Philadelphia to request the Medical Committee of Congress to clarify the limits and extents of his authority. His relations with Dr. Stringer and the Northern Department offered a typical instance in which he countered reports by several officers defining his responsibilities and made arrangements to visit Philadelphia: "I had received no such orders. As I thought proper regulations were wanting, to ascertain the respective limits of authority, intended by Congress to be vested in myself, and the several Directors, I requested leave to go to Philadelphia, to obtain an audience of a committee of Congress, on that subject, which I obtained."[34]

For Morgan, the desire to be justified by orders was, if not pathological, at least dispositional. Order was so intrinsic that to operate without adherence to rule-bounded discipline was inconceivable, as he expressed in juxtaposing his principled position to the regimental surgeons' "mischief." Demonized for modeling a fearsome resistance to corruption and fraud, he cast himself as one poised to unmask evil and prepared to endure its vicious slanders.

> Nor will the world be astonished to hear of a confederacy amongst persons of such similar tempers, against one who had set his face as flint

against their practices, and stood so much in their way, as having no other idea of duty, than what proceeded from an exact obedience to the orders of his superiors . . . and of which he had seen the good effects; as well as a firm resolution to stand immoveable against every attempt that might open a door to fraud and abuses in the department of which he was constituted head. Nor does he regret that he did so. From a fixt and steady adherence to these principles, he did not expect he should escape the tongue of slander, but was ever determined to conduct himself in such a manner as to be provided with an antidote to its venom, a consciousness of integrity and vouchers for his good conduct. That he has been calumniated on account of the faithful discharge of his duty, ought rather to be an occasion of joy, since that has enabled him to serve the public by unmasking a sett of evil minded persons, and placing them in full view, and thereby ranks him with men of the greatest merit, who have ever met with the reproach, and never could escape the slanders of the envious.[35]

Clarification like that solicited by Morgan was sought by others as well. Both Stringer and Shippen, for example, petitioned to be relieved of having to submit to Morgan's authority.[36] None, apparently, petitioned on their own behalf so well or so frequently as Morgan. Indeed, his appeals became a style of management so widely recognized that he was avoided when he applied for assistance to Samuel Adams of the Medical Committee, to Benjamin Rush when he was a member of that committee, and even to General Washington, who ultimately became cool to his demands.[37] At one point, Washington responded to Morgan's persistent requests that he acquaint himself with one of Morgan's voluminous reports: "How can you think I have time to read over such a bundle of papers?" Morgan's report of his own retort is characteristic.

I told him I was sensible of his situation, and how precious his time was; that the reason of my troubling him with so much writing, was that he might not be interrupted by long consultations, though on the most necessary matters; but be able to make himself master of the subject, when most at leisure to consider it, with the means before him: I informed him as briefly as possible, of the general contents, and what I had written to the Adjutant General, in whose abilities he placed great confidence; and concluded with a request, that if he should not have leisure shortly, to read them over himself, that he would refer them to Colonel Reed, or any other person he chose, to give them an account of them, that some orders might issue in consequence.[38]

Rush, by contrast, had not Washington's patience to stand still for Morgan's long-windedness. The Philadelphia physician allowed Morgan no time to "lay matters" before him in person, as the latter had with Congress.

> I met Doctor Rush in the street, and attempted for a moment, to detain him, till I could acquaint him with the present circumstances, and situation of affairs: He gave me no time: All he said was, that "he was glad I was come; it would take a great burden from his shoulders," and passed on. When I afterwards called upon him, at his house, to represent matters to him there, as a Member of the Medical Committee, for relief; the sum of his answer was, that "he would not, for ten times the consideration, go through the amazing toils and difficulties of my station."[39]

Morgan took few chances and certainly none that stretched his authority in an untenable direction. In a letter to Samuel Adams of the Medical Committee on the Northern Army's medical needs, he responded to the urgency of the situation with his typical caution. He was unwilling to supply the army in Canada "without fresh instructions or more ample power than I now have": "I cannot expect to receive instructions, on this matter, from General Washington; he supposes, that I understand the affairs of this department, and relies wholly on me for everything which relates to it. *But I neither durst, nor will I presume, to meddle in affairs, out of my province, or that are beyond the sphere, in which I suppose, I was designed originally, by Congress, to move.*[40]

Again, in July 1776, to Samuel Adams,

> I must not, I durst not transgress orders, or exceed my line of duty more than disobey, or go contrary to them. It is the same thing. I call for orders. I shall shrink from no fatigue: Say what is my duty, and to the best of my power, I will obey: But leave me not without orders. . . .
>
> I have not received the least answer, or instruction from Congress; nor can I give any assistance to that part of the army, without orders or power. Let them give me orders, whether limited or ample, they shall be obeyed. I will answer for my conduct. But do not make me nominal Gen. Director, and leave, me, at the same time, a destitute, a helpless one.[41]

His explanation regarding the regimental surgeons in the *Vindication* confirmed his sense of powerlessness and his inability or unwillingness to move without clear authorization: "being bound to act agreeable to my orders, it was not in my power to swerve from them."[42] He might as well have confessed it was not in his nature, for, as he later admitted, "nor could any consideration induce me to deviate from the commands of my superiors."[43] Whereas Morgan constituted himself as accommodating the desires of others where possible,[44] his core story was one of "adhering exactly to his orders"[45] whenever necessary, which for Morgan was on almost every occasion, for he never saw a situation which "necessity" could not embrace. Clearly, as he indicated when performing a duty against his best instincts, at the explicit direction of General Washington for instance, Morgan covered himself as a good soldier by carefully ascribing the responsibility upwards: "it was undertaken with all diligence and executed with all possible dispatch . . . it was by his Excellency's own order." He took even greater care when the act was not by his own hand, but within his area of responsibility: "by his commands, of which I had no knowledge at the time, when the General himself, and every other reasonable person, must be so far from condemning, that they cannot, in justice, but approve my conduct."[46]

Dr. Story

During his service as director general, Morgan navigated several significant feuds. The most dramatic played out around Dr. Story, a surgeon in Colonel Little's regiment whom Morgan was to examine for fitness, congruent with a general order from General Washington regarding the regimental surgeons. Story refused Morgan's authority over him outright in terms that, in Morgan's telling, would in civilian life have qualified him as a candidate for a duel: "On reminding him of the General's order, for examining the Regimental Surgeons, he behaved in a very insolent, and impertinent manner, giving me to know, 'that he had his commission already, no thanks to me, which was as valid, and of as good authority as my own, and that, truly, he would never submit to any examination of mine.' "[47]

Story was a party to later accusations against Morgan related to the latter's presumed insensitivity to the condition of the sick at regimental hospitals.[48] According to Morgan, Dr. Story was guilty of "making use of General Green's name, to sanctify his assertions, that the sufferings of the sick lay at my door."[49] Morgan attacked Story in several newspaper accounts in April 1777 for having repeated charges that Morgan had withheld hospital stores gathered from loyalist doctors in Boston. Morgan went further: "I came to

Boston on purpose to call upon the persons pointed out, as the principle authors of those reports, requiring them to make good that charge, and at the same time inviting any persons, who had any thing to offer against me, that regarded the faithful discharge of my trust, to step forth, and state their accusations."[50] Morgan wrote a letter to Story "calling on him to explain himself for taking such unwarrantable licence as he had done, assuring him that no man, be his rank what it may, should be suffered to do it, with impunity."[51] Called upon in person, Story denied "he had any thought of Dr. Morgan's having any intention to defraud the Continent,"[52] which Morgan apparently accepted in resolution of the matter.

Morgan's address to the public in the *Pennsylvania Gazette*[53] provided a construction of the affair that demonstrated how dangerously close to a duel Story had come before he stood down and how politic a choice he had made in taking a face-saving way out. Because Story met a letter of Morgan's with silence, Morgan felt himself justified in publishing the letter, and thereby publicly calling him out, arguing that no one was beyond his reach, however much they might distance themselves from him.

> I am informed that since your return to Boston, availing yourself of my imaginary distance from it, you have made more free with my reputation than any man may do, without being called upon to explain himself for taking such unwarrantable liberty. It is said you have asserted publicly, that the sufferings of the sick soldiers, during the last campaign, are to be ascribed to my management and to my having with held from them those stores they were intitled to draw from the General hospital to be taken care of, without which they could obtain none; and further, on being asked what motive you supposed Dr. MORGAN could have for the refusal, you replied, to stop the mens rations, and put the money into his pocket; you knew no other.
>
> In support of your general charge, you were pleased to refer the inquirer to General GREEN. I apprehend, Sir, you will find that gentleman will look upon himself but little indebted to you for making use of his name to sanctify any part of the charge; and till he shall adopt this spurious offspring, you must give me leave, in his behalf, as I have a high consideration and respect for him, to deny that he ever did, or ever will license you to presume on making free with his name to cloke or give weight to your insinuations, in prejudice of my fame.
>
> The names and character of gentlemen in posts of rank and public trust, are of a delicate nature. A person ought to be cautious how he sports with either. I WOULD SOONER PARDON THE MAN WHO SHOULD FIGHT VALIENTLY TO TAKE MY LIFE, than the SLAN-

DERER, WHO BY MISREPRESENTATION, SOUGHT TO BETRAY MY HONOUR. I am to insist, therefore, on your open, undisguised and unambiguous explanation of the above assertions and insinuations, that I may know to whom I am to look for the author; for I shall suffer no man, be his rank in life what it may, to fix that stain, which has been attempted upon the character I have had the honour to support, in quality of Director General. . . .

If, Sir, you fail in your charge against me, and instead of proving, only shift the accusation to the others, or leave it to rest on the footing of hearsay information, I must look to you as the author of it, and nothing less than your proof, or public retardation, will be considered by me as a suitable atonement for the injury you have offered me.[54]

For Morgan, a private assault on his honor eclipsed his medical responsibilities, even from a source considerably lower in rank and from a slander based on hearsay. Removing to Boston to face his presumed accuser and risking a public scandal in the press, Morgan spoke in the discourse of reputation and honor as an exemplar of social norms that trumped the orders and authority by means of which he had crafted the story of his military life.

Dr. Samuel Stringer

A second feud involved Dr. Stringer, director of the Northern Department, who declined as well to accept Morgan's authority. Stringer was appointed director of the hospitals of the Northern Department by a resolve of Congress, September 14, 1775, one month before Morgan was appointed director general. Morgan chose to put a positive spin on Stringer's request that Morgan supply the Northern hospital,[55] suggesting that Stringer thereby recognized the priority of the General Hospital. Nevertheless, at a time when not only Stringer, but General Gates, Colonel Anthony Wayne, and Dr. Jonathan Potts were desperately appealing for assistance to address the carnage in the Northern Army, and when General Washington had already ordered Morgan to provide whatever stores were possible,[56] Morgan was still defining himself in terms of protocol. In a letter to Stringer, June 24, 1776, Morgan framed the argument, "It never has been announced to me in what light I am to consider you." He posited the possibilities, "whether as Director of an Hospital, or Superintendent of the regimental Surgeons in Canada; or whether there is such a thing as a General Hospital."[57] Putting much too fine a point on it, Morgan bargained with Samuel Adams, a member of the

Medical Committee, for a credentials check: "I should be glad to know immediately: Till then, my hands are tied up, and the army suffering for want of help."[58] Morgan was hedging his bets between the speed he seemed to require and the pettiness of the clarification he was demanding in trying to confirm the commission and status of both Stringer and Dr. Potts.

> Upon looking into Dr. Potts' commission, I find he is appointed Physician and Surgeon in the department of Canada; but whether it be of a regiment, or in the Hospital, is not specified; nor does it shew whether it is the intention of Congress, to vest him with the power of a Director, in the General Hospital: Nor can I learn, what appointment Dr. Stringer has, or what is the nature of his commission.
>
> From all I am able to learn, every thing in the medical department, in Canada, displays one scene of confusion and anarchy: Nor have the Congress taken upon itself, to establish, or vested any person whatever, with a power sufficient to establish a General Hospital in Canada.
>
> The Congress cannot, in my humble opinion, be too speedy in determining what steps are to be taken for this purpose, and for settling a due subordination amongst the Surgeons there. It would be of particular use, that the intentions of Congress were made known in respect to Dr. Stringer and Dr. Potts, whether either of them is to be considered as Director, by appointment of Congress, and which of them; or whether they are both to be looked on, and acting by instructions from me.[59]

In his challenge to Stringer's commission, Morgan went so far as to demand that Congress declare whether or not the director general was the party with the authority to nominate surgeons in any part of the General Hospital and whether the Northern Department's director would not have been responsible to him. Upon receipt of a letter from Stringer declaring himself a senior officer, Morgan countered Stringer's construction that he "expected precedence, from that priority, or to take rank of me; and . . . that he never would be accountable to me, or to any person, but the Commander of the particular department where he was, or to the Commander in Chief."[60] Stringer referred to the votes in Congress that appointed him, which naturally led Morgan to request the actual votes from the secretary of Congress. In subsequent correspondence, Morgan exceeded his own pettiness by reminding Stringer of Congress's "Resolve" on the question of rank and preference and "asked him, if it was a matter of no importance, how it came to pass that the Congress, in their late resolves, had determined that the surgeons and mates of the hospital should take the rank of regimental surgeons and mates."[61] Stringer responded outside the frame Morgan had established, placing the dispute in a military context in which men of honor gave precedence to rank. Stringer denied familiarity with "courts and camps" and, as Morgan construed his words, "he doubted not that his way of thinking might appear as old fashioned to them, as their proceedings, at times, appear ridiculous to him, where rank stands for merit, and that fantastical thing called honour . . . supplys the place of virtue."[62] Morgan's insistence on precedence in the matter is framed in familiar terms: "I only wished to guard against breaking down those barriers, which were most likely to secure my rank and authority from innovations upon them."[63]

Stringer himself petitioned Congress for clarification of his status relative to Morgan, a petition that was resolved in Morgan's favor. Morgan was declared director general of "the American Hospital" while Stringer was declared director "in the Northern department, only."[64] Reinforcing Congress's "Resolve" of July 17, 1776, the determination required Stringer to submit regimental hospital reports to Morgan, while Morgan was not obliged to provide the regiment with hospital supplies.[65] Morgan nevertheless chose to do so, sending a token supply to General Gates which did little to address a desperate situation.[66]

Morgan and the Law

Morgan was dismissed by Congress in January 1777 without any kind of an inquiry or hearing. He was convinced the dismissal had been engineered by Shippen, who did, indeed, replace him as director three months later. Morgan instigated a campaign not to be reinstated but to be vindicated and pursued it in tandem with an effort by Benjamin Rush to court-martial his successor for corruption and dereliction of duty. Morgan's vindication campaign not only defended his conduct, as might well be expected, but contained an impassioned statement of the value to him personally and to the nation collectively of the protections that must be afforded to those subjected to what Morgan considered slanderous abuse at the hands of unscrupulous men. Reputation for Morgan was preeminent in his thinking, raising the specter of a great man brought low, the story of the Fall.

Will it be believed, that on no better evidence than the clamours and misrepresentations of interested men, they would have dismissed, from an office of the greatest trust, One, whose established character and their good opinion had called from private life, and exalted to that station; One, who, nevertheless, from his first stepping forth on the stage of action, had always met with public approbation and distinguished honours, both at home and abroad; who had served his country in posts of eminent trust and usefulness, with applause; that they would, on the first application, have sacrificed him to the crys of a faction?[67]

For Morgan the Fall was not merely that of a great man, but that of a great institution, Congress, and by implication a great nation and its laws. Morgan's defense was in many ways a treatise writ large on justice, the rights of man, impartiality, and providential punishment. He roamed broadly across the landscape of a democratic law to retrieve a legality founded, in the deepest sense, in the vision of a just world for a newly aborning nation. To begin, he interrogated the future, asking whether it could ever be believed that a body of men like those of the American Congress could "on any partial representation, without giving the person accused an opportunity of exculpating himself from the charges brought against him, or knowing what he was accused of; and without calling on him to offer what he had to say, why he should not be so dealt with; making themselves judges as well as hearers, pass sentence, as if all said, is proved?"[68]

Morgan's self-presentation required that he stand firm on the right of the accused to know the charges against him and be given the opportunity to defend himself. He posited a standard of proof by means of which judgment would not be passed until all the evidence had been heard and the charges had been proved. In his own case, Morgan argued, he had regularly asked to know the charges and to face his accusers. He alone had been brought forth and none others sought out "as if I was answerable not only for every supposed crime that could be alleged against any part of it, but for mere misfortunes."[69] Confirmed in his isolation, he demanded impartial judges, men who would not act both as judges and juries, as if everything presented was presumed to be true; and he required as a condition of such a hearing well-grounded charges that would justify even holding the hearing. Morgan construed himself as the chief obstacle to an impartial hearing, for he "stood in the way of an ambitious man," Shippen, who would elevate himself by means of Morgan's downfall: "either oblige me to bend, as a reed, before him, or, like a stubborn oak, to be torn up by the roots, for resisting the tempest; and to plant him on my ruin.''[70] As a man of "public approbation and distinguished honors," Morgan framed himself as not one to bend, nor to give way before a wind. If he was to fall, he would have to break or be broken, his foundations, like that of "civil Liberty," overthrown.[71]

Morgan's argument reached to the despotism by means of which honorable men were "immolated to the MISREPRESENTATIONS of others, or to the designs and wishes of a more SWELLING INTEREST." They were left without the protections of a trial to expose charges "founded on private pique, disappointed expectations, or secret resentment."[72] Was this not what the war itself was being fought to ensure, a liberty "Which can only be secured by impartial trials, before dis-interested Judges, where the accused person and the accusers, are brought face to face, and where full weight is given to the evidence in favour of the accused? What line is there betwixt this and DESPOTISM? At this rate, who is free from the fatal effects of influence?"[73] Was not this war a means of claiming "the essential right, as one of the main pillars of their Liberties?"[74] Or, Morgan argued, were Americans to fight foreign usurpation of man's rights only to find there were no laws to protect them from their own government?

Because he saw the threat as less to himself than to the nation and its institutions, that is, to Congress and the legal system, Morgan pictured it emanating from heaven itself.

> The best provision those men can make, for all events, who are above such compliances with the ways of the world, as may impeach their honour, or offer violence to their conscience; and to whom the judgment and approbation of the world is matter of but second consideration, is to have a firm confidence in Providence, that he will not suffer their innocency to be utterly oppressed, or notoriously defamed, and yet expect the gusts and storms of rumor, envy and detraction; to look on these as a *purgatory* he is unavoidably to pass through, and depend upon time, and the goodness of heaven for a vindication; and by constantly performing all the duties of his place and station with justice and integrity, prove to all men, how groundless these charges were, that men of secret designs have imputed to him.[75]

Morgan embraced the belief that heaven would not allow the innocent to go unredeemed, even if those whose secret designs had brought them low never paid the price of their malice. But while designing men might escape, Morgan warned that all must consider whether such a misfortune as had befallen him might not be their fate. Wielding the natural law standard of presumption of innocence much as a more pious man might frame the debate in terms of providential benevolence, Morgan implicated all men in his plight.

> Is it a misfortune, easily to be borne, that any persons should lay under a charge, which it was the duty of those, who are the authors of it, to have made good? Is it not consistent with the principles of equity, that every *accused person* should be deemed *innocent,* or judgment be suspended till guilt is proved? Let all consider, what mischief may happen to themselves, if, upon a general charge, without the mention of any one crime, a person is to be degraded from his rank and office; for who is secure from the consequences of such a precedent? Or, if men of secret designs can thus shelter themselves, by sacrificing those, who, from a sense of duty, remain immoveable against every effort to draw them aside from their duty, who is certain that he shall escape the danger?[76]

Like heaven's providence, the presumption of innocence might not, however, cover one accused as he had been, one whose right to self-defense had been denied. Reflecting an argument carried forward from British law, the accused was expected to speak or received no representation. Standing silent in the face of such accusations, Morgan argued, "will be considered, by most of mankind, as an argument of conscious guilt."[77] Having been denied a hearing, Morgan found himself incapacitated from a true defense, itself an undeserved punishment that a man, though innocent, was bound to endure: "It is to SCOURGE; it is to WHIP with SCORPIONS; *it is a punishment calculated only for GENEROUS MINDS, thus to rob men of their HONOURS;* it is to lay a stain upon them, which, though undeserved, a whole life is too short to efface the impression, without it be fully vindicated; and, to them, is worse than death."[78] This irremediable assault on a man's reputation prevented the accused from showing "to the world, how groundless the accusations were."[79] Those truly guilty of mismanaging or neglecting their duties, those who truly occasioned greater suffering among the sick and wounded "than was inevitable," were left unpunished. The people lost the opportunity that "the cause may be known, and a reasonable remedy applied."[80]

Losing confidence that he would find relief from Congress, the very body that dismissed him in the first place, Morgan expounded on a basic question posed in both religion and law: who should judge and in judging how would they know they were just. Why, he asked, would Congress not answer his appeal for a hearing?

> To what other cause can I impute it but their own reflexions, that there is not a set of men on earth, so free from the influence of their own passions, that a person may trust himself to their decisions, unheard, and to whom is it proper to appeal from their own decisions, thus made? For who are so free from bias, as not to have a secret wish to find, that, in passing judgment, they were just. Can it be their desire to find that man blameless, to whom they have behaved, as if they thought him otherwise? Would it not be a reflexion on their hasty judgment, when they have treated him, as guilty, to find him wholly innocent?[81]

The story pointed not merely to the pathologies of a human court, but to the implied absence of both divine law and the justice of a higher tribunal emptied of human imperfection and self-interest. Morgan nevertheless received the vindication he had earned from Congress after a hearing in June 1779.

The Regimental Surgeons

The difficulties Morgan experienced with the regimental surgeons had their roots in the relative positions of the parties, in much the same way as the difficulties between Shippen and Morgan had. In this case, however, Morgan was the one who was regarded as the late-comer and an outsider. Moreover, Morgan suffered from the disadvantage of representing centralized authority, that of Congress and the general command, while the regimental surgeons were appointed at the level of the regiment. The story at the local level was one of surgeons who were known and preferred by the men they cared for. They operated on a smaller level and were thus able to respond with greater flexibility and to maintain more healthful facilities. Many regimental surgeons had volunteered early in the conflict. They operated with relative autonomy, collected blankets, bedding, cloth, bandages, drugs, and medical chests locally. Many brought their own instruments with them. Whereas they were wedded to the regiments they served, their work went largely unexamined, which meant that the quality of care they offered and the skills and training they brought to their service were uneven and unmonitored.[82]

Morgan's job as director general was to organize a general hospital capable of taking in the sickest from the regimental hospitals. He was draped in the authority of General Washington who had assigned him to examine the regimental surgeons. The regiments could request medical supplies from him which, at his discretion, he could provide when possible. These supplies included only instruments and medicines, although Morgan tried to provide medical chests through a proposal he and the regimental surgeons presented to Congress.[83] The lines of authority were not clear, which gave rise to proliferating conflict that was never very effectively resolved. Several Congressional "Resolves," particularly those of July 17, August 20, and October 9, 1776, attempted to clarify responsibilities. Since interpretations differed depending upon which department or level of organization one came from—from the General Hospital, the Northern Department, the Flying Camp, the Medical Committee of Congress, or the General Command—even a Congressional "Resolve" led to conflicts that themselves required resolution.

Behind the organizational issues and conflicts over lines of authority, reputation and honor narrated the storyline that controlled how Morgan perceived himself. To have been dismissed without "an examination into my conduct," Morgan held, "might rather have prepossessed the world with an opinion, that there was some ground for those clamours against me."[84] Consistent with the value he placed on reputation, Morgan could not allow his name to remain blemished before the public.

> I can no longer, consistently with my reputation, defer it. The wounds that are given by the envenomed tongue of calumny are deeper, and more fatal than the sword; they destroy what is dearer to life, reputation and peace of mind blemishes on a man's public character soon fester, and if not speedily removed, will contaminate every thing about him, and infect the very air he breathes. He whose reputation is injured, is ever suspected; his society is shunned; he is looked upon as dangerous, as a walking pestilence. I must not therefore pass over, in silence, a proceeding which strikes so home at my honour. It would afford room for ingenious architects to raise a pile of plausible charges, which silence is no ways calculated to refute. Evil reports are apt to spread like wild fire, and even persons not easily inclined to it, by repeating and circulating a story, snow ball it from hand to hand, whence it cannot fail to accumulate; and where slanders have been suffered to take root, there are never wanting some persons, who will use all kinds of manure to quicken the growth.[85]

The architecture of the anti-Morgan narrative was one of story piled on story, elaborated into a shapeless festering confection. Morgan regarded himself, by contrast, as bound by a predictable structure of rules and expectations that reflected the essentials of a period definition of "honor." He responded quickly and forcefully to assaults upon his honor, which he valued as a fungible form of capital in social exchange. He held that attacks assaulted not merely a man's livelihood but the very quality of his life, and he rejected the view that public men must expect to meet with censure in such times. Morgan refused advice that he flatter himself that he attracted such attentions.

> They ought to content themselves with this remark, that men of worth, who are not only innocent, but whose conduct is meritorious, are most liable to be traduced by ignorant and designing men; that not *to meet with envy* and *back-biting* is a *frequent effect* of *compliances,* which argue a *weakness* unworthy of *confidence;* that my friends know I do not wish to be *popular* at such a *price,* but have rather courted the slanders of the *envious,* by a steady perseverance in my duty, than lay a train for the compliments of *flatterers,* by favouring their *dark purposes.*[86]

That others suffered invidious assaults was no comfort to him, and silence in the face of an attack was not in his nature. Morgan would not embrace counsel that suggested attacks upon him represented a form of flattery.[87] Rather, he would counter his slanderers in a public trial, before Congress if possible, in the press if necessary, or in both venues should the occasion require it. Morgan chose to take these base and malicious men, these villains, these "pests of every society"[88] before an impartial public, to which he appealed: "At this tribunal, no innocent person need fear to make his defence, nor to allow free scope to be given to that defence; where a man's conduct, and the motives of it being known, he has reason to hope for a candid judgment, free from prejudice or party."[89] Before this tribunal his vindication would expose "the true causes of the malevolence of the Regimental Surgeons against me."[90] His charges included abuse of hospital stores; his right to examine those "entrusted with the lives of the sick and wounded soldiery"; and the priority of General Hospital surgeons over regimental surgeons.[91]

Morgan rarely tired of raising the regimental surgeon issue, in one case attacking their "scheme of elevating themselves into greater consequence than the Congress ever intended to raise them, that of ranking with, and doing the duty of hospital Surgeons."[92] Cabals, conspiracies, schemes, and designs were executed, and acts were pursued "to frustrate the intentions of Congress, and to force me to a compliance with their measures." His own acts of resistance, Morgan asserted, were construed by his enemies as "unpardonable sins, which they were determined never to forgive or forget."[93] Morgan contended that he had resisted the regimental surgeons' neglect to report the sick to be admitted to the General Hospital. He cited among their schemes their spreading of "groundless suspicions" among officers and members of Congress and condemned their cynical efforts to entice him to act outside his orders by their mistreatment of the sick. Morgan reported poorly managed care whereby the regimental surgeons organized the hospitals "To retain as many sick, or nominally sick, as they pleased, on their lists, till the time of an action, and then to pour them all into the General Hospital, and to receive the wounded under their care, for the sake of trying experiments, and of performing operations, which some of them had never seen performed."[94] In a piece in the *Pennsylvania Gazette,* Morgan publicized yet other subterfuges.

> it is shameful that so many of the regimental Surgeons and officers contumaciously opposed, and carried the sick to places distant from the army, where they could obtain no succour; and that these Surgeons, under a pretence of taking care of them, instead of sending them to the General hospital, abandoned their posts, so that at the White Plains few were at their stations, by which many useful lives were lost, that might have been saved by skillful Surgeons, had they been present with their regiments, to dress the men on the field of battle, and then to send them to the General hospital for farther care, as they ought to have done.[95]

Whatever suffering occurred among the sick, Morgan was concerned that it be laid at the door of the surgeons and not "at my door, as one so wedded to his own plan, as not to yield to the united voice of all the Regimental Surgeons to come into their measures."[96] Unshaken in his certainty of the rightness of his own conduct, Morgan refused to yield to appeals to his humanity: "And, true it is, my perseverance in what I conceived to be my duty, and for the good of the service, was unshaken; nor could any consideration induce me to deviate from the commands of my superiors; although, had the Congress seen fit to alter their resolves, in some particulars, I should have thought it would have been for the better, as my letters fully prove."[97]

General Greene addressed directly the question of Morgan's sup-

posed inhumanity in a letter in which he tried, not entirely successfully, to give Morgan the benefit of the doubt:

> I remember great complaints were brought against you for withholding
> medicine from the Regimental Surgeons. It was said you pleaded in justi-
> fication of yourself that you were not authorized to do it as Director Gen-
> eral, neither were your stores equal to the demands made upon you, and
> that if you had issued agreeable to the applications, that had been made
> the General Hospital must have been without a proper assistance of
> medicine.
>
> However just your remarks they were unsatisfactory to the Army and
> gave rise to a great deal of censure and furnished a handle to insinuate
> that you were content so the sick did but die by rule. . . .
>
> On this account I could have wished you to have departed from the
> plan of the Hospital, and to have rested the justification of your conduct
> on the necessity of the case and the call of humanity that seemed to de-
> mand the measure.[98]

Whereas Morgan appeared to have inoculated himself against
Greene's adversion to his own possible misfeasance, he was clearly
responsive to comparable accusations against the regimental surgeons. The narrative he had constructed of the regimental surgeons
had been affected by reports of their absence without leave from
their posts and the sale of furloughs and discharges to soldiers.[99] In
November 1776 he sent out a circular letter to all regimental surgeons and mates of General Washington's army ordering them to
return to the General Hospital or their regiments immediately and
to furnish a certified list of all those sick who went out with them.
Morgan's reading was that "all those who are absent without leave,
must naturally be looked upon as deserters" and that all those "who
cannot give a regular and satisfactory account of the faithful discharge of their duty, necessarily subject themselves to an inquiry
into their conduct."[100] This text clearly informed Morgan's application to General Washington to authorize examinations of all regimental surgeons. The examinations only reinforced his general
disdain, as many resigned rather than submit and of those who un-
derwent "the test of inquiry" many revealed themselves to Morgan
to be "unlettered, ignorant, and rude to a degree scarcely to be
imagined."

> Some of them, I have been informed, and from what I observed, could
> readily believe, were never educated to the profession of physick, nor

had ever seen an operation of Surgery. . . . It would display a farce of the most ridiculous kind, to give the public an account of the learning and attainments, which some of them, whom I have had an opportunity of examining, have discovered; or to give a transcript of their reports. . . . And I observed, that it was generally the most ignorant, the most opinionated and the most disorderly, and irregular in their conduct, who were the most troublesome, and loudest in their clamours. These were the men, from whom I found the greatest opposition, to every regulation for introducing method, discipline and improvement, into the department of physick and surgery.[101]

That Morgan's own European and university-based training in medicine was well outside the experience of all but the most fortunate colonials did not surface as a consideration worth noting in Morgan's screed. Indeed, that the attainments of regimental surgeons reflected the training and experience most characteristic of colonial physicians (who, unlike those in England, performed mixed roles as physicians, surgeons, and apothecaries and were largely apprenticed into the medical trade) was given no credit or value.

In his concluding comments on the regimental surgeons in his *Vindication,* Morgan was careful to remind his readers that their accusations against him must count for little, indeed that their representation of him was unworthy, "however worthy it may be of the authors of it."[102] Whatever credit, he contended, they might gain by their attacks, time would unmask and they would, "By endeavouring to throw an odium on my character, fix an indelible mark on their own; and, perhaps, find that injustice so sweet to their taste, may, before it is digested, bring forth gaul and bitterness, and what they have sowed in deceit and folly, they may reap in remorse and disappointment."[103]

Morgan's perspective represented a core story that acted as an identity theme and provided an interpretive structure for self-presentation. Having cast himself in the role of a fallen hero seeking vindication, he redefined his enemies as conspirators against his good name and assassins of his reputation. Honor was sought beyond all else and was to be protected at all costs. His tale told of the dangers of undermining rank and the twin threats of acting without orders and failing to follow orders. Yielding to regional and local forms of order, or to cries for flexibility and humanity, was no more than to consort with disorder. Negotiating with subordinates or sharing authority became negative referents that signaled loss of respect and diminished status. If reputation, like hospital stores, was a form of material capital, Morgan would aggregate it, hoard it, and exploit it as a sign of power to offset the ambiguity of the authority he had been invested with. With such capital he would organize the story of his vindication and give it mythic significance as a tale of the hero who, having been perceived as fallen, returned home, if not to a hero's welcome, at the very least unscathed by dueling with demons.

Dr. John Brown Cutting and Morgan

After the fact of his dismissal, Morgan was not one to let go easily, as Shippen was about to discover. It would take Morgan, nevertheless, more than three years to convene a court-martial. In the meantime, Morgan located an interim target, Dr. John Brown Cutting, a young and inexperienced apothecary appointed to replace Andrew Craigie in the middle district after what Cutting referred to as Craigie's "most extraordinary and unparalleled dismission."[104] Cutting made the quintessential mistake, in Morgan's view, of abandoning hospital stores that had been committed to his care. Cutting determined to wait to expose Morgan in the press until Shippen had an opportunity to exonerate himself at his court-martial. With the acquittal, Cutter published the history of his intercourse with Morgan.[105] In it, he quoted Morgan's note to Cutting upon hearing from a gentleman that Cutting had claimed he "knew enough to break [Morgan]." "'When I have been first insulted I never will make any concessions for what I may be induced to publish on that account. If, therefore, you ever expect the least concessions from me, for what I have already written from the above motive, you must first make due reparation for your former injurious treatment of me. On that ground alone will I ever receive any further letter or message from you.'"

Cutter responded, "Conscious of no injustice I had ever done you, I could make no reparation, and as that 'was the ground alone upon which you would receive any further letter or message from me,' I took a gentleman of character, and called at your house in person three times, when I received the following note: 'Should Mr. Cutting call on me, if he has business, he is desired to communicate in writing, and to mention where he is to be met with, and he will receive an answer in the same way.'"[106]

Cutting's provocative attendance at Morgan's house and Morgan's request for a formal written challenge to a duel was first followed by Cutter's declining to write such a note, then by his reasserting his plan to publish his case in the press, and finally promising to take him to court.

> altho' the first sense of your unprovoked traduction of my character, had once nearly dissuaded me from awaiting the determination of civil justice on your malevolent libel, yet, reflection upon your unworthiness and your degradation from the stile of a gentleman, by the inconsistency, duplicity and littleness of your conduct, at present screens your person from hazard, since I am obliged to decline a mode of decision, wherein even success would not justify an offer to put myself in competition with you. At the same time rest assured, Sir, that your attempts to injure my character will no longer be suffered with impunity, but that after having vindicated my reputation to the public, I shall seek that justice from the laws of my country which I find it is vain to expect from the consciousness of a person destitute of generosity and truth.

Cutting proved as tenacious as Morgan, if a tad belated in his discussion of the events that transpired. In a second piece in *Pennsylvania Packet*,[107] he called into play Morgan's arrogance in taking for granted his fellow citizens and his condescension in thinking he could easily deceive them.

> I cannot say, Sir, whether "your fellow citizens could think it incumbent on you to pay any regard to the abuse of an angry man, who had chosen to treat them with a ragout of falsehood, virulence, gasconade and invective on you, highly seasoned with panegyrics on himself:" . . . That you would be highly contemptuous in your treatment of me, was what I expected, and could not complain of, but that you should suppose those very "fellow citizens" with whom you would wish to appear consistent, so mean in intellect as to be deluded by the worn out policy of affecting to treat with contempt and neglect *galling charges* which you could not disprove, is truly an honorable specimen both of your own ingenuity, and your respect for them.

Cutting might have seemed relatively small fry to Morgan, who quite possibly thought he would roll over, but Cutting was willing to go to the brink in his solidarity with Shippen and was unimpressed with Morgan's sense of his own importance. Citing the contradiction between an initial certificate from Morgan stating that the apothecary had "given entire satisfaction" and Morgan's later savaging of Cutting to vindicate himself, Cutting played the two positions against one another in racial terms: "They are both your own children, Doctor, and I trust, voluntarily begotten. One of them to be sure, is rather of a *dusky hue* for the offspring of a *white,* and I think it would be better for you to disclaim the bantling, or acknowledge it the conception of something *Black:* For I am afraid you will never be able to *white-wash* it, and am sure neither contempt or neglect will ever annihilate it. I will not say you was 'angry' when you got that *Black child,* though you was a little 'stung.'"

Cutting had cunningly chosen to put the passage in an off-color and racially tinged light, using the term "bantling" (a corruption of the German for "bastard") and referring to the "Black child" and the inability to "white-wash it." He noted that Morgan's dignity rested on teaching boys to spread plasters in battle and "in religiously denying yourself the society due to your learned honors, to associate with servants and Negroes for their patriotic aid to pull down your adversary." He then added a postscript by T. Matlack referring to Morgan's brother and sister-in-law from the West Indies who had left their child in Philadelphia with Morgan. He noted Morgan's intention to leave the city, claiming that "he had been informed Morgan intended leaving the country and settling in the West Indies when the British evacuated Philadelphia, and only changed his plans on receiving assurance from Dr. Rush, of help in a contemplated attack on Dr. Shippen."[108] The brother's child, Morgan's association with Negroes, the black population of the West Indies, and the inappropriateness of Morgan's relations with the British enemy implied bastardization, illegitimacy, crossing racial and political lines, cover-ups, and "passing" for white. Cutting's innuendoes transformed Morgan's framing of the event from straightforwardly oppositional and adversarial dueling terms to blurred values, dissimulation, and boundary breaking that would have both disturbed and dishonored a man of traditional morality.

An auger of what was to come, the Cutting feud placed Morgan on the distaff side of a future in which his values no longer had much of a role to play. His "black and white" terms were now ambiguified; his rules, his order were now transformed to respond to the complexity of a social order that had replaced violence and force as a means of persuasion. Morgan had been asking all along for impartiality and public justice without realizing how alien they were to his framing of events. In a short note to the editor of the *Pennsylvania Packet,* Mr. Dunlap, Morgan could only refer to Cutting's comments as "such incoherent and incomprehensible jargon, and such barefaced falsehoods and unsupported assertions."[109] Cutting, for all Morgan could imagine, was no more than a surrogate for Shippen, "one of those insects who have been hatched in the sunshine of his corrupt administration of the hospitals." Cutting's apt rejoinder held that Morgan's "thirst of revenge for imaginary wrongs has engrossed your soul; it was entirely natural" that he would take anyone who analyzed his conduct and his heart to be under the influence of one who "intended most inhuman injury." Morgan, he warned, had best hope this insect "does not prove of that species" who shall disclose "truths which shall make his very ears to tingle."[110] The world was in transition to a legal order of more inclusive and responsive values that relied less on the social norms of individual reputation and honor than Morgan was prepared to admit.

WILLIAM SHIPPEN

Whereas Morgan appeared to preoccupy himself in feuds with collateral individuals like Story, Stringer, and Cutting, the central players in his script were in reality the regimental surgeons as a group and William Shippen as his successor. Even as he argued his right to a defense under the law, Morgan was preoccupied to an almost obsessive extent by the assault on his reputation raised by the regimental surgeons. Certainly it was this issue that predominated in the working documents—letters, orders, analysis—that made up the 158-page appendix to the *Vindication* he wrote to defend himself after his dismissal. Morgan only mentioned Shippen in the 43-page "Prolegomenon" to that report and in a later *Memorial to Congress*. In those documents, he shifted his focus to an attack on Shippen, personalizing his defense by identifying Shippen as the singular force behind his fall. Dr. Barnabas Binney, in a letter to another doctor, regarded Shippen as having "laid himself shockingly open to Morgan, the most implacable, revengeful man under the Heavens." The good Dr. Binney found the medical profession itself remarkable for its "obtrusive, brazen pretenders," at a time when "surgeons and villains are synonymous terms."[111]

Two parallel storylines suggest themselves as we move from considering Morgan's tenure as director general and the feuds that contributed to his dismissal, to Shippen's tenure in the same position. The first occurs as a result of the treason trial of the first director general, Benjamin Church. Church was appointed on July 25, 1775,[112] and by September was already being investigated because of conflicts with the regimental hospitals. Having conducted coded correspondence with the British, he was arrested and convicted of treason before the investigation was completed.[113] Morgan himself was accused after his dismissal as director general of fraternizing with the enemy in Philadelphia during the British occupation of that city. In his defense, he did not deny that he had considered leaving America for the West Indies with the British.[114] The second storyline reminds us that Shippen played the same hand in replacing Morgan as director general of the Continental Army hospitals as Morgan played in founding the medical school in Philadelphia and eclipsing Shippen's existing efforts to establish a school. Both men prepared an elaborate plan in private, secretly shopping it around to parties of influence and winning their superior commissions essentially on the basis of the promise of their plans.[115]

Shippen Replaces Morgan as Director General

Shippen initially held a temporary appointment to a unit newly created after the military campaign had already begun, an appointment that Morgan felt degraded his own position. As a man who stuck to the rules, Morgan argued that it was "contrary to the rules and discipline of war" to place Shippen "on an equal, or, to say the truth, a preferable footing"[116] with him. That Congress "should interfere with my power, and superior appointment of Director-General"[117] was, for Morgan, something he was unwilling to admit. That it was nevertheless what Congress had in fact intended led him to conclude in his characteristic fashion that not only was the "whole power" of the medical department of the army thrown "into the hands of an inferior officer" but that Morgan was once again put in a position where "my hands were so tied up by resolves of Congress, and general orders, as to leave little freedom for proper exertions."[118]

From the outset, Morgan figured Shippen's underhanded attempts in line with "his interest with a particular set." Shippen's ambitions interfered with Morgan's department and "with a view to promote his design of succeeding me."[119] Morgan construed Shippen as a "Machiavellian," a man without regard for right or wrong, for rank or inferior position. In his view, Shippen was determined "to couzen and deceive, so long as it answered any purpose, and might contribute to what he desired upon motives, how foreign so ever; and then that failed, further to serve his purposes, to compel submission, by force."[120] In counterpoint, Morgan figured himself as a man dispossessed "of the powers of action" and yet made accountable "for misfortunes beyond human reach to prevent, and for the misconduct of others; to transfer my stores, my hospitals, my surgeons and officers, to another; and yet to blame me for the consequences: who is so blind as to see no design in all this, or so wilful, as to ascribe the whole to mere accident?"[121] Invoking imagery of the Fall, Morgan constructed himself as an unsuspecting innocent, cast down with the complicity of Congress "breaking down the separating wall of distinction" outside the bounds of lawful inquiry and due process, [by those who] hatched their plans in the darkness of their secret purposes."[122]

Morgan's story incorporated Shippen's desire "to continue in the service, as he thought it a more gentlemanny life, than that of a drudging private practitioner."[123] To do so, Morgan represented, he would have to make himself a place. Shippen's troops, raised for a limited service, were due to be released in a few months; his appointment would itself terminate shortly. The construction proposed by Shippen's subordinate, Dr. Foster, according to Morgan, was that Shippen would be gone "unless he could carve out some place that he could be pleased with, in the mean while, that would put him on a better establishment."[124] Morgan initially depicted himself as amenable to Shippen's further service so long as "he could remain in it, without elbowing me out of any thing that appertained to my place."[125] Morgan amended this section of the *Vindication*, however, in his subsequent *Memorial to Congress* where, upon second thought, he added the following language: "At the very Time he was secretly calumniating me to Congress, & misrepresenting the state of the sick under my Care, by Insinuations full of Falsehood and Deceit, with a view to traduce my Character, to abridge & share, or usurp my Authority."[126] Already in play, Morgan's hospital stores was the prize whose possession would determine who would survive. Morgan understood clearly that he was in end-game: "to be deprived of the only resources I had left me, those of my own providing, and of my own saving, with extreme difficulty and hazard, to be at the sole command of another, a junior, and inferior officer, appeared to me to be an unreasonable demand."[127]

Whereas General Washington, as Morgan recounted, had reinforced the latter's position with a promise that the stores "were to remain under my direction," the general was superseded by a vote of Congress. While the stores were delivered to the director of the Flying Camp, Morgan had already tipped his hand should his superiors fail to back him: "to be stripped of the rank of a Director-General, and the power of my station, and to be left but the shadow of a Director . . . to be rendered the mere dependent of a junior and subordinate officer, was what I never would submit to. Sooner than be subject to such controul, or give up the stores and hospitals, which by the General's orders I had established for the sick of his own army, when I had no convenience for providing others, I would give up my commission."[128]

Morgan could hardly have been surprised when his bluff was called and he was discharged as director, having cried wolf once too often. Still, he chose to go out with a howl. The last paragraph of the *Memorial* indicted Shippen and set the terms for the battle to be waged upon Shippen's ascension to the position of director general. Morgan planned to turn the tables and call for a court of inquiry, a formality he had been denied. In this case, he hoped a court-martial would find Shippen guilty on all charges. In implied contrast to Shippen, Morgan laid out his own career, at the same time anticipating his charges against Shippen.

I have done my Duty with Zeal and Fidelity as a Servant of the Publick: I have taken no Toll out of the Sums which have passed through my hands; I have withheld no Stores from the sick entrusted to my Care; nor dissipated them by a lavish Compliance with the unauthorized Demands of those, who wished to make a Tool of me to answer their own sordid Purposes. . . . I never, by dark and secret Suggestions, have attempted to wound the Fame of those placed in Authority above me, to asperse and vilify, in order to get them degraded and displaced, that I might raise myself to their envied situation. I have not for that Purpose trampled upon all order and subordination, neither thro' my private Plans of aggrandizement, nor through my Inattention to Business, nor has the Country been alarmed with the Progress and Fatality of putrid Fevers bred by crouding the sick too much together in close Rooms, or by shuttering them up to starve and famish. The high Roads and Places of the Fields have not been converted into Sepulchres of the dead, from my *Soliciting a Charge I was not qualified to execute;* nor have Church yards been made fat with the numbers of the dead whose Blood cries to heaven for Punishment of my neglect.[129]

Morgan's medicolegal brief against Shippen read out a range of accusations from simple profiteering, complicity, and subversion to the more complex charges of medical malpractice and administrative malfeasance. His metaphorical brief deployed images of bleeding corpses applying to the heavens for justice as they transformed fields and death-fattened church yards into wholesale burial grounds. Charging forward on both fronts, Morgan toggled between two realities—the actual and the metaphorical—convinced that Shippen would be convicted if not in an earthly at least in a heavenly court.[130]

Rush's Role

Benjamin Rush, then physician general for the Middle Division Hospitals, had begun collecting evidence against Shippen from as early as the summer of 1777, only a few months after Shippen's appointment as director general in April.[131] Congress, meanwhile, had not asked Rush to provide it with evidence until April 1778, a full year after the appointment: "We wish to proceed in this business so as to obtain the most perfect information of the malpractices, if there are any, of the Director General and to this end we desire that you will be pleased to ascertain the procedure and transmit to us the charge and upon oath, the evidence you have or can procure against him; also the names of the witnesses and places of residence."[132] Prepared to provide evidence, Rush specified a request for a court-martial and offered to act as prosecutor.

> I have written to the committee appointed to inquire into Dr. Shippen's conduct in the hospital and have requested a court-martial for that purpose, as being the way which Congress have ordered in a resolution of the 11 of April 1777 for trying all the officers of the hospitals. As Dr. Shippen has no superiors or equals in rank in the medical department, I take it for granted that the court will consist of general and field officers. I have promised to appear as his prosecutor in behalf of my country and of those unfortunate people whose sons, husbands, and fathers have been sacrificed by his ignorance, negligence, and injustice in our hospitals. I hope the event of the trial will show that I have had no personal malice against him, and that the "want of harmony" between us has had no share in the distresses and mortality of our soldiers.[133]

When it appeared that Shippen would not be court-martialed and that all Rush could hope for was a committee of Congress, which he considered would be biased in favor of Shippen, Rush became reluctant to provide any evidence. He told Morgan "that if the Congress would send a committee to the hospitals or order a court of inquiry to be held, I would produce proofs of all the facts I had related and of many more of a more heinous nature. This proposal had no effect upon the committee. They treated the complaints I made of the sufferings of their brave soldiers with neglect, and were easily persuaded to believe that all their misfortunes arose from a misunderstanding between Dr. S. and me."[134] Thus, Rush reported to Morgan "that I never brought any direct charges against Dr. Shippen and that no trial or acquittal ever took place."

Rush was not prepared to admit he had been collecting evidence against Shippen himself. As we see from a letter to Daniel Roberdeau, member of Congress, he claimed to have focused on amending the powers of the director general rather than generating testimony against Shippen: "I had no personal resentment against him and therefore took no pains to collect vouchers of his ignorance—negligence—or injustice. A change in the system (such as I wish for) I was sure would place the sick and the public beyond the reach of suffering from those vices."[135] Rush had written three months earlier to Congressman William Duer. He noted that "Dr. Shippen has taken pains to represent my complaints of the sufferings of the sick as intended to displace him."[136] In his own defense, Rush offered to resign and in fact did so on January 30, 1778. He followed his resignation immediately with a letter to Shippen in which he covered himself.

> nothing but the remembrance of an early connection with you, a tenderness for your worthy family, and in particular an affection for your amiable and promising son Tom, prevented my collecting and producing vouchers of the abuses of our hospitals which would ultimately have ended in your dishonor. The illiberal censures you passed upon my conduct before the committee of Congress did not force from me several anecdotes of your conduct (properly attested) that would have shown more than a 100 other things the extreme danger of the medical system. The one I mentioned (a *suspicious* one only) was intended to show that nothing but a change of the system would do justice to the sick, be safe to the directors or purveyors, and agreeable to the surgeons.[137]

Rush followed the polite forms of protocol to a fault, even as he avoided the implication that he was cowed by Shippen's representations of him or that he feared a court-martial himself.

Shippen's Court-Martial

With all the side-stepping and strategizing that informed the Shippen court-martial, the actual charges made against him by Morgan are a good place to start. Shippen had an advantage over Morgan who complained in his own dismissal that he never had the opportunity to know what he was charged with or to face his accusers.[138] Shippen was charged with five counts of abuse: fraud in the handling of hospital stores; speculating on hospital stores; failing to maintain regular accounts of expenditures; neglect of hospital duties; and conduct unbecoming an officer.[139] Morgan's attacks against Shippen put the most emphasis on the charges involving hospital stores, including the record-keeping charge. His reaction was entirely predictable, given his pride in accumulating stores, his maintenance of stocks at the General Hospital, and his resistance to orders that would have required him to turn his stocks over to the Northern Department, regimental hospitals, or the Flying Camp. For Morgan, hospital stores at the General Hospital represented capital through which he could assert and exercise the authority he believed should have been vested in the director general's rank. More than material capital, Morgan's astute and disciplined management of those stores gave him, in his own eyes, symbolic standing as a man of honor and one who stood in defense of the rule of law. That Shippen should be charged with fraud and speculation related to hospital stores was particularly important to Morgan. Morgan had never gottten over the attacks by Shippen and others against him for his presumed hoarding of and profiteering from stores. He felt only barely redeemed by General Greene's lukewarm defense of his conduct in this area.

Shippen admitted to the speculation in hospital stores charge. Even if Congress did later find that conduct "Highly improper and justly reprehensible," he held it was not illegal conduct.[140] Indeed, Congress judged there was insufficient evidence to establish guilt on that count. On three of the remaining counts Shippen was acquitted, while the conduct count was found to be groundless. Nevertheless, as Morgan made clear in his continuing attacks on Shippen in the *Pennsylvania Packet,*[141] Congress resolved following the court-martial that "It is of the utmost importance, to prevent further waste and embezzlement of hospital and other stores, and no adequate provision having been hitherto made for the just punishment of those crimes, the delinquent shall, in future, suffer death, or such other punishment as shall be directed by a General Court Martial."[142]

Morgan interpreted the new order as a direct rebuke to Shippen; as he editorialized to his readers, "They deemed a simple reprehen-

sion for offences so atrocious as yours, to be a mere burlesque punishment, so very inadequate was it to your crimes; therefore chose to
omit that: but immediately after resolved, that selling hospital stores,
etc. is a capital crime, and made it punishable with death, or otherwise, according to the nature and circumstances of the offence;—a
resolution that reflects greater reproach and disgrace upon you,
than any punishment whatever could have done."[143]

Irrespective of Morgan's ire at Shippen's acquittal and of Congress's apparent recognition of the scope and criminal nature of the
waste of hospital stores, Morgan's interpretive framework for explaining Congress's action revealed as much about Morgan's story
of reputation and honor as it did about malfeasance in office. Shippen was in any case court-martialed in August 1780, acquitted in
September, and reappointed as director general in October. Just
three months later, in January, he voluntarily resigned his commission; like Morgan, he received the vindication from Congress he demanded.

The Story of the Court-Martial

Shippen's court-martial expressed a dominant theme quite different from the obsession with orders that ran through Morgan's *Vindication*. Like Morgan's, Shippen's story was institutionally based, but
in a strategic sense. Shippen manipulated Congress's investigation
from a subject position, at least in Morgan's construction of that position, that contrasted with Morgan's dependence upon being authorized. A second difference arose from the dominant content of
the stories. Morgan's story expressed an obsession with defending
himself against accusations by the regimental surgeons, focusing on
the hospital stores. Shippen, by contrast, evaded having his story
turned to Morgan's use. Rather, he refused to rise to Morgan's bait.
He remained silent and thereby avoided having to appear before
Congress. He excused himself by asserting the importance of his
presence among the wounded, a site—the hospital—where Morgan
claimed Shippen was rarely seen. Shippen, moreover, only offered
his own vindication, unlike Morgan, after he had been cleared by
the court martial.

Shippen's silence should not be taken to suggest that Shippen was
uninvolved in his defense. Rather, Shippen did not step down from
his post while he was being tried, as his accuser had demanded. Instead, by continuing as director general (unlike Morgan who was dis-

missed well before he received a hearing), he could shape the potential testimony of subordinates. They were, after all, dependant upon his good will for supplies, their assignments and orders, perquisites of their positions, and such recommendations as promotions. Shippen was in an optimal position to offer inducements likely to massage testimony that might be forthcoming. In addition, he retained the ability to handle physical evidence—like the hospital records and the returns of the sick and wounded—that might be called into evidence. Simply by remaining on as director general during the court-martial he created a certain sense of inevitability about its outcome, having retained as he did privileged access to relevant information, the ability to ensure that critical testimonies did not conflict, and the ability strategically to appear and disappear at will. The court-martial's verdict, in any case, had ultimately to be ratified by Congress. The same inertia that operated during the court-martial to keep Shippen on in his position as director general was likely to encourage Congress simply to endorse the court-martial's verdict. The spirit of decision-making most likely to determine the final vote appeared to be reflected in a letter from John Armstrong, member of Congress, to General Horatio Gates: "The General having thrown the decision of the matter upon Congress, we are now tormented with reading the large bundle of rubbish and testimony but have not yet come to the Doctor's defense; it will probably end, indeed must end, in approving the sentence of the court-martial."[144]

Private Prosecution

The court-martial raised two central legal issues, one that related to whether Morgan was prosecuting the case and the other to witness testimony and evidentiary standards. Both Shippen and Morgan referred to the complainant, Morgan, as a "prosecutor," a representation that Morgan not only preferred but petitioned Congress to endorse. The conflation in a military context of official and private prosecution,[145] of criminal and civil formats, is itself remarkable if only because it calls to our attention the negotiated state of political and legal relations. Private prosecution relied upon an older model of the law in which victims gathered evidence and pursued their complaints in their own time and at their own expense. The accused was expected to speak on his own behalf, largely without counsel, and defend himself absent the presumption of innocence, carrying to a large extent the burden of proof. Judges assumed responsibility to advocate for the accused.[146]

Morgan arrived at the compounded position of plaintiff-prosecutor as the result of two congressional resolves, November 16 and December 24, 1779, which presumably responded to letters he had sent to Congress.[147] Morgan noted that in the former "Congress was pleased to resolve that in cases not capital, depositions might be given in evidence provided the prosecutor and the person accused were present at the taking of same but no provision was made to receive depositions as evidence, if the adverse party had reasonable notice of the time and place and should neglect to attend."[148] Morgan was apparently granted pseudo-prosecutorial status when the judge advocate could not attend a deposition, legitimized by the judge advocate's allowance that Morgan could act in the latter's "name and stead":[149] "The Judge Advocate informed me in due time, that if depositions are to be taken over again it was not within his power to attend; his presence being required in camp, and he would therefore authorize me in his name and stead to cite Dr. Shippen to attend the taking of such depositions."[150]

Presumably Morgan was thereby enabled to examine the witnesses and make up the depositions, a considerable enhancement of his contribution to the proceedings. Morgan reserved to himself in this capacity the authority to deliver witness summons, set the times, dates, and places of depositions, and notify the accused, all without the input or presence of a representative of Congress.[151] He adopted the attitude that his own private accusations carried a weight comparable to legal charges, to the extent that, in a letter to Samuel Huntington, president of Congress, he assumed the tone of a judge advocate, making clear that he had served Shippen notice of the charges when Shippen complained he had not been officially charged.[152]

Morgan's interest lay in Shippen coming fully prepared to make a defense at trial that would result in a speedy trial. Shippen's efforts to avoid preparing a defense he took to be an "endeavor to wear out his prosecutor."[153] In line with that goal, Morgan had particularly asked General Washington to suspend the then-director general which, on the face of things, would oblige Shippen to take time to prepare his defense. More importantly, it would prevent him from interfering from a position of power with witnesses. In the mantle of private prosecutor, Morgan argued the essential unfairness of his having to assume the responsibility not only to provide evidence that proved the charges but to do so "opposed to a man holding in his hands the means to bribe and seduce witnesses."[154]

For all his interest in protecting legal process, Morgan seemed not to have been much bothered at playing the roles of both plaintiff and prosecutor. Whereas he was a stickler for having the defendant present at depositions, a privilege he had not enjoyed himself, having been deprived of a hearing, Morgan did not feel constrained from influencing, even constructing, witness statements and, by some later testimony, coercing it where possible. The lack of boundaries that characterized Morgan's conflated roles created a legal ambiguity that would undermine the proof he would need to make good his charges.

Morgan was well aware that his performing a pseudo-prosecutorial role was a point of contention for Shippen and that Shippen considered Morgan "never named or recognized by Congress as his prosecutor."[155] In a letter to his brother-in-law Richard Henry Lee, Shippen referred to Morgan as "supposing himself to be the Prosecutor as well as persecutor."[156] Shippen's resigned skepticism about Morgan's newly endorsed role leeched into a preferred view of his adversary as persecutor:

> My persecutor is now made a Deputy Judge Advocate and we will set off in four or five days to go around the circuit and make the poor people again give their former attestation; this is the most curious piece of business ever undertaken. He gives me much trouble;—the matters happened so long ago and at so many places, and he is so meanly industrious.There is hardly an action in two years that I am not obliged to explain. If you can recollect any person who wrote or complained to Congress of his [Morgan's] malconduct and the suffering of the sick under his care, do write of them to me by the first post. . . .
>
> It is very mortifying to have every boy, formerly my pupil, asked what he knows against the Director General; but I must go through with it.[157]

The conflation of "persecutor" and "prosecutor" recurred throughout correspondence surrounding the court-martial and was picked up by Shippen's supporter Lee who wished Shippen "successful discharge from persecution."[158] Indeed, for those, like Lee, who saw the prosecution of a director general of the continental army hospitals in the middle of a war more than merely a distraction, the jockeying between Morgan and Shippen was disconcerting. Lee referred to it as "an atom compared with North America," which was in his view the larger stakes, that is, the war itself. Nevertheless, even for Shippen's brother-in-law the legal complications were troublesome for a new nation. They suggested a legal system perhaps less worthy than the one being overthrown, a system run by jurists who were hardly in charge and thereby potentially unable to yield a speedy trial much less evenhanded justice. As Lee, with some justification, queried, "It (your proposed proceedings) appears to me a new mode of judicial proceedings, for the prosecutor to be the evidence taker—although the defendant be present—because if they differ concerning the propriety of any insertion [evidence], who is to determine? Or is either of the parties to decide for himself against the other?"[159]

A developed legal order would have provided not only for due process but for rules of evidence, including corroboration of testimony, probable cause, credibility tests, exclusion of testimony and evidence, extenuation of guilt, and qualifications with the use of presumptive and circumstantial evidence. Such standards were only partly exemplified in the court-martial, where standards of proof and court processes were in flux. The independence of courts from the political process was not yet in evidence; there was neither a strong sense of a right to a trial nor a guarantee that the charges against one be proved. In parts of the law, the use of the truth as a defense was questionable, particularly where the charges had to do with public disorder and slander.

Witness Depositions and Testimony

The handling of witness testimony was also in flux as new legal standards were developing. Hearsay as opposed to personal knowledge, the value of expert testimony, with its potential for conflicting testimony and conflicts of interest, the need for corroboration, rules for taking depositions, and the relative value of signed depositions as opposed to oaths taken in court were all potentially at issue in the Shippen court-martial. For Morgan, the whole history of generating affidavits to prove his charges expressed Shippen's manipulation of the legal process and the ill-formed state of legal principles and processes that obtained in the court-martial. Congress's failure to afford Morgan himself due process when it dismissed him without announcing charges or holding a hearing seemed no less satisfying. In neither case, it began to appear, was Morgan to participate in a process where a court would assure that charges would be proved.

In a letter to Samuel Huntington, Morgan tried to capitalize on

Rush's earlier effort against Shippen to remind Congress that it had agreed then to assure the testimony of witnesses. A resolve by Congress at that time[160] obliged witnesses to testify, paid expenses for such testimony, and ensured that parties in one state would be obliged to testify in another state. Depositions were allowed so long as the accused had reasonable notice of time and place, so that he might attend.[161] Morgan made the case that Congress had insufficient time in the present instance to pass a law "that can oblige anyone to leave his boundaries to give evidence in another state."[162] Nor did any law exist in Pennsylvania, where the witnesses he wished to interview resided. Morgan asked that Congress renew its earlier "Resolve" for the purposes of his charges against Shippen. At the same time, he was irritated that he had to accept the burden of persuasion in the value and use of depositions since a resolve he had himself solicited on November 16 gave depositions less weight before Congress than they held in some states: "In many states, depositions are deemed good evidence in courts of law if the person accused has had reasonable notice of the time and place and then neglects to attend. Unless that is the meaning of Congress by the said resolve, it is in the power of the accused person to evade the force of evidence by absenting himself, though he received due notice."[163]

Morgan's suspicion of evasions was prescient for Shippen did indeed disappoint him by disregarding his notices and failing to appear. Depositions collected under these conditions, Morgan opined, would be less than pristine: "If I should proceed [on the journey] and he not attend, and the depositions on that account be considered as ex parte evidence, I had better save myself any further trouble unless Congress, in its wisdom, will point out a mode of rendering testimony of witnesses effectual and obtainable."[164] Whereas he would entertain revisiting the witnesses in Shippen's presence prior to re-starting the proceedings, Morgan was reluctant "after the court was appointed . . . [to] beat the ground over again."[165]

The journeys of which Morgan spoke put him to considerable time and expense. He had to endure the hardships brought on by winter weather, poor accommodations, and bad roads, since witnesses were dispersed and the circuit he would have to travel was extensive. Shippen never held out much hope for circuit riding as he made clear three weeks into the court-martial in a letter to Lee. Morgan, he offered, "cited me to attend [the taking of such depositions] through the deepest snow of the winter which he broke for two hundred miles and was one day dug out and once froze in his saddle."[166]

Once the court-martial opened in March 1780, it became clear that not only were the journeys onerous but that such a means of collecting evidence was to become a legal sticking point on which Shippen could hang his case. Depositions would require clarifications, open up opportunities for challenges to testimony, and permit delays. Shippen's approach was to challenge whatever testimony was collected as improperly generated and therefore not legally valid. To encourage further delays, he asserted that charges had not been properly presented to him. He excused himself for not appearing before Congress because his services were required by the sick and wounded for whom he was responsible to provide care. When the charges were specified, Shippen sought an adjournment to ensure his presence when depositions were taken by Morgan, asked for time to prepare his defense, and demanded that Morgan's affidavits not be admitted by the judge advocate as they did not constitute legal testimony. Morgan, in a letter to president of Congress Huntington, characterized Shippen's behavior in terms that suggested he found little to admire in the seeming justice afforded by the process of the court-martial: "I cannot but consider the conduct of Dr. Shippen to evade trial as a temporizing expedient, unworthy of an innocent man and a man of honor to endeavor to wear out his prosecutor by obliging him to sacrifice that time which is necessary that he employ for the support of his family, in an irksome pursuit after justice and to weary him with expenses and delays."[167]

Whereas Shippen ultimately agreed to attend Morgan's circuit riding to gather witness testimony, he had earlier attempted to undermine that testimony. As he admitted to Lee, he had "sent a friend around to interview the same persons and obtain certificates from nine-tenths of them, to the effect that they knew nothing against Dr. Shippen and did not mean to injure his character but that Dr. Morgan had earnestly and meanly importuned them to depose something or other."[168] Better advised by his friends, Shippen tried another tack which left him no alternative but to attend Morgan in a new round of peregrinations.

it was whispered among my friends that I was on slippery ground and that my certificates might be of no use and not legal testimony; in short that if I convinced their [the court's] honor and conscience that I was innocent, they could not acquit me because the testimony was not legal.

Upon this, I thought I was running too great a risk, as some weak, wicked or angered person might have been persuaded to swear falsely (against me) and [I] begged his [Morgan's] affidavits might not be admitted; urging five reasons against them and begged time to [better] prepare my defense, and to take all these dearly earned oaths over again.[169]

Morgan described the same set of events in the following terms:

The resolution of Congress of Dec. 24th last relative to admitting depositions of persons not in the line of staff of the Army to be read as evidence in trial not capital before court martial, was laid before the court and Dr. Shippen then made no objection to that resolve; whereupon some depositions were read in support of the first charge. Next day, finding he could not stand before the force of such evidence and the testimony in other depositions which I was prepared to produce, Dr. Shippen moved the court that no more depositions be read against him, pleading that he not only was not present at the taking of same, although he could not deny having had sufficient notice beforehand of the time and place of their taking, had he chosen to attend, but he alleged that I was never named or recognized by Congress as his prosecutor; that he was not under arrest at the time, nor served with the charges.[170]

The stories told by both men featured Shippen as the primary actor and absented Morgan as an active agent. To the extent that Morgan appeared at all it was as an objectified party to be resisted. Shippen's telling provided an insider's view of a subject who sought counsel, was situation-dependent and self-reflexive. In a summary sense, Shippen constructed himself as a strategic player improvising resolutions. Morgan, by contrast, an outsider, displayed Shippen as isolated, single-minded, and in control. Capable of moving others, Shippen was, in Morgan's story, calculated and driven.

A public disgrace once it played out on the pages of the *Pennsylvania Packet* after the court martial, the court's inability to ensure even fundamental fairness in handling evidence, in particular the witness depositions, is indicative of the condition of legal standards in the court-martial. The underlying problem with witnesses testifying was expressed in a piece in the *Pennsylvania Packet* by Thomas Bond, assistant director of the military hospitals, which was included as part of Shippen's vindication in the press. Bond's testimony had been reported by Benjamin Rush, whom Bond accused of being a discredited reporter for having given conflicting explanations of his own reasons for leaving the military medical department. Bond denied having offered the testimony Rush attributed to him.

The FEAR of being DISMISSED was, as doctor Rush then acknowledged, the reason of his resignation. It now suits his calumniating view to forge new and totally opposite reasons, and to attempt to impose them on the public, in which attempt it has been luckily in my power to detect him.

Having thus shewn that Dr. Rush is capable of LYING in the WORST SENSE of that approbrious WORD. It is unworthy of me to take any notice of the pretended conversation concerning doctor Shippen, which he has imputed to me, but to observe that this mention of it was prompted by the same malignant spirit which has so shamefully actuated doctor Rush thro the whole of his disgraceful writings, and carries in it the strongest marks of an unprincipled man.[171]

Beyond notice that conversations would be taken out of context, lied about, or put to someone else's use, Bond's piece offered a quote from Horace that served as a warning to all those who would offer testimony against their friends:

> He who malignant tear an absent friend,
> Or when attack'd by others don't defend;
> Who trivial bursts of laughter strives to raise,
> And courts of prating petulance the praise;
> Of things he never saw, who tells the tale,
> And friendship's secrets knows not to conceal:
> This man is vile, here, Roman, fix your mark;
> His soul is black, as his complexion's dark.

Shippen offered his own low opinion of the techniques and the sources used to malign him, suggesting, like Bond, that nobody likes a "rat": "It would be trifling with the patience of the public to enter into the incompetency of the witnesses doctor Morgan produced, and the low arts he employed, to draw from poor ignorant people certificates and depositions which, had they understood them, they could never have given. It is sufficient to say, that as these arts were not practicable with more proper and competent witnesses, he was obliged to have recourse to those who deserve no credit."

The larger issue, however, was neither so obvious nor so simple. The questions of law related to witness testimony were very much in evidence. Perjury, coercion, outright lying, interested witnesses, collusion, witness tampering, and the standards of evidence for witness testimony were all implicated to one degree or another. What possible value, for example, was the court to place on witnesses who had been coached or had their scripts written for them? Both Shippen and Morgan were plagued by such considerations. Morgan accused Shippen, for example, of selling food from hospital stores and then seeding the testimony of his witnesses with favorable recollections: "You have the modesty to assert, that you are only accused of selling four pipes and an half of wine, and three tierces of sugar. To cover the affair of wine, you make all your witnesses ring over the same tune about five or six pipes which you so frequently told them (not to forget) that you bought them of Mr. Nesbit."[172]

On a similar note, involving Shippen's failure to keep competent records, Morgan attacked the quality of the evidence provided by Shippen's witness.

> When doctor Rush had so recently remarked in the Packet of November 21st, on the unblushing "manner in which many of your witnesses performed the evolutions you had taught them," was it simple effrontery, or downright stupidity, that induced you to put the matter beyond the reach of doubt, by exhibiting to the public so striking a proof, in the questions and answers of the said Cutting? The books of the treasury prove that previous to his setting out for Boston, on your errand, you drew a large sum from thence, besides the order for sixty-seven thousand dollars [referred to previously as "an order of the United States on the loan office"]. How did he know the money you gave him was not public money? without choaking at the oath he had taken, he glibly swallowed the whole of a very complex question, which it was impossible for him, or any mortal but yourself to answer, with, "you did." Perhaps you told him it was your own money: but did that make it so.[173]

Concerned that evidence and witnesses "have been laid aside and rejected" by resolves of Congress, Morgan contended that even as a deputy of the judge advocate, he was hampered in his pursuit of justice:[174] "Although I acted by deputation from the Judge Advocate General, to attend and cross-examine witnesses, where he could not attend himself, I was not allowed to explain any matters in Court, as they arose, though no other person knew the circumstances, nor was I permitted to give my testimony as a witness, although sworn by the Court as a witness and the only one in support of the fifth charge."[175]

Shippen's own legal skills were apparently well served in the court-martial, above all in his presentation of witnesses. Indeed, Morgan complained of Shippen's clever manipulation of witnesses and his evasion of court rules: "Much have I to say on the artifices and chicanery of which you made use, to elude the cross examination of Mr.

Thomas Smith and other witnesses; of your examining your witnesses out of court, and producing their testimony thus taken in evidence before the court, when none of the members had the least
opportunity of cross-examining them contrary to a fixed rule of that
very court, and to the resolves of Congress."[176]

Morgan's criticism of Shippen's handling of witnesses reflected,
as well, reluctant admiration for his adversary's fluidity.

> you cannot deny, the manner of your examining your witnesses was to
> put them a string of artful complex questions, to which those that you
> had properly trained, generally answered categorically, as you wished
> them; or if left to themselves and the answer did not please, out went
> both question and answer. I will illustrate this latter assertion with an
> example to the point, in your examination of that honest witness doctor
> Craik, whose regard to truth revolted against some of your questions;
> and I will subjoin the evidence of doctor Thomas Bond, junior, on the
> same question: and what you have omitted of his testimony about your
> books.[177]

Examples of actual trial testimony provided some insight into the
difference between Morgan and Shippen's handling of witnesses.
Morgan cross-examining Dr. Tilton, for example, appeared straight-
forward and literal with the witness.

> Q: Was the director general at Trenton when you arrived, and did you
> represent to him the ill consequences of putting your men in barracks
> where it was reported that putrid fevers prevailed, and what did he say?
> A: I did represent it to him, and that, very earnestly. I forgot particularly
> what it was he said, but he put me off, and I could get no other place.
> Q: Do you know whether other quarters could be provided for your
> wounded men at Trenton, than those unhealthy barracks, had the direc-
> tor general taken care for that purpose.
> A: I know there were houses enough to be had, and that the director
> general had power to put them any where.
> Q: Do you know of any particular instance of the sick suffering and
> dying, from neglect of the director general?
> A: In my narrative I have already declared, that I think the principal
> source of the fatality, of the sick, at Trenton and Princeton, where I pre-
> scribed, was owing to neglect in the directorial branch of the hospital.
> Q: When Dr. Shippen was purveyor, did the sick suffer for want of wine
> and sugar?
> A: At Princeton wine was of an inferior quality and in sparing quantity,
> and the sick did suffer for want of it; and all the stores have been greater

plenty, since the purveyorship was taken out of Dr. Shippen's hands, than before. When I was sick I was obliged to procure Madeira wine else where.[178]

Shippen, by contrast, personalized and asked leading questions in his examination of Doctors Craik and Bond. He tried to negotiate Craik's response even as he was unable to move Bond to be more responsive to his questions.

> Doctor Shippen's question to doctor Craik.
> "Did I not always appear to you, anxious for the welfare of the sick and wounded very attentive to the duties of my station; and frugal in the expenditure of public money?"
> Answer by doctor Craik.
> "No! I beg pardon, sir, I cannot answer that question."
> Doctor Shippen in reply.
> "I believe it is very true, now I think of it, you had not so good opportunity of knowing it as some others I shall have occasion to examine so, JUDGE, we may pass over that question for the present."
> The answer of doctor Thomas Bond, junior, to the same question, was thus given,
> "I always thought you very anxious and humane, attentive enough in business, but rather too frugal."
> Question by doctor Shippen.
> "Did not the two books I gave you to look over, contain all my accounts against the public?"
> Answer.
> "I don't know."
> Question.
> "Did you not see credits given for transportation wagons?"
> Answer.
> "I did see one or more; but for what purpose I don't know."[179]

With the importance given to witness testimony in the court-martial, it is unsurprising that many witnesses wished to have their depositions revisited with the intention of correcting or even outright denying them. Dr. Samuel Finley, for one, had signed his original certificate at Rush's request[180] only to reopen his testimony within weeks[181] to make numerous corrections. He subsequently asserted that he had not meant to cast reflections on the director general. Finley claimed that Shippen did not know what quantities of wine had been issued from hospital stores and that he paid for whatever meats he took for himself, the costs being no more than sixteen dollars. Shippen always wrote true returns of the sick and either he or another officer visited the hospital almost every day. Finley, in sum, did not "think any of our distress arose from any want of conduct in the Director or any officer of the hospital."[182] Finley's withdrawal of critical parts of his certificate clearly undermined Rush's effort to use it, as he had intended, to support "the negligence, injustice, and falsehood of the Director General."[183] The prosecution was further injured by the testimony at court-martial of a hospital steward named Scott, who was present when the certificate was signed by both Finley and W. W. Smith. Scott testified that he overheard "when the gentlemen were going to sign it, that Dr. Rush said, 'We will bring the Shippens down,' upon which Dr. Smith signed it, and said he would join with all his heart."[184]

The self-interest displayed by Rush and W. W. Smith was countered by that of Colonel Moylan and Thomas Smith who gave evidence for Shippen. Morgan presented their certificates as of no avail, since one's motive was transparently to save the bacon of his "'dear Billy,' and the other of his own dear cousin."[185] In their cases, the testimony extended beyond mere interest to potential perjury.

> their opinion, that a person who has the handling of public money, may warrantably speculate in the stores of his department. . . . [is] a curious doctrine to support, at a time, when the citizens of these states are oppressed and born down with taxes, accumulated upon them by the malpractices of defaulters and speculators in public offices. I have a higher opinion of the integrity and honor of those worthy gentlemen, than to imagine they were ever capable, themselves, of reducing their speculative opinions to practice, for their own benefit.[186]

A second kind of testimony that proved problematic was that provided by witnesses who were later to claim they were coerced. Robert Jewell was one such witness. He revoked his testimony in the following declaration, included as part of Shippen's vindication.

> Doctor Morgan offered me a certificate to sign, which he had ready drawn up, reflecting on the character of doctor Shippen, which was not true. He importuned me much to sign it; I refused: he then begged I would draw one up myself as near it as I would. I told him I knew nothing against doctor Shippen: I would sign nothing. He urged and persuaded me much to do something, and added You know Mr. Jewel, you are under obligations to me, and ought to oblige me so far. At length he obtained a deposition before justice Adcock, in which I did not mean to

reflect on doctor Shippen's character as director general or an honest man.[187]

Morgan responded to Jewell's published declaration in a subsequent issue of the same newspaper.

> The fact is, I waited upon Mr. Jewell with a memorandum of what Doctor Rush had informed me (and he had received it from Mr. Jewell, himself) I shewed it to him, and he corrected it. He moreover told me he was ready to appear and give evidence to those facts whenever he was called upon by proper authority, but would not sign it. He said he had nothing personal against you, but would declare it to your face, but he would not sign it, you not being present. He then talked like an honest man; but after he had seen you, he changed his note: says he "Doctor Shippen has used me very handsomely, and I will not appear against him." Referring to his voluntary promise, and the duty he owed to that country, whose bread he lived upon, as a public officer I said he was under obligations to appear.[188]

The opposed stories of Jewell's testimony pitted Morgan against Shippen, the former figured coercing a witness and the latter bribing him. In one story, Morgan was portrayed as a man to whom some obligation was owed, calling in a debt. Jewell, pressured to deliver, was first presented with a prepared document for his signature, then "begged" to create his own version to the same effect. In the presence of a justice, Jewell was finally brought to deliver a deposition that he did not mean to be used as Morgan apparently used it.

The story of Shippen's involvement told a tale of Jewell not as a man "opportuned" to provide involuntary testimony but as an active agent who offered information against Shippen that Morgan received at second hand and which Jewell sought to confirm and correct. Jewell appeared in charge of his own testimony to the point that he would not trade off signing a deposition for meeting Shippen face to face as an accuser. His resolve was tested when he did in fact face Shippen, an event constructed as collusion when Shippen, in Jewell's words, "used me very handsomely."

The extent of the difference between Morgan's apparent threatening of Jewell and Shippen's handsome treatment was rather predictable, that is, the difference between an old boss and a present boss, a relationship in which one master simply replaced another. The nature of the difference, although both appealed to perjury, was that Shippen, for all his power to do harm, relied upon his ability to reward. Morgan, having lost the power to reward, relied upon a form of punishment, the use of force, that had no authority behind it.[189] A warning of this kind had not only less appeal than a reward, but it ultimately left the decision to the witness who could choose to take it as advice so long as the likelihood of harm was absent. Shippen's more indirect approach had the advantage of gauging Jewell's possible response face-to-face, so that he was less likely to overplay his hand and could resolve the issue with a wink and a nod, leaving future considerations vague and delayed by an implied understanding, more like a business proposal than a bribe event.

The representation of both Shippen and Morgan in this set of stories was consistent with the objectively distant quality of Morgan's questioning of Dr. Tilton in the court-martial and Shippen's strategic and personable interrogation of doctors Bond and Craik. As duelling stories, they reprise as well the narration of the two men collecting witness depositions, where the stolid Morgan was countered by the slippery Shippen, the former reliant on formal argument and the latter on conspiring with and influencing others.

Dr. Bodo Otto, a German emigrant, provided one of the most disturbing instances of witness tampering, an instance that covered misrepresentation, language differences, a degree of coercion, opportunism, and interpretation. In this case, the original certificate was simple enough. Solicited by Rush, Otto certified he had applied to Shippen for supplies "but he received them in such small quantities and so out of time that they did the sick but little good."[190] In addition to providing the certificate, Otto made the following request to Rush for supplies he lacked: "I beg I may be supplied with articles in the inclosed list, which things stand in very necessity of—I shall take the greatest care to do my duty in the important office here to which you were pleased to appoint me, and all orders shall be punctually obeyed by, respected sir, your obedient and very humble servant, BODO OTTO, Surgeon."[191]

Whether Rush suggested Otto write such a request or not is unclear, although Rush would not have been a party to whom Otto would normally make such a request. In any case, Rush interpreted Otto's certificate in a response to Shippen as an application that proved "that he applied to you for them to no purpose; for he well knew that it was no more my business to furnish these articles than it was to provide beef and flour to the army." Ever one to push events to their limits, Rush expressed the hope that the attorney general would take note of the deposition, certain that "He knows the name and punishment of his [Otto's] crime."[192]

In response to the certificate, Shippen presented a counter from Otto under oath that abrogated it: "Dr. Otto, a senior surgeon, when a paper was shewn and read distinctly to him, drawn up by Dr. Rush, and he was asked whether he signed his name to it, and whether the facts certified by him were true, answered thus on oath: 'I signed my name to one part of it, but not to the other, to the best of my recollection. The facts in that paper I do not acknowledge as true, or to have been assented to by me, but I must have been imposed to sign it."[193]

Shippen added, cavalierly, that "Dr. Otto is an extremely excellent officer, is not master of English, and a very polite man."[194] Otto's biographer, James E. Gibson, concluded that Rush, who was a master of English, had composed the certificate for Otto's signature and purposefully left it sufficiently ambiguous that Otto could sign it without hesitation. A native reader, nevertheless, could read into it an accusation of negligence against Shippen,[195] which left Otto open to a charge of perjury in Rush's mind as he rushed headlong to make his case. As Morgan warned Rush in a letter about the court-martial, not only did Otto disavow the certificate and claim to have been imposed upon to sign it, but Rush's interest was divulged when the judge advocate produced the original document following Otto's testimony. Morgan advised Rush, "The certificate is in your handwriting. He [Dr. Otto] had given testimony in direct opposition to the facts therein set forth. . . . On this declaration I found Shippen prepared to triumph. He intimates he shall in the course of examining other witnesses, show more of this [kind of] work. I think it my duty to inform you of these particulars."[196]

In a later letter, Morgan added that "Dr. Shippen is making great use of Dr. Otto's statements, in his harangues and frequent references to you. He asserts he shall show more forgery, etc. which, in his language, 'must ever bless our character.'"[197] For his part, Rush was quick to add that Shippen's role in the Otto affair was itself suspect. He reported that "When I showed these certificates to Dr. Shippen at York Town, he looked at them with a sneer and said in the presence of a Committee of Congress that he could prevail upon the old fellow to sign a counter-certificate. At that time I thought it impossible, for I had the highest opinion of Dr. Otto's probity as well as his industry and humanity, in his profession. In the course of his evidence before the court, he showed that Dr. Shippen was better acquainted with him than myself."[198]

Otto, feeling himself ill-used, published his own letter to Rush in *Pennsylvania Packet* in which he admitted to feeling "himself injured in his honor and reputation." The slight was particularly painful because, as Otto said, the source of his injury was a person "engaged in the service of his country as a public character, and of course accountable for his conduct." Otto was especially concerned by the reference Rush had made to punishing Otto for his crime.[199] A good servant of the people caught in an ugly battle of egos, Otto intimated an end-of-career sensitivity to his legacy as a doctor and as a man.

> The plain and obvious design and intent of which is (as far as your power and influence extends) an endeavor to blast my character and credit, by representing me to the public as guilty of the most odious and disgraceful offense to society.
>
> A charge or accusation of this kind in such a public manner (however weak and ineffectual in itself), must naturally excite the most keen sensation in a feeling mind; and I can, with satisfaction say, that in the course of seventy years' journey through life with its various changes and vicissitudes, both in Europe and America, I have never experienced an instance of similar treatment.[200]

Leaving aside the question of the likelihood that the German doctor was able by himself to pen a letter so "masterfully" written, Otto laid claim here under oath to what he "knew to be the truth, and to what I shall always religiously and truthfully adhere." Otto expressed his expectation to be at all times "held accountable at a proper tribunal," suggesting not merely military accountability but heavenly accountability as well. He regarded himself as uninfluenced by "prejudice or party" and energized "by love of justice and humanity . . . in the honest and conscientious discharge of my duty of which the envenomed sting of slander cannot deprive me." Of all the witnesses in Shippen's court-martial, Otto might well have been the most abused and least dishonored by it.

One final witness requires discussion in this case, a figure, Patrick Garvey, who could not be more opposite to Otto. With Garvey, we extend our discussion beyond witness testimony to standards of material evidence. Garvey's testimony was tied to that of Thomas Bond who demonstrated his reluctance to certify regularity in Shippen's bookkeeping. Morgan raised the issue with Shippen: "Upon this slender foundation, without producing your books, as, I suppose, they were not then transcribed, and suited to invalidate the testimony which appeared against you, the whole flimsy superstructure of your defence upon book keeping is built."[201] According to Otto's biographer, Shippen did submit his records when he finally resigned in January 1781, seven months after he was acquitted in June 1780 by the court-martial. Although Bond's testimony suggested that Shippen kept adequate books,[202] Morgan found the standards of evidence outrageously lax: "Nor was Dr. Shippen obliged to produce his books. . . . A Commissary's declaration of his having had an order from a Surgeon, whether written or verbal, without any receipt or other proof of the orders being comply'd with, was deemed the only proper and sufficient voucher for the expenditure of hospital stores. Yet, it was proved on the oaths of the Physicians and Surgeons General, that their orders as well as those of the Surgeons, were often disregarded by the Commissaries, and refused, or only partially complied with."[203]

Between the court-martial acquittal and Shippen's subsequent resignation, a notice appeared in the *Pennsylvania Packet* that appeared to support Morgan's criticism of the court-martial's standards. It appeared over the name of Garvey, apparently without encouragement from either Morgan or Rush, and certainly without their open sponsorship in the newspaper. Garvey provided an affidavit that suggested considerably more chicanery than Shippen ever admitted or, more importantly, than Morgan suspected. Garvey added the following ingredient to the mix.

> In January of 1780, Dr. William Shippen, Jr., Director General, applied indirectly to me to settle his books. The gentleman who made the application, informed me that Dr. Shippen made particular inquiries respecting my ability to settle accounts; my character, and asked him if I was a person in whom he might confide, remarking that he had neglected taking receipts, etc., and finally that the purpose for which he wanted me was to transcribe his books. For this service, he said Dr. Shippen would give One Hundred Guineas if I would undertake the task.
>
> The gentleman told me he was struck with astonishment at the proposal, yet was determined to inform me of it. I told him I detested Shippen and his money and would have nothing to do with him.[204]

Equally interesting was a notice, anonymously submitted, that appeared in the same issue to the effect that "a Friend to Truth," having discovered that Garvey's affidavit was to appear, wished to have printed as well a certificate regarding the witness's present status. The notice warned that Garvey had been "charged with being a spy." The anonymous informant's intent was to impeach him "that the public may not be imposed upon by such a witness." The certificate provided was endorsed by the "Gaoler" of the Philadelphia Gaol: "I do hereby certify that Patrick Garvey was committed to the gaol in the City and County of Philadelphia on the 22nd of November last, being charged with treasonable and dangerous practices to the State and remains in custody this day as committed by His Excellency, Joseph Reed, Esq., President of the State of Pennsylvania."[205]

Morgan weighed in on the issue, unfazed by the fact that he had himself been accused, at least in the press, of fraternizing with the enemy. Neither did he consider that his isolation from the American troops after his own dismissal made first-hand information about Shippen's affairs unlikely. Shippen put it that "As Dr. Morgan remained in the city with the enemies of his country all this time he was quite ignorant of my conduct, and was obliged to ask information and assistance of Dr. Rush, before he could plan his prosecution."[206] Taking the opportunity to respond to the Garvey notice, Morgan went on the offensive.

> The deposition of Mr. Garvey shews the plain reason why you chose to carry a load of hospital stores to your trial, in preference to your books. It likewise shews the reason why you concealed yourself with some of your select witnesses at Dr. Bond's country seat, four miles from town, and spent several weeks there previous to your trial, with your new advocate and book-makers to alter your books for the inspection of the auditors of accounts, till the house took fire, and brought you all to light. Not having it in your power to compleat your plan there you applied to Mr. Garvey for assistance, whose spirited answer drove you to look out for other help. By what means you worked through this shameful business, it is probable time will soon discover and the dirt come out.[207]

Outraged at Congress's subsequent endorsement of the court-martial acquittal, Morgan gave Shippen notice that the issue of the books would be pursued and that he still expected a prosecution under civil law.

> When I first impeached you for trial by a court martial, I earnestly demanded of Congress to secure your books to prevent erasures and false entries: my application for that purpose was then in vain. But I once more give notice, that if Congress will direct you to be delivered up and

prosecuted by civil law, and will immediately secure your books, and direct a committee to attend the business, as they did in a similar case, and by means of the books thus secured, proved the charge; I am willing to give them my assistance, and have no doubt, you will be convicted of other frauds and embezzlements (not yet known to the public) on new and fresh evidence providentially offering.

The heavy reliance on witness testimony, particularly depositions—which could not be effectively subjected to cross-examination, even if they were taken with both the defendant and the prosecutor present—was a characterizing feature of the Shippen court-martial. To its detriment, the proceeding was suspect for the lax and irregular way in which depositions were collected and admitted, so that their status as legal testimony was consistently under scrutiny. Signed testimony was opposed to testimony under oath and written testimony was opposed to live testimony in court. Questions were raised about testimony that was prepared for signature, or forged, as opposed to that written by a witness, testimony that was sworn falsely, taken under false pretenses, revised, or revoked in addition to that which was influenced, coerced, or bribed.

Witness tampering and coaching became issues as did reluctant and hostile witnesses. The intention of testimony and its interpretation as well as self-interested testimony and conflicts of interest posed problems, as did the absence of corroboration and evidentiary support for testimony. Whether testimony was from a qualified witness, firsthand, or hearsay and whether a chain of custody existed for evidence suspected of having been altered or that should have been sealed or otherwise protected were issues as well. And if the prospect of all these problems was not daunting enough, the court-martial had to deal with amateurish and prejudicial examinations and cross-examinations of witnesses that tried the patience of the court. In a case so dependent upon witness testimony, Shippen's court-martial was bound to undermine confidence in legal process. That a verdict reached under such conditions would fail to be embraced for its legitimacy was hardly surprising. Neither was Congress's endorsement of the acquittal sufficient to render the verdict determinate.

The court-martial began as feud and would end as a feud, even to the point of anticipating a duel between Rush and Shippen. That a duel did not actually eventuate surprised even Rush, who expressed his belief that a duel would be forthcoming in a letter to Daniel Roberdeau, member of Congress: "The patience with which Dr. Shippen heard the hints I gave of his peculation, and his declining to call upon me for public or private satisfaction for what I said of him before the committee of Congress, were sufficient to convince any man that my insinuations were well-grounded."[208] The extension of the feud would not end in a duel, but neither would it end with the court-martial. It would continue, this time before the public and in the press.

Trial by Press

Rush and Morgan had waited more than three years to bring Shippen to judgment. The court-martial before Congress lasted three months. The trial by press that followed lasted four months. Unsatisfied with Shippen's acquittal, Rush and Morgan pursued the newspaper war as a form of vigilante justice, with little hope of a court prosecution. Rush addressed Shippen in the *Pennsylvania Packet,* expressing the sentiment that the three years had been

> borne, in silence, with the suspicion of having accused you unjustly, and of sacrificing the public good to private resentment. I was satisfied that an appeal to the public, (for I always suspected the resources of your office would enable you to baffle every attempt to bring you to punishment by the ordinary course of law) would do justice to my complaints, and shew you in your proper colours to your country. I hope my fellow citizens will ever be tenacious of this invaluable check upon the decisions of our courts, as well as the proceedings of our legislatures. A free paper is the surest detection of fraud and corruption: the virtue and liberties of America, and the liberty of the press must stand or fall together.[209]

Putting aside the irony of Rush's use of the fourth estate to pursue his enemies, given his suit against the journalist William Cobbett in 1799 on a charge of abusing the powers of the press in much the same way, Rush defended freedom of the press as a tool of public democracy: "Let tyrants and public defaulters cease to complain of the freedom I have taken with the votes of Congress. The enemy knows full well that a free press is the engine of liberty, and all their hopes of conquering us are in vain, while that bulwark of freedom exists among us. . . . They sicken at the sight of those publications, which point out the defects in the administration of our governments, and expose the folly and tyranny of our rulers."

On behalf of his case, Morgan too offered an encomium to a free press.

> I congratulate you, my fellow citizens, upon the invaluable privilege of a free press, which I consider as the palladium of liberty, the scourge of knaves, the terror of despotism, and the refuge of the oppressed. By means of it, driven as I have been, by an act of tyranny, into exile with the enemy, as David was by the persecution of Saul, I have, nevertheless been enabled to cite doctor Shippen before your impartial bar, and compelled him to attend, however reluctantly, although intrenched in power, and guarded by the arts of bribery and seduction, he has long affected to treat your opinion of him with silence and contempt.[210]

From the very outset of his attacks in the press, Morgan had been clear that his use of the medium was as a surrogate court, albeit a court without walls. His intent was to tell his story in a public forum, to shed light on the court-martial evidence, and to expose Congress's failure to convict an enemy of the people. He would leave his opponent no place to hide. Morgan's only consolation for Congress's verdict was that the evidence was now in the hands of the people: "I rest assured that the discerning public is now too well acquainted with the facts and the character of the deponents to be diverted from its passing judgment according to evidence, or to be imposed upon either by invectives or assertions; and that the declaration of disinterested witnesses upon oath, will be considered as the pillars of truth, not to be shaken by cavil, or intemperate abuse, thrown out, either upon the witnesses, or the prosecutor in behalf of the public."[211]

Beyond their objective of outing Shippen, Morgan and Rush accomplished little by publishing the trial facts. At points they suggested that a civil trial should ensue, at others that Congress should re-indict, and elsewhere that public ignominy might be punishment enough. Morgan's appeal to the free citizens of the nation was in any case a warning to his fellow citizens lest they should attempt to hold the powerful to account by exercising their right of private prosecution: "Nor is any man to expect in that case, to escape the stabs of secret and open enemies, actions at law, and a combination against him of the agents and dependants of the person prosecuted. He must also lay it to his account to take the whole weight and expence of the prosecution on his own shoulders, and with all the embarrassments that can be thrown in his way."[212]

The private prosecutor, he warned, had become the persecuted.

In the absence of the verdict Morgan had hoped for and the unlike-lihood of a court trial, a public trial by press was, it appeared, the most justice he could hope to have.

Morgan's story had come to a less than propitious end. It began as a tale of a fallen man who sought the resurrection of his reputa-tion and honor. His redemption was to have come at the cost of the sacrifice of the conspirator who had led his enemies against him. Instead, he became himself an exile like David, a Judas-goat perse-cuted in his righteous fight and who, blamed by the public for hav-ing exposed such a sore wound in the national psyche to public review, would die alone and broken, feeling himself reviled by the very nation he had been so intent on rescuing from an evil at its core.

Francis Hopkinson's Court of Honor

The last exhibit and capstone piece of the Shippen court-martial and trial by press was a satire by Francis Hopkinson, then a Philadel-phia lawyer and subsequently an admiralty judge. It appeared in the last issue of the *Pennsylvania Packet* to include material on the case.[213] The cessation of material thereafter was abrupt, a factor attributable not so much to Hopkinson's proposal as to the opportunity it pro-vided the printer John Dunlap to withdraw gracefully from the alter-cation, which had by then clearly abused the public's patience.

Calling for the establishment of a "High Court of Honour," Hop-kinson's entry was addressed to "Mr. Printer" and was signed "Cala-mus," a Latin term for a reed used for writing.[214] Hopkinson pitched his piece to the publisher by suggesting the proposal would save him and his newspaper time and money. Although the author avowed that his intent was much greater than the mere saving of money, it did not escape his notice that by means of his project, "when a gen-tleman finds himself so disposed, he may vilify and abuse his friend and neighbor at the very reasonable expence of *two shillings;* where-as it costs the Lord knows what to get a column or two of scandal inserted in your paper."[215] Not only was the author's proposal sim-pler and cheaper than other legal alternatives, but he saw possibili-ties of "considerable improvement" for his country with the establishment of such a court: "How much bloodshed—how much inkshed, would be spared? How many difficult points of honour, and nice questions of ceremony would be judicially determined? How many private animosities would be checked in the first stage, and brought to issue before the blood became heated by argument and altercation?"[216]

In Calamus, Hopkinson masqueraded as a figure with "a tolerable education in the charity-school belonging to our university,"[217] having been bound over by his parents to a scrivener who put him to the task of writing out "deeds, leases, wills, etc."[218] Setting up by himself following his apprenticeship, he was pleased to report that "my employers frequently applied to my judgement in difficult cases [and] . . . that my advice contributed not a little to support their worship's official reputation." With no prospect of reward but with hopes of gaining the reputation of being its author, Calamus proceeded to proffer an "ingenious and salutary" scheme: "Let there be a new court of justice established, under the name and stile of *The High Court of Honour*." The author detailed his proposal with the care one would take in drafting legislation or a contract, consistent with his training by the scrivener. The court would consist of twelve men elected by freemen of all degrees and quality, excepting only slaves and strangers to the city or county, nine of those selected forming a quorum and a majority determining the judgment. The court's jurisdiction would be over "all matters of controversy between man and man, of what kind soever they be, provided no property real or personal shall come in question." It would have the authority to render decisions "on differences in opinion—points of honour—ceremony—rank and precedence in all cases of affronts—flights—abuse—scandal, slander, and calumny—and in all other matters of contest; except as before excepted."[219]

In the high court of honour, one would not be allowed counsel; indeed, "No council shall be admitted in this court," contrary to the tendency of the times. Such rough justice as honor required, it appeared, was to be delivered without the interference and tricks of lawyers and outside earshot of judges. Judges and lawyers were men known to steer juries and to reverse jury verdicts of which they disapproved. Rather, "the parties shall personally plead their own causes" and must "make good [the] charge or charges against the *accused*."[220] Should one bring trifling charges to the court or fail to make good on those charges, the court would inscribe the accuser's name in the Rascal's Record. The nature of the disincentive became clear when one considered that once one's name was entered in the Record, it was "there to remain from generation to generation. World without end. *Amen!*"[221]

Calamus assigned a clerk to keep a large bound book to be entitled "*The Rascal's Record,*" which was open to inspection for a given fee. The book was to serve as an official registry to memorialize a guilty verdict. The Record was not, however, merely a repository of names for public inspection, but a publicly inscribed punishment. Being publicly named was a punishment intended to replace other reprehensible means of conflict resolution, so that if "any person or persons shall presume to decide any point of honour, contest, or squabble, by duel, or by appeals to the public, in any newspaper, hand-bill, or pamphlet, such offence shall be deemed a contempt of the high court of honour: and the party or parties so offending shall be rendered infamous, by having their names respectively entered in the *Rascal's Record.*"[222]

Taken in these terms, the offense lay not in dishonoring another but in putting dishonor to the test of a duel or a trial by press. The means of deciding a point of honor was being tried here, so that the infectious and outrageous use of the press to advertise one's case was itself before the court. By the same argument, the court tried abuses of codes of honor that required men to defend their reputations by risking their lives. Since duels were outside the law, to win was the same as losing. Parties were open to the judgment of the high court if they won a duel and open to injury or death if they lost.

Hopkinson had devised a scheme to address what he understood to be an excessive condition in his native city Philadelphia, in which a tradition of litigiousness and uncivil abuse of one's enemies prevailed. Indeed, the form in which one was to render a declaration in his High Court was modeled on the kind of language that appeared routinely in newspaper assaults on citizens by whom others felt they had been wronged. The boilerplate language could act as a "blank form of declaration with which to institute a suit":[223]

> Know ALL MEN, by these presents, that I A.B. of the city of Philadelphia—do announce, pronounce, attest, and declare, that my friend and fellow citizen C.D. of the same city _____ is a rogue, a rascal, a villain, a thief, and a scoundrel: that he is a tory, a traitor, a conspirator, and a rebel: That he is a forestaller, a regrator, a monopolizer, a speculator, and a depreciator: That he is a backbiter, a slanderer, a calumniator, and a liar. That he is a mean, dirty, stinking, sniveling, sneaking, pimping, pocket-picking-d——d son of a bitch. And I do further declare, that all and every of the above appellations are intended, and ought to be taken, construed, and understood *in the most opprobrious sense of the words.*[224]

Hopkinson argued for predictability, certainty, and neutrality to move beyond petty conflicts and personal affronts to questions of public interest. Satirizing the libelous disputes that had come to characterize legal charges and counter charges, he recognized that the old nonlegal order was no longer functional. Having been made ludicrous, honor and dishonor would be displaced as valued forms of reputational capital from the public venue and relegated to the domain of rascals. This move left the courts and the press free to take up issues of substance and import. Moreover, it allowed for reform of abuses arising from the chicanery of lawyers and judges, it anticipated reforms that presumably offered more effective representation to parties involved in lawsuits, and it provided for greater independence of juries.

Hopkinson's high court satire put the American legal system on notice that feuds like those engaged in by Morgan, Shippen, and Rush had to be reigned in. The risk to the new nation was too great to be borne. The descent into internecine feuding, marked at its low point by the events of the Morgan/Shippen feud, needed to be reversed. Such disputes threatened to undermine the stability and order that the legal system had to deliver if the nation was to gain the confidence of the people and if the courts were to be accessed for dispute resolution. Standards of evidence, witness testimony, the role of the prosecution, individual rights of due process, facing one's accuser, and having charges proved against you were all implicated in the transition, pointing the way for disputants to move from the nonlegal order to a legal order, a move already in transition in the Shippen court martial.

Looking at the world of eighteenth-century medicine through the prism of its narrative constructions—the stories it tells and those that are told about its practices and practitioners—and through the social norms and nonlegal order that characterized that world, has provided an opportunity to capture the profession like an insect in amber. Medicine had, after all, created a form of being out of the conditions in which it was set but which crystallized it, leaving it no space in which to develop without shattering its case or replacing it with another. The legal order that was represented by establishing medicine as a profession, capitalizing on a scientific paradigm, and making use of a formal model for dispute resolution would place feuds within a different, more official order capable of controlling their effects more efficiently and yielding greater stability and predictability to the operations of medical culture. It would no longer be enough to rely upon honor and reputation as safeguards. Personalization of rewards and punishment would have to yield to a distribution of resources and deterrents that looked more like fairness and, even, justice. Hopkinson got it right when he cut off the Morgan-Shippen-Rush trial by press with a satire. Medicine had become an object of ridicule and its players had been reduced to performers staging a tale of fury told, as Hopkinson might have put it, by rascals and scoundrels. They might not have warranted the appellation of pimps and pocket-pickers, but they had clearly been reduced to back-biters and slanderers.

Notes

INTRODUCTION

1. Anthony Giddens, *The Constitution of Society: Outline of the Theory of Structuration* (Berkeley: University of California Press, 1984), xxi; Roger Cooter, "'Framing' the End of the Social History of Medicine," in *Locating Medical History: The Stories and Their Meanings,* ed. Frank Huisman and John Harley Warner, 315 (Baltimore: Johns Hopkins University Press, 2004).

2. George Everett Hastings, *The Life and Works of Francis Hopkinson* (New York: Russell & Russell, 1926), 236–37, 309.

CHAPTER 1. THEORY

1. Kenneth Allen De Ville, *Medical Malpractice in Nineteenth-Century America: Origins and Legacy* (New York: New York University Press, 1990), 225.

2. Ibid., 4.

3. Ibid., 1.

4. *Lowell v. Faxon* (1824) 5. See Charles Lowell, *Authentic Report of a Trial before the Supreme Judicial Court of Maine, for the County of Washington, June 1824* (Portland: C. Lowell, 1825).

5. De Ville, *Medical Malpractice,* 16.

6. *Lowell v. Faxon,* in De Ville, *Medical Malpractice,* 17.

7. Carol J. Greenhouse, "Nature is to Culture as Praying is to Suing: Legal Pluralism in an American Suburb," *Journal of Legal Pluralism* 20 (1982): 17.

8. Ibid., 29.

9. Dov Cohen and Joe Vandello, "Social Norms, Social Meaning, and the Economic Analysis of Law: Meanings of Violence," *Journal of Legal Studies* 27(1988): 567, 570.

10. Ibid., 571.

11. Ibid., 575, 584.

12. Warren F. Schwartz, Keith Baxter, and David Ryan, "The Duel: Can These Gentlemen Be Acting Efficiently," *Journal of Legal Studies* 13 (1984): 325, note 16.

13. David Harley, "Honour and Property: The Structure of Professional Disputes in Eighteenth-Century English Medicine," in *The Medical Enlightenment of the Eighteenth Century,* ed. Andrew Cunningham and Roger French, 138–64 (Cambridge: Cambridge University Press, 1990). Harley suggests that informal disputes be given more attention as they "offer glimpses of rules, beliefs and values which are normally unspoken, despite presenting severe problems of representativeness"

(139). The real interest in disputes, he contends, is in the politics and ideology, economics, tensions between rival groups, and efforts to influence the public (140–41), as in England where such groups as Dissenters, Whigs, Jacobites, Papists, and Quakers, were often at the heart of a dispute. But more than anything else, physicians' honor, status, and reputation—which have been regularly overlooked—have been decisive in keeping disputes, feuds, and even duels alive (144).

14. Schwartz, Baxter, and Ryan, "The Duel," 328–29.

15. Ibid., 335–36, 343.

16. Ibid., 339–40, 345.

17. Greenhouse, "Nature is to Culture," 18–20.

18. Ibid., 20.

19. Ibid., 28.

20. Greenhouse 30.

21. Resolution was critical in quarrels that involved hospitals as the political, ideological, and religious differences that arose there could paralyze an institution. Indeed one conflict in England in 1792 resulted in the publication of a work on medical ethics by Thomas Percival that was to have wide distribution in both England and America (Harley, "Honor and Property," 156–57). Nevertheless, except for the threat of duels, "there was no restraint on the level of hostility and dispute behavior did not exorcise the grievances" (160). What Harley makes quite clear is that disputes were rarely settled without the death or departure of one of the principals (156, 160). He makes the point that it is valuable to consider disputes outside of settlements, for settlements tell us more about maintaining the status quo than about the variety of extra-legal mechanisms, social change, and uncertainty that is present in a dispute.

22. Schwartz, Baxter, and Ryan, "The Duel," 338.

23. Ibid., 338–39. Whether publicly advertised in the press or more privately contained, feuds often expressed themselves recklessly as a form of "chicken." People of reputation were more likely to engage in such behavior when their opponents were smaller fry and the game more like cat and mouse over smaller stakes with less risk involved. Whether players of status captured significant community advantage even under those conditions is questionable.

24. Ibid., 344.

25. Ibid., 345.

26. Harley makes the point that the truth of an accusation is not necessarily important to discern, for what the accusation itself represents is revealing about behaviors that the group wishes to endorse or condemn ("Honour and Property," 140).

27. Schwartz, Baxter, and Ryan, "The Duel," 335.

28. De Ville, *Medical Malpractice,* 1–4.

29. Linda Myrsiades, "A Language Game Approach to Narrative Analysis of Sexual Harassment Law in *Meritor v. Vinson,*" *College Literature* 25, no. 1 (1998): 201–2, nn. 2 and 3, 223; Jean François Lyotard and Jean Loup Thebaud, *Just Gaming,* trans. Wald Godzich (Minneapolis: University of Minnesota Press, 1985) 23, 27–28; Bill Readings, *Introducing Lyotard: Art and Politics* (New York: Routledge, 1991), 102.

30. Pierre Bourdieu, *Outline of a Theory of Practice,* trans. Richard Nice (Cambridge: Cambridge University Press, 1977), 81. In a rewrite of Marx, "we write his-

tory, but not in texts of our own choosing"; Nick J. Fox, "Is There Life After Foucault? Texts, Frames and Differends," in *Foucault, Health and Medicine*, ed. Alan Peterson and Bryan S. Turner, 48 (London: Routledge, 1997).

31. Michel De Certeau, *The Practice of Everyday Life*, trans. Steven Rendall (Berkeley: University of California Press, 1984), xiii–xiv.

32. Ibid., xi, xii.

33. Usufruct is "a right to use another's property" which would otherwise go unused; Bryan A. Garner, ed., *Black's Law Dictionary* 7th ed. (St. Paul: West Group, 1999), 1542. See Morton J. Horwitz, *The Transformation of American Law, 1780–1860* (Cambridge: Harvard University Press, 1977), 54–58;William J. Novak, *The People's Welfare: Law and Regulation in Nineteenth-Century America* (Chapel Hill: University of North Carolina Press, 1996), 40–43, 46.

34. If we act consistent with the idea of judgment that is largely unknowable and always just over the horizon, our dilemma is clear: we are faced with the chore of finding determinative law within an indeterminative justice, of trying to represent an unknowable law. Myrsiades, "A Language Game," n. 5, 223; Lyotard and Thebaud, *Just Gaming*, 83; see Charles Altieri, "Judgment and Justice under Postmodern Conditions; or, How Lyotard Helps Us Read Rawls as a Postmodern Thinker," in *Redrawing the Lines: Analytic Philosophy, Deconstruction, and Literary Theory*, ed. Reed Way Dasenbroc, 65 (Minneapolis: University of Minnesota Press, 1989); Joan Williams, "Critical Legal Studies: The Death of Transcendence & The Rise of the New Langdells," *New York University Law Review* 62 (1987): 493–94. Lyotard and Thebaud, *Just Gaming*, 16–18; Jean Francois Lyotard, *Peregrinations: Law, Form, Event*, trans. Cecile Lindsay (New York: Columbia University Press, 1988) 8, 20–27.

35. See Eric A. Posner, *Law and Social Norms* (Cambridge: Harvard University Press, 2000); Paul W. Kahn, *The Cultural Study of Law: Reconstructing Legal Scholarship* (Chicago: The University of Chicago Press, 1999); Robert C. Ellickson, *Order Without Law: How Neighbors Settle Disputes* (Cambridge: Harvard University Press, 1991).

36. According to Bourdieu, such concealment constitutes "misrecognition" or "misconception." Richard Terdiman, "Translator's Introduction" to Pierre Bourdieu, "The Force of Law: Toward a Sociology of the Juridical Field," *Hastings Law Journal* 38 (1987): 813.

37. Ibid., 178.

38. Ibid., 179.

39. Ibid., 179–80.

40. Ibid., 181–82.

41. Ibid., 183.

42. Ibid., 184.

43. The fiction of permanence is maintained in Michel Foucault in his sense of the power of social norms as an ubiquitous force that exerts control over heterogeneous practices. It diffuses itself through them at the local level to create a "carceral society," a society we find regulated through professions like medicine and law as it had earlier been regulated through religion. Foucault, as discussed by De Certeau, "The Practice of Everyday Life," 48; Bryan S. Turner, "From Governmentality to Risk: Some Reflections on Foucault's Contribution to Medical Sociology," in *Foucault, Health and Medicine*, ed. Alan Peterson and Bryan S. Turner, xi–xii (London: Routledge, 1997); Deborah Lupton, "Foucault and the Medicalisation Critique," in

Foucault, Health and Medicine, ed. Alan Peterson and Bryan S. Turner, 95 (London: Routledge, 1997). Foucault negates the fixity of rules while he asserts a disciplinary grid that is something like an ossified habitus—without the negotiated quality of Bourdieu's habitus. For De Certeau, the "field of force" that exists is like a text which the reader inhabits and in which he insinuates himself, making his own changes and thereby asserting his agency (xvii, xxi). For Foucault, however, the activities of agents are merely "the surface manifestation of a deeper power/knowledge" (Fox, "Is There Life," 37) linked as one entity so that, power requiring information and information implying power, they are mutually reinforcing (Fox, 36–37; Turner, "Governmentality," xiii).

44. One form of regularity, Pierre Bourdieu's "habitus," is constituted as social dispositions "written into the body" that offer a "feel for the game," reproduce its rules, and shape possibilities for action. Should this commonsense world fail to orchestrate social reality, should it meet resistance as a statement of similar experiences, social norms step in to provide sanctions and enforcement. Edward Gieskes, *Representing the Professions: Administration, Law, and Theater in Early Modern England* (Newark: University of Delaware Press, 2006), 28–29, 32; Bourdieu, *Outline of a Theory of Practice,* 80.

45. Gieskes, *Representing the Professions,* 43–44.

46. Ibid., 49–51.

47. Ibid., 252.

48. Bourdieu, "Force," 805.

49. Gieskes, *Representing the Professions,* 57.

50. Ibid., 66.

51. Bourdieu, "Force," 831.

52. Ibid., 832.

53. Ibid., 833.

54. Ibid., 832–35.

55. Ibid., 845. As Bourdieu would put it, "Unlike two players who, for lack of agreement upon the rules of their game, are condemned to accuse each other of cheating every time their comprehension of the game diverges, the actors involved in an undertaking governed by specific rules know that they may *count* on a coherent and inescapable norm. They therefore may calculate and predict both the consequences of adherence to the rule and the effects of transgressing it" (849).

56. Bourdieu, *Outline of a Theory of Practice,* 78; Gieskes, *Representing the Professions,* 32.

57. Kahn, *Cultural Study,* 36.

58. Ibid.

59. Ellickson, *Order Without Law,* 284.

60. Ibid., 284.

61. Ibid., 236.

62. Ibid., 157.

63. Ibid., 137, 140.

64. Ibid., 150, 153.

65. Ibid., 173.

66. Ibid., 180.

67. Ibid., 133–34, 184, 207, 232, 236, 240.

68. Ibid., 207–11, 228.

69. Ibid., 210–12, 217.

70. Ibid., 208, 213–16, 219, 228, 239, 232.

71. Posner, *Law and Social Norms,* 4; Ellickson sees the nonlegal and the legal orders mixing as a way of minimizing costs; *Order Without Law,* 249.

72. Ellickson, *Order Without Law,* 250; see Posner, *Law and Social Norms,* 4.

73. Ellickson, *Order Without Law,* 252; Posner, *Law and Social Norms,* 8, 221.

74. Ellickson, *Order Without Law,* 257.

75. Ibid., 250–52, 256.

76. Posner, *Law and Social Norms,* 12, 149.

77. Ellickson, *Order Without Law,* 249, 252, 254, 256–57; Posner, *Law and Social Norms,* 3, 150, 153.

78. Ellickson, *Order Without Laws,* 181–82, 250–54, 257; Posner, *Law and Social Norms,* 115, 177.

79. Posner, *Law and Social Norms,* 5.

80. Ibid., 218.

81. Ibid., 5–7, 13.

82. Ibid., 22, 27, 30, 37.

83. Posner in any case thinks it does not have intrinsic value.

84. Posner, *Law and Social Norms,* 44.

85. Ibid., 31,40–41, 43, 88, 90, 149.

86. Ibid., 88.

87. Ibid., 91.

88. Posner 91.

89. Ibid., 91–93, 105, 108–9.

CHAPTER 2. MEDICAL HISTORY

1. Lawrence L. Conrad, Michael Neve, Vivian Nutton, Roy Porter, and Andrew Wear, *The Western Medical Tradition: 800 BC to AD 1800* (Cambridge: Cambridge University Press, 1995), 371.

2. Ibid., 25, 59–60, 64.

3. Ibid., 374–75.

4. "Police" was the term used to describe the assumption by the state of responsibility for public health through public agencies and rules and regulations.

5. See John B. Blake, *Public Health in the Town of Boston, 1630–1822* (Cambridge: Harvard University Press, 1959); John Duffy, *The Sanitarians: A History of American Public Health* (Urbana: University of Illinois Press, 1990); George Rosen, "The Fate of the Concept of Medical Police, 1780–1890," *Centaurus* 5, no. 1 (1957): 97–113; George Rosen, *From Medical Police to Social Medicine: Essays on the History of Health Care* (New York: Science History Publications, 1974).

6. See John Harley Warner, *The Therapeutic Perspective: Medical Practice, Knowledge, and Identity in America, 1820–1885* (Cambridge: Harvard University Press, 1986); Philip Cash, Eric H. Christianson and J. Worth Estes, eds., *Medicine in Colonial Massachusetts, 1620–1820* (Boston: Colonial Society of Massachusetts, 1980); Richard Harrison Shryock, *Medicine and Society in America, 1660–1860* (New York: New York University Press, 1960); Richard Harrison Shryock, *Medicine in America: Historical Essays* (Baltimore: Johns Hopkins University Press, 1966).

7. Patricia A. Watson, *The Angelic Conjunction: Preacher-Physicians of Colonial New England* (Knoxville: University of Tennessee Press, 1991), 1.

8. Ibid., 37, 44.

9. Ibid., 3.

10. Ibid., 37.

11. Ibid., 4.

12. Divines often had difficulty collecting a full salary from their pastoral duties, so that acting as physicians provided necessary additional income. During a time of restlessness or contentiousness in a congregation and in times of anti-clericism and dissenting, divines found they had to move from church to church. A second occupation not only provided some financial stability but made a medical divine a more attractive choice for a congregation or town that might not be able to afford a physician, to the point that a church might appreciate the ability of a divine to bring in extra income (Ibid., 5, 46–47, 52–53, 56–65).

13. Ibid., 42–43.

14. Divines were more likely than regular physicians to pick up and share knowledge of home remedies, herbal and Indian medicine, suggesting greater fluidity in practice by mixing vernacular and formal medicine. Certainly they were more attuned to local practices and sources of herbal remedies than were physicians who studied in Europe and relied upon European medicines (Brock, "North America," 202). Indeed, the natural affinity of divines for a local style of medicine led in many cases to their deserting the church to become medical practitioners (Watson, *Angelic*, 69).

15. Warner, *Therapeutic*, 17. As servants of the poor, divines were expected to provide medical service as a religious act to their congregants, particularly those who could not afford to pay (Watson, *Angelic*, 39; Brock, "North America," 198). Accepting a fee from the poor would have put clerics in a compromising position that confused religious duty with self-interest, whereas taking from the rich was considered appropriate (Watson, *Angelic*, 44–45). Physician-divines, as a result, complicated the ability of professional physicians to charge a fee, leading to accusations of opportunism and greed. Divines were certainly in the right place to perform as physicians, since they routinely visited the afflicted. So long as physicians practiced hands-off medicine based on rational theory, educated divines found themselves able to perform credibly as physicians. Moreover, many pursued dual careers, taking up both medicine or law and theology as students (Watson, *Angelic*, 38, 41, 44, 50; see Brock, "North America," 197).

16. Richard Cooke, 1834, as quoted in Chester R. Burns, *Medical Ethics in the U.S. before the Civil War* (PhD diss. Johns Hopkins University, 1969), 259.

17. Physician-divines became less common as practitioners had to make a choice between professions and the only significant carryover was in missionary medicine (Watson, *Angelic*, 146). As divines began to have less influence, physicians rose in prominence for those seeking explanations of disease (145).

18. Warner, *Therapeutic*, 19–20.

19. L. H. Butterfield, ed., *Letters of Benjamin Rush* (Princeton: Princeton University Press, 1951) 2: 807.

20. As quoted in Warner, *Therapeutic*, 18.

21. Ibid., 17–20.

22. Benjamin Rush, *Sixteen Introductory Lectures to Courses of Lectures Upon the Insti-

tutes and Practice of Medicine, With a Syllabus of the Latter (Philadelphia: Bradford and Innskeep, 1811) lecture 5, 122.

23. A. Hitchcock, 1859, as quoted in Burns, *Medical Ethics,* fn4, 243.

24. Letter to John Dickinson February 16, 1796, in Butterfield, *Letters,* 2: 770.

25. Rush, *Lectures,* lecture 5, 121–22.

26. Rush, *Autobiography,* 233.

27. Ibid., 337.

28. Ibid., 193.

29. Ibid., 222.

30. As quoted in George Rosen, "Political Order and Human Health in Jeffersonian Thought," *Bulletin of the History of Medicine* 26 (1952): 37; Nathan Goodman, *Benjamin Rush: Physician and Citizen, 1746–1813* (Philadelphia: University of Pennsylvania Press, 1934), 208.

31. Bob Arnebeck, *Destroying Angel: Benjamin Rush, Yellow Fever and the Birth of Modern Medicine* http://www.geocities.com/bobarnebeck/fever1793.html chap. 2, p. 3.

32. Benjamin Rush, *Medical Inquiries and Observations,* 4th ed. (Philadelphia: Johnson & Warner, 1815) 3: 126; Arnebeck *Destroying Angel,* chap. 2, p. 3.

33. Arnebeck, *Destroying Angel,* chap. 2, p. 4.

34. John C. Greene, *American Science in the Age of Jefferson* (Ames: University of Iowa Press, 1984), 12–13.

35. See Sally F. Griffith, "'A Total Dissolution of the Bonds of Society': Community, Death and Regeneration in Mathew Carey's *Short Account of the Malignant Fever,*" in *A Melancholy Scene of Devastation: The Public Response to the 1793 Philadelphia Yellow Fever Epidemic,* ed. J. Worth Estes and Billy G. Smith, 258–59 (Philadelphia: College of Physicians of Philadelphia, 1997); Greene, *American Science,* 19; Burns, *Medical Ethics,* 242–45.

36. Burns, *Medical Ethics,* 265–66.

37. Margaret Pelling, "Medical Practice in Early Modern England: Trade or Profession?" *The Professions in Early Modern England,* ed. Wilfrid Prest, 111 (London: Croom Helm, 1987); Edward Gieskes, *Representing the Professions: Administration, Law, and Theater in Early Modern England* (Newark: University of Delaware Press, 2006), 59.

38. Rosemary O'Day, "The Anatomy of a Profession: The Clergy of the Church of England," in *The Professions in Early Modern England,* ed. Wilfrid Prest 28 (London: Croom Helm, 1987); see Rosemary O'Day, *The Professions in Early Modern England, 1450–1800: Servants of the Commonweal* (London: Longman, 2000).

39. Wilfrid Prest, "Introduction," *The Professions in Early Modern England,* ed. Wilfrid Prest (London: Croom Helm, 1987), 12.

40. Ibid., 14.

41. John Morgan, *A Discourse Upon the Institution of Medical Schools in America; Delivered at a Public Anniversary Commencement, Held in the College of Philadelphia May 30 and 31, 1765* (Philadelphia: William Bradford, 1765), 38–39.

42. O'Day, *Professions,* 20–25.

43. Ibid., 21.

44. As quoted in ibid., 258.

45. O'Day, *Professions,* 33, 263.

46. Pelling, "Medical Practice," 94.

47. G. B. Warden, "The Medical Profession in Colonial Boston," *Medicine in Colonial Massachusetts, 1620–1820,* ed. Philip Cash, Eric H. Christianson, and J. Worth Estes, 152–56 (Boston: Colonial Society of Massachusetts, 1980).

48. O'Day, *Professions,* 33, 186, 257.

49. Warden, "Medical Profession," 148, 151, 157.

50. Gieskes, *Representing the Professions,* 24, 34.

51. Warden, *Therapeutic,* 151.

52. Prest, *Professions in Early Modern England,* 7.

53. Pelling, *Professions in Early Modern England,* 114.

54. See Karl Marx's introduction to *The Method of Political Economy* where he discusses ascending to the concrete as a way of complicating the simple abstract (the general) and returning to complexity (the individual).

55. The business of medicine appears as a large part of his tenth lecture to his students and is touched upon in three others, lectures five, six, and nine.

56. Rush, *Lectures,* lecture 10, 233.

57. Ibid., 233–37.

58. Ibid., 253.

59. Ibid., 237.

60. Ibid., 238.

61. Ibid., 241.

62. Ibid., 243.

63. Ibid., 241.

64. Ibid., 242.

65. Ibid.

66. Ibid., 249.

67. Ibid., 249–50.

68. Rush admittedly liked the personal drama of medicine and the prospect of being held in high regard as he rescued his charges from the jaws of death:

> To snatch the chief magistrate of a country, on whose life a whole nation depends for the continuance of its safety and repose, from an untimely grave; to arrest a malignant fever in its progress to death, in the father, and a consumption in the mother of a numerous family of children; to restore the deranged faculties of the mind in an only daughter; to resuscitate, from apparent death by drowning, an only son; to behold the tears of joy in the relations of the persons who have been the subjects of these cures, and to receive from them their almost idolatrous expressions of gratitude and attachment! How exquisite the pleasure to a physician! (Rush, *Lectures,* lecture 9, 226)

69. Ibid., lecture 10, 252.

70. See Mary E. Fissel, *Patients, Power, and the Poor in Eighteenth-Century Bristol* (Cambridge: Cambridge University Press, 1991), for the patient's perspective.

71. Rush, *Lectures,* lecture 9, 216.

72. Rush nevertheless presents his students with a paean on medicine that suggests his own professional pride in being a physician as well as his hopes for its future. Success in the medical business, he claims, is like "a high prize in a lottery": "the chances of success are greatly in favor of the physicians who deserve it. The union of the wisdom of the serpent, with the simplicity of the dove, does not produce more solid advantages in any human pursuit, than it does in medicine"; Rush,

Lectures, lecture 10, 254. Acknowledging all the distress he feels when he has failed as a healer, Rush "includes all those painful feelings which are excited by doubts of the nature of our patients' diseases; by the occurrence of new or alarming symptoms; by the unexpected and disagreeable effects from our medicines; by the anxious inquiries of the relations and friends of the sick, with respect to the issue of their diseases; by our own apprehensions of censure, in case of their fatal termination; and lastly, by our constant fears, of doing too little or too much for their recovery." Rush, *Lectures,* lecture 9, 220.

73. Ibid., lecture 9, 214.
74. Fissell, *Patients, Power,* 34–35.
75. Ibid., 42, 44, 50, 63, 68.
76. Ibid., 2, 171. Fissell studied Bristol, England, a town which she considers common in critical ways to the medical scene that existed in eighteenth-century Philadelphia (12–14).
77. See Watson, *Angelic,* 97–121.
78. Fissell, *Patients, Power,* 175.
79. Ibid., 181.
80. Ibid., 172–73.
81. Ibid., 184.
82. Ibid., 195.
83. Ibid., 148, 166–69.
84. Ibid., 152–53.
85. See Julian Martin, "Sauvages's Nosology: Medical Enlightenment in Montpellier," in *The Medical Enlightenment of the Eighteenth Century,* ed. Andrew Cunningham and Roger French 111–37 (Cambridge: Cambridge University Press, 1990).
86. Fissell, *Patients, Power,* 158–159.
87. Ibid., 170.
88. Benjamin Rush, *An Autobiography of Benjamin Rush: His "Travels Through Life" Together with His Commonplace Book,* ed. George W. Corner (Princeton: Princeton University Press, 1948), 18.
89. Ibid., 89.
90. Conrad, Neve, Nutton, Porter, and Wear, *Western Medical Tradition,* 375, 410. Nosology sorted "diseases into classes, species, and varieties, as in botany and zoology" to create a disease taxonomy (409).
91. Rush, *Autobiography,* 87.
92. Conrad, Neve, Nutton, Porter, and Wear, *Western Medical Tradition,* 378. John Brown sponsored the unitary idea (called Brunonianism) that there was only one disease in many varieties.
93. Rush, *Autobiography,* 87.
94. Ibid., 91.
95. Ibid., 92.
96. Ibid., 348.
97. Ibid., 350.
98. Ibid., 94.
99. Ibid., 97.
100. Ibid., 96.
101. Rush, *Lectures,* lecture 15, 341.
102. Ibid., 343.

103. Ibid., 345.

104. Ibid., 346.

105. Ibid., 347.

106. Ibid.

107. Ibid., 348. Of all the topics in a twenty-two-page lecture on acquiring knowledge (lecture 15), Rush devoted only one paragraph to experimentation. Conversation, by contrast, was taken a bit more seriously, commanding two and a half pages of text. In another lecture (lecture 10), experimentation was referred to in a paragraph as an unjust cause of losing business.

108. Ibid., 352–53.

109. Ibid., 353.

110. Ibid., 357.

111. In spite of the many errors of physicians who have offered theories and systems (in particular Rush discussed the errors of Brown, Boerhaave, Cullen, Stahl), Rush was reluctant to admit that reputable physicians had, like him, "acknowledged the fallacy of principles in medicine" (Rush, *Lectures,* lecture #1, 10). Where they deserved to be followed, Rush would follow them and where they did not, he would depart from them. In lecture one, the most personally revealing of his lectures, Rush concluded with a humility about medical knowledge that in some ways added up the struggles of a lifetime fraught with conflicts grown out of ambition as well as good intentions:

> A zeal to promote the union and interests of our medical schools, has, I fear, been mistaken by me, for knowledge and talents, equal to my present undertaking. I feel my incapacity for it. The physiological controversies, which compose so great a part of the medical instruction given in all universities, have, for many years, been wearing out of my mind, and I have yet much to learn of the discoveries and improvements of modern times in that branch of medicine. But whatever may be the issue of my present attempt, I shall continue to assert, should I fail of fulfilling your wishes, that principles in medicine, are the only safe and certain guide to successful practice. (16)

112. Rush, *Lectures,* lecture 15, 359.

113. Ibid., 360.

114. Ibid., 361.

115. Ibid.

116. Ibid., lecture 1, 3.

117. Ibid.

118. Ibid., lecture 1, 4.

119. Ibid.

120. Ibid., 5.

121. Ibid., 6.

122. Ibid., 7.

123. See Greene, *American Science;* John Bender and Michael Marrinan, eds., *Regimes of Description in the Archive of the Eighteenth Century* (Stanford: Stanford University Press, 2005).

124. Shryock, *Medicine in America,* 240–49.

125. Conrad, Neve, Nutton, Porter, and Wear, *Western Medical Tradition,* 210, 387–89.

126. Audrey P. Davis, *Medicine and Its Technology: An Introduction to the History of Medical Instrumentation* (Westport, CT: Greenwood Press, 1981), 62, 65.

127. Ibid., 88.

128. Conrad, Neve, Nutton, Porter, and Wear, *Western Medical Tradition*, 350, 389–90, 397, 399.

129. As quoted in ibid., 391.

130. Ibid., 297, 434.

131. Paul Starr, *The Social Transformation of American Medicine: The Rise of a Sovereign Profession and the Making of a Vast Industry* (New York: Basic Books, 1982), 156; Conrad, Neve, Nutton, Porter, and Wear, *Western Medical Tradition*, 435.

132. Conrad, Neve, Nutton, Porter, and Wear, *Western Medical Tradition*, 319–22.

133. Watson provides examples of poetry on iatrochemical medicine (the chemically-based alchemical theory of Paracelsus, fifteenth century ACE), a major influence on eighteenth-century medicine:

> From God it [alchemy/divine grace] cometh, and God maketh it sensible To some
>   Elect, to others he doth it denay. . . .

> This parallisme shewes
> That the Regeneration of Man and the Purification of Mettall haue like degrees of
>   Preparation and Operation to their highest Perfection.
>   William Blomfild (d. 1575), (102)

> [that man will depart this world]
> nothing else but dross
> And sinner reprobate,
> That is not purify'd
> By passing through the fire.
>   Michael Wigglesworth (1717), (102–3)

> This [the "tincture" of Christ] is the famous Stone
> That turneth all to gold:
> For that which God touch and own
> Cannot for lesse be told.
>   George Herbert, (103–4)

> God Chymist is, doth Sharon's Rose distill.
> Oh! Choice Rose Water! Swim my Soul herein.
> Let Conscience bibble in it with her Bill.
> Its Cordiall, ease doth Heart burns Causd by Sin.
> Oyle, Syrup, Sugar, and Rose Water such.
> Lord, give, give, give; I cannot have too much.
>   Edward Taylor (1642–1729), (103)

> Gold in its Ore, must melted be, to bring
> It midwift from its mother womb: requires
> To make it shine and a rich market thing,
> A fining Pot, and Test, and melting fire.
> So do I Lord, before thy grace do shine
> In mee, require, thy fire mee refine.
>   Edward Taylor, (104)

The boasting Sparyrist (Insipid Phlegm,
Whose words outstrut the Sky) vaunts he hath rife
The Water, Tincture, Lozenge, Gold, and Gem,
Of Life itselfe. But here's the Bread of Life.
I'le lay my life, his Aurum Vitae Red
Is to my Bread of Life, worse than DEAD HEAD.

                                                    Edward Taylor, (104)

134. Conrad, Neve, Nutton, Porter, and Wear, *Western Medical Tradition*, 421–25.

135. Duffy, *The Sanitarians*, 8.

136. Warner, *Therapeutic*, 1.

137. Ibid., 4–6.

138. See, for example, Benjamin Henry Latrobe, *View of the Practicality and Means of Supplying the City of Philadelphia with Wholesome Water* (Philadelphia: Zachariah Poulson, Jr., 1799).

139. See William J. Novak, *The People's Welfare: Law and Regulation in Nineteenth-Century America* (Chapel Hill: University of North Carolina Press, 1996); Duffy, *The Sanitarians;* Blake, *Public Health.*

140. Rosen, "Fate," 100.

141. Rosen, "Political Order," 35.

142. Rosen, "Medical Police," 101.

143. Ibid., 107.

CHAPTER 3. QUACKS AND CORPSES

1. Daniel E. Williams, "Gadding About Quack Like: The Science of Deception and the Practice of Physic in the Narrative of Henry Tufts," in *The Body and the Text: Comparative Essays in Literature and Medicine,* ed. Bruce Clarke and Wendell Aycock, 77 (Lubbock: Texas Tech University Press, 1990).

2. The caterwauling among physicians diminished the cultural authority of medicine itself as a field in which no one won and all lost so long as physicians continued to feud in public. One famous London feud was captured in a poem published in the *Public Ledger* (September 30, 1776) by a pseudonymous author who took the name Galen, the ancient physician largely credited with fostering the medical theory of the balance of four humors—blood, phlegm, black and yellow bile. The feud occurred between an eminent London physician John Lettsom and a German quack Theodor Myersbach, who was known for his urine-casting, or urine-gazing, to diagnose disease; Roy Porter, *Health for Sale: Quackery in England 1660–1850* (Manchester: Manchester University Press, 1989), 29–30. See also Porter, "The Eighteenth Century," *The Western Medical Tradition: 800 BC to AD 1800,* ed. Lawrence I. Conrad, Michael Neve, Vivian Nutton, Roy Porter, and Andrew Wear, 371–475 (Cambridge: Cambridge University Press, 1995). Galen, who regarded both men as disreputable fellows, depicted them in bumptious debate.

Pray, who are my betters?
Why I am—yes, I Sir,
You mistake in good French, but in English you lie, Sir,
I appeal to this friend, I submit to another

Why thou Talk'est like a fool, neither one thing nor t'other.
I will and I won't, and you can't and you dare not.
Either this Judge or that Judge, by heav'n I care not:
He'll pronounce thee an ass, my good friend, never fear it,
If he proves you a fool, I'll be happy to hear it.

Friend says,
Gentlemen,
At a club once established,
For drinking and dining,
Two amazing wits
Were determined on shining

They contended,
Who most like a blackguard could quarrel,
Who scolded the best
Was to bear off the laurel.

They curs'd and talk'd
Bawdry,
And shouted and thunder'd
And so equal their parts,
The spectators all wonder'd.

And the umpire himself,
Vow'd no Billingsgate whores,
Sirs, could ever come near'em.

With one it was art,
And the other 'twas nature,
But that both were such blackguards,
He never saw greater.

Now permit me to say,
That it's hard to determine
In a case that concerns, Sirs,
Such physical vermin:

But I think ye both quacks,
Who prescribe in the dark, Sirs,
By trusting to p———s p———s [piss pots],
And opium, and bark, Sirs.

As quoted in Porter, *Health*, 214–215. Lettsom had himself been parodied for a quack who bled and blistered in a jingle that left him no better off than his piss-prophet counterpart:

I, John Lettsom,
Blisters, bleeds and sweats 'em;
If after that they please to die,
I, John, lets 'em.

As quoted in Herbert Silvette, *Doctor on the Stage: Medicine and Medical Men in Seventeenth-Century England* (Nashville: University of Tennessee Press, 1967), 7.

3. As quoted in Porter, *Health*, 199–200.

4. See Charles E. Rosenberg, *Explaining Epidemics and Other Studies in the History of Medicine* (New York: Cambridge University Press, 1992), 32–73.

5. Porter, *Health*, 210.

6. As quoted in ibid., 209.

7. Ibid., 198.

8. Regulars turned to the market to experiment in medicine and to advertise to expand their practices and to sell their discoveries. The kind of competition made possible in the commerce of an open medical marketplace was what would come to be regulated by medical licensing to control medical malpractice and to build the cultural authority of medicine. It also represented, however, an economic engine capable of growing a new medical tradition able to break from the monopolistic practices of regular medicine with its licenses, proper degrees, affiliation with medical societies, or approved apprenticeships as means of restricting membership to its network of members.

9. April 25, 1780, L. H. Butterfield, ed., *Letters of Benjamin Rush* (Princeton: Princeton University Press, 1951) 1: 251. Rush respected true empirics, who "were restrained from perverting their judgments, and impairing the success of their practice, by their great experience, and singular talents for extensive and accurate observations." But "common empirics," or quacks, were not so advantaged: "They cure only by chance; for, by false reasoning, they detract from the advantages of their solitary experience." He faulted their credulous patients and their own zeal in exaggerating their cures and denying their mistakes: "Quacks are the greatest liars in the world," he wrote, "except their patients." Benjamin Rush, *Sixteen Introductory Lectures to Courses of Lectures Upon the Institutes and Practice of Medicine, With a Syllabus of the Latter* (Philadelphia: Bradford and Innskeep, 1811) lecture 1, 9.

But far from being chastened by accusations of quackery, Rush continued to learn from and associate with irregular physicians. Training poor blacks to do his bleedings and going on calls with quacks, he capitalized on a new pool of patients and presumably spread his own gospel of purging and bleeding at the same time.

> I frequently exposed myself to reproach from the regular bred physicians by attending patients with quacks, and with practitioners of slender education. I justified this conduct by saying that I rescued the sick from the hands of ignorant men, and gave them a better chance of being cured, and at the same time instructed them in a regular mode of practice. I am satisfied I did good by my condescention, and that many poor people owe their lives, and one practitioner in Philadelphia owed his fortune in part to it.

Benjamin Rush, *An Autobiography of Benjamin Rush: His "Travels Through Life" Together with His Commonplace Book,* ed. George W. Corner, 106 (Princeton: Princeton University Press, 1948).

10. Rush cited several forms of "quackery" which assaulted the reputation of the profession, such as flattering patients with the promise of unearned qualifications, quick cures, and low fees to gain customers. Deceptive or dramatic therapies and publication of fictional cures were cause for concern, as were attacks upon physicians disliked by those whose favor one sought or undeserved attacks upon popular or new remedies; Rush, *Lectures*, lecture 10, 245–46.

11. Ibid., lecture 9, 211–12.

12. Esther Schor, *Bearing the Dead: The British Culture of Mourning from the Enlightenment to Victoria* (Princeton: Princeton University Press, 1994), 9–12.

13. Michael Sappol, *A Traffic of Dead Bodies: Anatomy and Embodied Social Identity in Nineteenth-Century America* (Princeton: Princeton University Press, 2002), 29–30.

14. See David Charles Sloane, *The Last Great Necessity: Cemeteries in American History* (Baltimore: Johns Hopkins Press, 1991).

15. Sappol, *Traffic*, 5, 31.

16. Ruth Richardson, *Death, Dissection, and the Destitute* (London: Routledge and Kegan Paul, 1987), 12, 14–15.

17. Ibid., 20–21.

18. Ibid., 8–9; Sappol, *Traffic*, 16.

19. Richardson, *Death*, 22–23.

20. Ibid., 18–19.

21. Ibid., 25.

22. Sappol, *Traffic*, 4.

23. Ibid., 4; on the poor see Mary E. Fissel, *Patients, Power, and the Poor in Eighteenth-Century Bristol* (Cambridge: Cambridge University Press, 1991); Billy G. Smith, *The "Lower Sort": Philadelphia's Laboring People, 1750–1800* (Ithaca: Cornell University Press, 1990); Gary B. Nash, "Poverty and Poor Relief in Pre-Revolutionary Philadelphia," *William and Mary Quarterly* 33, no. 1 (1997): 3–30.

24. *Rex v. Lynn* 1788, as cited in Sappol, *Traffic*, 101; see Richardson.

25. Sappol, *Traffic*, 100–101.

26. Ibid., 101, 103. Objections were raised about the assignment of corpses to dissection as an extension of a sentence of death. At the same time, fewer crimes were attached to a sentence of execution. Crimes like arson and burglary, for example, were no longer capital crimes after 1796. Moreover, increased attention was given to formal funeral practices that memorialized the dead, including services, gravemarkers, coffins, and dedicated plots of land. Declining numbers of corpses assigned for dissection and sentiments honoring the dead thus steadily decreased the availability of corpses for medical study just as the proliferation of medical schools was getting under way (110).

27. Richardson, *Death*, 36.

28. Quoted in ibid., 179.

29. Ibid., 51.

30. As Richardson makes clear, "poor people were routinely imprisoned, transported and even hanged for the smallest of crimes against property" (137).

31. Not until 1867 was Philadelphia, along with Pittsburgh, covered by a Pennsylvania act to legislate controls on the anatomization of corpses; Sappol, *Traffic*, 123.

32. Richardson, *Death*, 183, 204–206.

33. Ibid., 186–87, 208.

34. The journalist William Cobbett, a defender of the poor, bitterly resented that, since dead bodies were not treated in the law as real property, theft of human corpses was not technically a crime. The theft of livestock, by contrast was "a capital felony, punished with DEATH" (quoted in Richardson, *Death*, 58). He told of country people forming clubs to form "a fund for defraying the expense of watching the graves of relations" (quoted in ibid., 58, 83). Cobbett's deeper objection was one

of class prejudice, as he indicated in his opposition to legislation that would allow the sale of bodies of the poor to provide medical schools with sufficient supplies of corpses: "The bill exposes to the odious sale none but the bodies of the poor; and this the labouring poor very clearly perceive. They well know that the bodies of the rich will never be sold . . . that the rich do not go to poor houses and hospitals . . . that the rich are not unclaimed when they die" (quoted in ibid., 193).

35. Ibid., 184.

36. Medical schools increased from four in 1800 to more than 160 by the end of the century, and they doubled between 1865 and 1890; Sappol, *Traffic*, 2, 5.

37. Whitfield J. Bell, Jr., *John Morgan Continental Doctor* (Philadephia: University of Pennsylvania Press, 1965), 137.

38. Philip Cash, "The Professionalization of Boston Medicine, 1760–1803," in *Medicine in Colonial Massachusetts, 1620–1820,* ed. Philip Cash, Eric H. Christianson, and J. Worth Estes, 78 (Boston: Colonial Society of Massachusetts, 1980).

39. Bell, *John Morgan*, 144.

40. As quoted in ibid.,146.

41. Jean Deveze, *Enquiry;* as quoted in John Lane, "Jean Deveze (1753–1826? [*sic*]): Notes on the Yellow Fever Epidemic at Philadelphia in 1793," *Annals of Medical History* n.s. 8 (1936): 211.

42. As quoted in William Currie, *Memoirs of the Yellow Fever, Which Prevailed in Philadelphia, and Other Parts of the United States of America, in the Summer and Autumn of the Present Year, 1798* (Philadelphia: John Bioren, 1798), 73.

43. Richardson, *Death*, 52–55.

44. Ibid., 162–63.

45. Sappol, *Traffic*, 124.

46. Ibid., 113–17.

47. Ibid., 115.

48. As quoted in ibid., 116.

49. Sappol reports seventeen riots over dissection from 1785 to 1855 (3).

50. *Pennsylvania Gazette*, November 11, 1762.

51. Betsy Copping Corner, *William Shippen, Jr.: Pioneer in American Medical Education,* (Philadelphia: American Philosophical Society, 1951), 101–3.

52. *Pennsylvania Gazette*, September 26, 1765.

53. Ruth Richardson reports that grave robbers had preferences, including Jewish bodies, because they were buried quickly and had not decomposed. Corpses buried in the flimsy coffins of the poor were preferred as well, in this case because they were easy to extricate from the ground (*Death*, 62–63). Professional body snatchers hired women to represent themselves as relatives and claim bodies at the workhouse, saving poor relief the cost of another funeral (64). Rival gangs would inform on each other, which kept prices from being driven down by competition (66), and bodies would often be broken down to sell off by parts, with teeth (which dentists would use for dentures), heads, fetuses, and children earning a premium (67, 72). As an industry, grave robbing appears to have attracted people who treated it as a business rather than as a criminal enterprise, many of them associated with hospitals or graveyards as their primary employers (70). Those in hospitals took liberties in robbing the hospital "crib," the poor burial ground for those who died in the hospital. Indeed, the trade-off for someone committed to the workhouse was denial of a proper funeral and the prospect of dissection (178). In other

cases, a scam called the "resurrection rig" obtained corpses by attending to the ringing of church bells or frequenting ale-houses to pick up news of a passing and then purchasing the corpse from the undertaker (79). Still other gangs engaged in "burking," a term used to refer to those who murdered people on the streets to provide corpses (87, 101, 131–41, 192–97). The term itself is derived from William Burke, who was suspected of having murdered sixteen poor people in Edinburgh and was tried, executed, and publicly dissected in 1829 (133). Some considered that passage of the Anatomy Bill of 1832 in England would undermine the high prices that made burking profitable, ensuring that bodies of the poor would be provided as an alternative supply, a cynical form of supply-balancing that mediated laissez-faire capitalism and the public welfare (209–10).

54. Sappol, *Traffic*, 116.

55. As quoted in Corner, *William Shippen, Jr.*, 102.

56. Richardson indicates that graves that did not get robbed were more often those in private burial grounds, buried in deep graves, or in coffins that were metal or had security provisions built in. Some had iron bars connecting the head and foot panels, spring catches on the inside of the lid, or double rows of nails. Some had one coffin inside another, iron straps around coffins, or screws which, once set, could not be unscrewed (*Death*, 81). Trip-wires attached to guns were placed in graveyards, and attendants were hired to watch over graves. Bodies were sometimes given a delayed burial so that they were too putrified to be worth stealing (83).

57. See Sloane, *The Last Great Necessity*.

58. As quoted in Sappol, *Traffic*, 107.

59. Ibid., 118.

60. Ibid., 118–19, 120–21. See Richardson, *Death*; Fissel, *Patients, Power.*

61. Samuel Thomson, *Learned Quackery Exposed; Or, Theory According to Art, As Exemplified in the Practice of the Fashionable Doctors of the Present Day* (Syracuse: Lathrop and Dean, 1843), 33.

62. Sappol, *Traffic*, 108.

63. Ibid., 109.

64. Pauline Maier, "Popular Uprisings and Civil Authority in Eighteenth-Century America," *William and Mary Quarterly* 3rd ser. 27 (1970): 16–17.

65. Ibid., 4.

66. Ibid., 5.

67. Ibid., 5–12.

68. Ibid., 13.

69. Ibid., 18.

70. Ibid., 19–21.

71. Ibid., 24.

72. Ibid., 26, 34.

CHAPTER 4. MEDICAL FEUDS IN PHILADELPHIA

1. David Harley, "Honour and Property: The Structure of Professional Disputes in Eighteenth-Century English Medicine," in *The Medical Enlightenment of the Eighteenth Century*, ed. Andrew Cunningham and Roger French, 138–64 (Cambridge: Cambridge University Press, 1990). Harley, writing on professional disputes

in eighteenth-century England, raises the prospect that medical disputes were particularly resonant during the early years of establishing a practice. A critical source of disputes was the anti-competitive practice of denying consults to outsiders, that is, to those who did not graduate from Oxford or Cambridge (Harley 145), those who studied at Edinburgh or a European university, or who were not members of the Royal College of Physicians. This is not to say that with the greater rewards of an established practice disputes diminished, for monopolistic practices continued under those circumstances as well. Indeed, it was the latter kind of disputes that was more likely to lead to cases that fed into the legal system, while the former stayed at the level of informal mechanisms and social norms.

2. "Continuing an ancient Philadelphia tradition, medical feuds added spice to the world of the nineteenth-century physician . Major doctrinal variance, or picayune infractions (real or imagined) of a punctilious code of etiquette, could equally spark a verbal free-for-all. Intensifying the excitement was the small size and clannishness of the profession, almost all of whose members could participate in, or at least actively observe, the donnybrook." Irwin Richman, *The Brightest Ornament: A Biography of Nathaniel Chapman, M.D* (Bellefonte: Pennsylvania Heritage, Inc., 1967), 145.

3. Benjamin Rush, *An Autobiography of Benjamin Rush: His "Travels Through Life" Together with His Commonplace Book,* ed. George W. Corner (Princeton: Princeton University Press, 1948), October 15, 1789, 180.

4. Ibid., July 11, 1808, 322–23.

5. James E. Gibson, *Dr. Bodo Otto and the Medical Background of the American Revolution* (Springfield: Charles C. Thomas, 1937), 185–86; Betsy Copping Corner, *William Shippen, Jr.: Pioneer in American Medical Education* (Philadelphia: American Philosophical Society, 1951), 106–26; Whitfield J. Bell, Jr., *John Morgan Continental Doctor* (Philadelphia: University of Pennsylvania Press, 1965), 106–7, 124–25, 132–49.

6. Bell, *John Morgan,* 137–38.

7. Ibid., 143.

8. Ibid., 157.

9. Ibid.; Alyn Brodsky, *Benjamin Rush: Patriot and Physician* (New York: St. Martin's Press, 2004), 95.

10. Gibson, *Dr. Bodo,* 299–300; Brodsky, *Benjamin Rush,* 255, 258–59.

11. Corner, *William Shippen, Jr.,* 112–15; Bell, *John Morgan,* 178–239; Gibson, *Dr. Bodo,* 190–300.

12. The drawings were by the same artist, van Rymsdyk, who illustrated William Hunter's famous work on anatomy to be published in 1774. Pennsylvania Hospital, founded in 1751, was the first hospital in America. See Benjamin Franklin, *Some Account of the Pennsylvania Hospital,* 1817. rpt. (Baltimore: Johns Hopkins University Press, 1954); William H. Williams, *America's First Hospital: The Pennsylvania Hospital, 1751–1841* (Wayne: Haverford House, 1976).

13. Quoted in Corner, *William Shippen, Jr.,* 98–99.

14. Ibid., 99.

15. William Hunter in the 1740s began his own private school of anatomy in London which was to become a medical school "offering courses in anatomy, chemistry, surgery and medicine until its closure in 1833." Rosemary O'Day, *The Professions in Early Modern England, 1450–1800: Servants of the Commonweal* (London:

Longman, 2000), 232. Hospitals in London took paying students associated with affiliated physicians, surgeons, and apothecaries from as early as 1702 and it was at St. Thomas's in 1759 that we find William Shippen taken on as a pupil "viewing surgical operations, walking the wards, and taking private courses" (O'Day 233).

16. Bell, *John Morgan*, 106–7.

17. Ibid., 110, 159.

18. Quoted in ibid., 117.

19. John Morgan, *A Discourse Upon the Institution of Medical Schools in America; Delivered at a Public Anniversary Commencement, Held in the College of Philadelphia May 30 and 31, 1765* (Philadelphia: William Bradford, 1765), 34; see Bell, *John Morgan*, 124–25.

20. Morgan, *Discourse*, 35.

21. Ibid., 35.

22. Ibid., xx.

23. Ibid., xx.

24. Ibid., xxi.

25. Ibid., xxii.

26. Ibid.

27. Ibid., 31.

28. Ibid., 34.

29. Letter to the Trustees, September 17, 1765, quoted in Bell, *John Morgan*, 132.

30. *Pennsylvania Gazette*, September 18, 1766.

31. Ibid., September 26, 1765.

32. Notices in the *Pennsylvania Gazette* on October 13, 1768; September 20, 1770; September 5, 1771; and October 24, 1771.

33. Letter January 24, 1771, quoted in Brodsky, *Benjamin Rush*, 95.

34. *Freeman's Journal*, 3 October 1781 and 10 October 1781; see Brodsky 260.

35. Among his supporters he included Doctors Samuel Griffitts, Philip Physick, and William Dewees, whereas other physicians tended to fall in and out of Rush's graces, at intervals departing from and later returning to his heroic bleeding and purging or the Brunonian theory of Dr. John Brown (which proposed the unity of all diseases and the necessity of stimulating or sedating the nerves) that he endorsed.

36. Lawrence L. Conrad, Michael Neve, Vivian Nutton, Roy Porter, and Andrew Wear, *The Western Medical Tradition: 800 BC to AD 1800* (Cambridge: Cambridge University Press, 1995), 378.

37. Rush, *Autobiography*, 81–82.

38. Benjamin Rush, *Sixteen Introductory Lectures to Courses of Lectures Upon the Institutes and Practice of Medicine, With a Syllabus of the Latter* (Philadelphia: Bradford and Innskeep, 1811), lecture 10, 238.

39. Conrad, Neve, Nutton, Porter, and Wear, *Western Medical Tradition*, 378–379.

40. June 21, 1807, in T. J. Randolph, ed., *Memoir, Correspondence, and Miscellanies from the Papers of Thomas Jefferson* (Charlottesville, 1829), 4, 91–94; quoted in Richard Harrison Shryock, *Medicine and Society in America, 1660–1860* (New York: New York University Press, 1960), 73.

41. Jefferson, quoted in Shryock, *Medicine and Society*, 73.

42. Letter to John Dickinson, October 11, 1797, L. H. Butterfield, ed., *Letters of Benjamin Rush* (Princeton: Princeton University Press, 1951), 2: 793.

43. Rush, *Autobiography*, 83.

44. Benjamin Rush, *An Address on the Slavery of the Negroes in America* (Philadelphia: John Dunlap, 1773), 30.

45. Rush, *Autobiography*, 88.

46. Letter to John Adams, September, 1810, Butterfield, *Letters*, 2: 1060–61.

47. Rush was sensitive about fortuitous explanations for success dependant not upon one's merit, but one's connections and others' power and wealth, which were therefore not to be depended upon as a stable component in building a business. In a lecture he noted the patronage of a powerful family, political party, or religious society and physician connections from medical work in the army, which represented for Rush bridges he had largely burned in the practice of his profession; Rush, *Lectures*, lecture 10, 237–45.

48. Ibid., *Autobiography*, 79.

49. Ibid., 83–84.

50. Ibid., 84.

51. Ibid., 102.

52. Ibid., 88–89.

53. Rush felt that the regard in which the public held physicians discouraged physicians from giving their best advice for fear of being driven out of the profession. Referring to "the false judgment which the public form of the characters of physicians," he explained,

A disposition to employ new medicines is often ascribed to a dangerous spirit of innovation. That bold humanity, which dictates the use of powerful but painful remedies, in violent diseases, is branded with the epithet of cruelty; while an accommodation of remedies, to the changes induced in diseases by a difference in the season, and of the habits of sick people, is attributed to caprice, and a want of stability in the principles of medicine. . . . this intolerant spirit discovers itself chiefly in the clamour and persecution which always follow a physician's declaration of the existence of a malignant or contagious disease, in the city in which he resides. Many physicians have been driven into voluntary banishment by this clamour; and we read of one, who, in consequence of such a declaration, was compelled to save his life, by a rapid flight to a church.

Rush, *Lectures*, lecture 9, 213–14.

54. Rush, *Autobiography*, 89.

55. Letter to Wistar, November 18, 1793, in Bob Arnebeck, *Destroying Angel: Benjamin Rush, Yellow Fever and the Birth of Modern Medicine*, http://www.geocities.com/bobarnebeck/fever1793.html, appendix 5, p. 2.

56. William Currie, *Memoirs of the Yellow Fever, Which Prevailed in Philadelphia, and Other Parts of the United States of America, in the Summer and Autumn of the Present Year, 1798* (Philadelphia: John Bioren, 1798), 78.

57. Harley, "Honour and Property," 139, 145.

58. John Lane, "Jean Deveze (1753–1826? [*sic*]): Notes on the Yellow Fever Epidemic at Philadelphia in 1793," *Annals of Medical History* n.s. 8 (1936): 220.

59. Ibid., 209, 218.

60. For the history of the organization of the hospital, see *Minutes of the Proceedings of the Committee, Appointed on the 14th September, 1793, by the Citizens of Philadelphia, the Northern Liberties, and the District of Southwark, To Attend to and Alleviate the Sufferings of the Afflicted with the Malignant Fever Prevalent in the City and Its Vicinity*

(Philadelphia: City of Philadelphia, 1848); in particular, see September 19 to 22, 1793, 25–36.

61. Lane, "Jean Deveze," 204.

62. September 21, 1793, *Minutes,* 33.

63. Quoted in Lane, "Jean Deveze," 221.

64. Quoted in ibid.

65. Benjamin Rush, *An Account of the Bilious Remitting Yellow Fever, as It Appeared in the City of Philadelphia, in the Year 1793* (Philadelphia: Thomas Dobson, 1794), 319.

66. See here Lane, "Jean Deveze," 218–19, referring to Rush's general neglect as animosity and to LaRoche's comment that "Dr. Rush states that at one time, there were but three physicians able to do their duty out of their houses. Our celebrated countryman must have forgotten the French physicians who never ceased to attend to their professional duties." R. La Roche, *Yellow Fever Considered in its Historical, Pathological and Therapeutical Relations Including a Sketch of the Disease as It Has Occurred in Philadelphia from 1699 to 1854* (Philadelphia: Blanchard & Lea, 1855), 1: 73.

67. Jean Deveze, *An Enquiry into and Observation Upon the Causes and Effects of the Epidemic Disease, Which Raged in Philadelphia From the Month of August Till Towards the Middle of December, 1793* (Philadelphia: Parent, 1794), preface.

68. Quoted in Lane, "Jean Deveze," 220; Deveze, *Traite de la fievre jaune* (Paris: Comte, 1820), 14.

69. *Federal Gazette,* September 12, 1793; Butterfield, *Letters,* 2: 660–61.

70. Rush, *Autobiography,* 97.

71. Letter to John R. Coxe, September 19, 1794, Butterfield, *Letters,* 2: 750.

72. Rush, *Autobiography,* 98, 103.

73. Letter to John Redman Coxe, September 19, 1794, Butterfield, *Letters,* 2: 752.

74. Rush's son John did in fact go mad (Brodsky, *Benjamin Rush,* 348), a possible link to the madness charge against his father as it suggests that Benjamin Rush was mentally dysfunctional and that the son inherited his father's "madness."

75. Quoted in Butterfield, *Letters,* 2: note 3, 791–92.

76. Letter to John Redman Coxe, April 28, 1796, Butterfield, *Letters,* 2: 775.

77. Historical Society of Pennsylvania, Rush manuscript, vol. 29, cover page, nos. 92–94.

78. Charles Caldwell, *Autobiography of Charles Caldwell, M.D.,* ed. Harriot W. Warner (New York: Da Capo Press, 1968), 239.

79. Ibid., 232.

80. Ibid., 241.

81. Ibid., 245.

82. Ibid., 245–46 .

83. Ibid., 289–90.

84. Ibid., 234.

85. Ibid.

86. Ibid., 293.

87. Conrad, Neve, Nutton, Porter, and Wear, *Western Medical Tradition,* 378.

88. Caldwell, *Autobiography,* 294–95.

89. Historical Society of Pennsylvania, letters May 24, 27, and 28, 1796, Rush manuscript, vol. 29, nos. 62–66.

90. Rush, *Autobiography*, 96.

91. Letter to James Rush, December 22, 1809, Butterfield, *Letters*, 2: 1030.

92. Caldwell, *Autobiography*, 293.

93. Harriet W. Warner, "Introduction," in Caldwell, *Autobiography*, xxiii.

94. Caldwell, *Autobiography*, 230–31.

95. Ibid., 292.

96. Ibid.

97. Letter dated December 14, 1809, Rush manuscript, vol. 29, no. 67.

98. Quoted in Irwin Richman, *The Brightest Ornament: A Biography of Nathaniel Chapman, M.D.* (Bellefonte: Pennsylvania Heritage, Inc., 1967), 62.

99. Letter to John Adams, September 8, 1810, Butterfield, *Letters*, 2: 1060–61.

100. Historical Society of Pennsylvania, Rush manuscript, vol. 29, no. 75; see Richman, *Brightest Ornament*, 55–63.

101. Richman, *Brightest Ornament*, 62.

102. Letter December 5, 1807, in ibid., 63.

103. Historical Society of Pennsylvania, Rush manuscript, vol. 29, no. 77; see Richman, *Brightest Ornament*, 63.

104. Quoted in Richman, *Brightest Ornament*. 156.

105. Where errors were related to his medical theories and teaching, rather than medical school politics or his medical practice, Rush nevertheless presented himself as amenable to self-correction. In a lecture to his students, he made a personal commitment that should he "be so unfortunate as to teach anything, which subsequent reflection or observation should discover to be erroneous, I shall publicly retract it. I am aware how much I shall suffer by this want of stability in error, but I have learned from one of my masters to 'esteem truth the only knowledge, and that labouring to defend an error, is only striving to be more ignorant.'" Rush, *Lectures*, lecture 1, 13.

106. Historical Society of Pennsylvania, August 27, 1797, Rush manuscript, vol. 29, no. 92.

107. Ibid., draft of a letter by Rush, August 28, 1797, manuscript, vol. 29, no. 94.

108. Ibid., draft of a letter by Rush, August 29, 1797, Rush manuscript, vol. 29, no. 97.

109. Ibid., draft of a letter by Rush, August 28, 1797, manuscript, vol. 29, no. 94.

110. Quoted in Richman, *Brightest Ornament*, 157.

111. William Cobbett, *Porcupine's Works; Containing Various Writings and Selections, Exhibiting a Faithful Picture of the United States of America; of Their Governments, Laws, Politics, and Resources; of the Characters of Their Presidents, Governors, Legislators, Magistrates, and Military Men; and of the Customs, Manners, Morals, Religion, Virtues and Vices of the People* (London: Cobbett and Morgan, 1801), 231; Cobbett, *The Rush-Light* (New York: William Cobbett, February 15–August 30, 1800) 1: 225; *Porcupine's Gazette*, October 7, 1795.

112. Quoted in Cobbett, *Rush-Light* 1: 228.

113. Ibid., 1: 229.

114. Ibid., 1: 230.

115. Ibid.

116. Cobbett, *Rush-Light* 1: 231.

117. Letter to Brockholst Livingston, March 5, 1800, Butterfield, *Letters*, 2: 817.

118. Cobbett was brought to trial by Benjamin Rush in 1799 for the former's

attacks against his extreme purging and bleeding practices in Philadelphia yellow fever epidemics. He was fined the then-exorbitant sum of $5000, although commentators had held that the suit had little chance of success. It appears that the libel charges made against Cobbett in the trial were, in the end, given less weight by the jury than public print exchanges on press freedom and medical malpractice and political arguments (Cobbett was a British citizen at a time when Thomas Jefferson was running for president as a pro-French republican and when Rush, as a Philadelphia physician, was a local favorite, a signer of the Declaration of Independence, and a prominent republican). See Winthrop Neilson and Frances Neilson, *Verdict for the Doctor: The Case of Benjamin Rush* (New York: Hastings House, 1958).

119. Letter to Brockholst Livingston, March 5, 1800, Butterfield, *Letters,* 2: 817.

120. Rush, *Autobiography,* 288.

121. Letter to Brockholst Livingston, March 5,1800, Butterfield, *Letters,* 2: 816.

122. Rush, *Autobiography,* 295.

123. Richman, *Brightest Ornament,* 147–51, 164, 159. According to David Harley, disputes in England were comparable in many ways to those in America. They occurred, for example, under similar conditions: "new economic relationships and new strategies of practice, the wider distribution of a variety of credible qualifications and the desire of a widening circle of consumers to receive cures from a reputable source" (Harley, "Honour and Property," 160). As in America, disputes in England arose over stealing patients, refusing consultations, ungentlemanly behavior, practicing in a combination of roles rather than strictly as a surgeon, apothecary, or physician, blackballing a physician from serving at an infirmary, assignments at hospitals, ostracizing new practitioners, spreading false reports, interfering with subscriptions to voluntary infirmaries or hospitals, complaints about a physician's medical practices, condescending to rural practitioners, using patronage connections against other physicians, or publishing an appeal to the public in a private matter. Harley considers that in England confrontations over honor rather than property were most at issue in disputes, although patients and hospital positions were indeed forms of property to a physician. Moreover, just as in America, professional disputes had the effect of undermining public confidence in the medical profession at a time when increased competition meant that public wrangling would carry an economic price (158). Of particular importance were those disputes that played out as trials in the press. In England, perhaps more than in America, an elite group of physicians found it difficult to express disapproval of disputes that involved inferiors, given the implications of a code of honor consistent with their status. Harley suggests that the absence of their disapproval made it unlikely that disputes would ever be silenced.

124. John Harley Warner, *The Therapeutic Perspective: Medical Practice, Knowledge, and Identity in America, 1820–1885* (Cambridge: Harvard University Press, 1986), 52.

125. Ibid., 51–53.

126. Plain Truth, *A View of the Absurd Practice, in the Yellow, or Bilious Fever, Addressed to the Inhabitants of Philadelphia* (Philadelphia: John Bioren, 1803), 7.

127. Ibid., 3–5.

CHAPTER 5. MEDICAL FEUDS IN THE ARMY

1. See Terence C. Davies, "American Medicine During the Revolutionary Era," *Journal of the Medical Association of the State of Alabama* 6 (1976): 34–36; Ann

M. Becker, "Smallpox in Washington's Army: Strategic Implications of the Disease During the American Revolutionary War," *Journal of Military History* 68, no. 2 (2004): 381–430; C. M. Gilman, "Military Surgery in the American Revolution," *The Journal of the Medical Society of New Jersey* 57 (1960): 491–96; C. Jelenko, "Emergency Medicine in Colonial America: Revolutionary War Casualties," *Annals of Emergency Medicine* 11, no. 1 (1982): 40–43.

2. John Morgan, *A Vindication of His Public Character in the Station of Director-General of the Military Hospitals, and Physician in Chief of the American Army* (Boston: Powars and Willis, 1777), iv.

3. Ibid., v.

4. Ibid., iv.

5. Letter to George Washington, February 1, 1777; Morgan, *Vindication*, 6.

6. Whitfield J. Bell, Jr., *John Morgan Continental Doctor* (Philadelphia: University of Pennsylvania Press, 1965), 181, 185.

7. *Pennsylvania Gazette*, May 14, 1777.

8. Bell, *John Morgan*, 199, 211.

9. Ibid., 189–94.

10. Ibid., 197.

11. Morgan, *Vindication*, 30–31.

12. Ann Becker's portrait of General Washington's vacillation on inoculating the American army for smallpox is a case on point. Becker indicts not only Washington and the military command structure but the army's medical department for failing to support a systematic approach to an epidemic that did more than British military might to guarantee colonial failures in battle (Becker, "Smallpox," 422–24). American soldiers themselves secretly self-inoculated in a ground-level action to protect themselves in the face of military orders that made such acts punishable by death and in the absence of the medical knowledge, techniques, and precautions to do so safely (414–15). They thereby wrested control of their own health from the very military authorities and medical personnel supposed to protect them in one of the most disruptive medical crises of the war. Becker demonstrates that disease had the status of a military weapon in more than one way. Both the in-fighting within the American medical establishment described in this chapter and stratagems of the British risked the health of the revolutionary army. The way the British army handled its own smallpox inoculation and dispersed contagious refugees suggested that it saw an opportunity to infect American colonials just as it had used smallpox as a biological weapon to devastate Indian tribes during the Seven Years War (400–402).

13. Morgan, *Vindication*, 25.

14. Ibid., 26.

15. Letter to George Washington, February 1776, in Morgan, *Vindication*, 33–34.

16. Ibid., 34.

17. Nathanael Greene, "Letter of Nathanael Greene to Dr. John Morgan, 1779," January 10, 1779, *Pennsylvania Magazine of History and Biography* 43 (1919): 78–79.

18. *Pennsylvania Gazette*, May 14, 1777.

19. Ibid.

20. Bell, *John Morgan*, 184.

21. Ibid., 189.

22. Ibid., 201.

23. Ibid., 204.

24. Greene, "Letter," 78–79.

25. Morgan, *Vindication,* 36.

26. Ibid., 34.

27. Ibid., 43.

28. Ibid., 34.

29. Ibid., 43–44.

30. Ibid., 36.

31. Ibid., 35.

32. *Pennsylvania Gazette,* May 14, 1777.

33. Morgan, *Vindication,* 45–47.

34. Ibid., 48.

35. *Pennsylvania Gazette,* May 14, 1777.

36. Morgan, *Vindication,* 30–31.

37. Bell, *John Morgan,* 148, 204, 208.

38. Morgan, *Vindication,* 78.

39. Ibid.,148.

40. Letter to Samuel Adams, June 25,177[6], Morgan, *Vindication,* 52.

41. Letter to Samuel Adams, July 1776, Morgan, *Vindication,* 69–70.

42. Morgan, *Vindication,* 85.

43. Ibid., 86.

44. Ibid., 116.

45. Ibid., 115.

46. Ibid., 133.

47. Ibid., 84.

48. The issue of the number of deaths that resulted from the sick and wounded taken to military hospitals was a serious concern that affected war-readiness for the army as a whole. Becker's review demonstrates that reports of deaths in the American revolutionary army varied considerably. Reports ran from John Adams's claim of ten killed by disease to every one killed in battle (he actually contended it was "ten times more terrible than Britons, Canadians, and Indians together," quoted in Becker, "Smallpox," 420), U.S. War Department statistics that put sickness and disease at 10,000 out of 250,000 men who served in the army (391), and the historian Howard Peckham's claim that almost 7,000 died in battle compared to 18,000 in camp and prison, to war troop strength returns that, at one point in 1778, saw figures from disease run as high as 35% of the total force (392). Benjamin Rush reported "that while the risk of being killed in battle was 2%, the risk of dying if hospitalized was 25%" (Jelenko, "Emergency Medicine," 42).

49. Morgan, *Vindication,* 109.

50. Letter to a friend, April 17, 1777, ibid., xiii note.

51. Morgan, *Vindication,* xiv note.

52. Ibid.

53. *Pennsylvania Gazette,* May 14, 1777.

54. Ibid.

55. Bell, *John Morgan,* 190–191.

56. Ibid., 190–94.

57. Quoted in ibid., 190.

58. Letter to Samuel Adams, June 25, 177[6], Morgan, *Vindication,* 51.
59. Ibid., 50.
60. Morgan, *Vindication,* 149.
61. Ibid., 151.
62. Ibid.
63. Ibid.
64. Congressional Resolve, August 20, 1776, ibid., 30.
65. July 17, 1776 order, Morgan, *Vindication,* 28–29; Bell, *John Morgan,* 193–94.
66. Morgan, *Vindication,* 193.
67. Ibid., v–vi.
68. Ibid., v.
69. Ibid., xxvi.
70. Ibid., xxvii.
71. Ibid., xviii.
72. Ibid.
73. Ibid.
74. Ibid.
75. Ibid., xvi.
76. Ibid., xviii.
77. Ibid., xvi.
78. Ibid., xix.
79. Ibid., xvii–xviii.
80. Letter to George Washington, February 2, 1777, ibid., 21.
81. Morgan, *Vindication,* viii.
82. Bell, *John Morgan,* 181, 184–87, 194–96.
83. Morgan, *Vindication,* 64–66.
84. Ibid., xi.
85. Ibid., ix–x.
86. Ibid., xv.
87. This argument was used unsuccessfully on Benjamin Rush as well when he was contemplating suing William Cobbett, the journalist, for slander.
88. Ibid., xlii.
89. Ibid., xliii.
90. Ibid., 84.
91. Ibid., 84–85.
92. *Pennsylvania Gazette,* May 14, 1777.
93. Morgan, *Vindication,* 86.
94. Ibid., 113.
95. *Pennsylvania Gazette,* May 14, 1777.
96. Morgan, *Vindication,* 86.
97. Ibid.
98. Greene, "Letter," 79.
99. Morgan, *Vindication,* 104–5.
100. Ibid., 106.
101. Ibid., 103.
102. Ibid., 156.
103. Ibid.
104. Letter to Morgan from Cutting, July 26, 1780, in July 29, 1780, *Pennsylvania Packet.*

105. *Pennsylvania Packet,* July 29, 1780.
106. Ibid.
107. Ibid., August 6, 1780.
108. James E. Gibson, *Dr. Bodo Otto and the Medical Background of the American Revolution* (Springfield: Charles C. Thomas, 1937), 275.
109. *Pennsylvania Packet,* August 8, 1780.
110. Ibid., August 12, 1780.
111. Quoted in Gibson, *Dr. Bodo,* 261.
112. Shippen had apparently been offered the directorship by General Washington before it was offered to Church, but felt unable to accept (Bell, *John Morgan,* 179). As his brother-in-law Richard Henry Lee indicated, "I well know, that before Dr. Morgan's appointment to the directorship, you expressed yourself against taking that office, and that it plainly appeared to Congress"; May 7, 1780, quoted by Gibson, *Dr. Bodo,* 255. This testimony is absent from the published version of the Lee letter in Richard Henry Lee, "Selections and Excerpts from the Lee Papers, *The Southern Literary Messenger* 30 (May 1860): 345.
113. Howard Lewis Applegate, "The Medical Administrators of the American Revolutionary Army," *Military Affairs* 25.1 (1961): note 15, 3.
114. Bell, *John Morgan,* 211.
115. Whitfield J. Bell, Jr., "The Court-Martial of Dr. William Shippen, Jr., 1780," *Journal of the History of Medicine and Allied Sciences* 19 (1964): 219–21; Applegate, "Medical Administrators," note 28, 5–6.
116. Morgan, *Vindication,* xxi.
117. Ibid., xxii.
118. Ibid., xxiii.
119. Ibid., xxiv.
120. Ibid., xxvi.
121. Ibid., xxv.
122. Ibid., xxviii.
123. Ibid., xxxii.
124. Ibid. Shippen himself was anxious to re-write the record on his presumed conspiracy to solicit the position when Morgan held it. Shippen "inquired of R. H. Lee if there was anything in the records to show that he was behind Morgan's discharge. Lee replied negatively, probably 'forgetting' his brother-in-law's letters of 1776 and 1777" (Applegate, "Medical Administrators," note 28, 5). Such revisionism appears to have been contagious, as we find Benjamin Rush and his heirs actively engaging to excise from his private papers and other publications aspersions on General Washington that he had injudiciously committed to paper when he and Morgan were actively collaborating to organize a court-martial of Shippen for his performance as director general.
125. Morgan, *Vindication,* xxxii.
126. Quoted in Bell, *John Morgan,* 218.
127. Morgan, *Vindication,* xxxiv.
128. Ibid., xxxv.
129. Quoted in Bell, *John Morgan,* 219.
130. When the court-martial cleared Shippen and Morgan undertook to try him in the press, Shippen appealed to Congress to publish the court record. The court records were not published and have not been located. *Pennsylvania Packet,* September 23, 1780.

131. Gibson, *Dr. Bodo,* 205–6.

132. April 7, 1778, quoted in ibid., 223.

133. Letter to Jonathan Bayard Smith, April 20, 1778, L. H. Butterfield, ed. *Letters of Benjamin Rush* (Princeton: Princeton University Press, 1951) 1: 213. This letter refers to a letter sent to William Henry Drayton, Samuel Huntington, and John Banister on the same day. The recipients of that letter were members of the committee appointed on April 3 to investigate Shippen.

134. Letter to John Morgan, June 1778, Butterfield, *Letters,* 1: 226.

135. Letter to Daniel Roberdeau, March 9, 1778, ibid., 1: 204.

136. Letter to William Duer, December 8, 1777, ibid., 1: 174.

137. Letter to William Shippen, February 1, 1778, ibid., 1: 196–97.

138. Bombarded with an unremittingly hostile series of attacks from Morgan, Shippen had as well to deal with Benjamin Rush, who had decided to assist Morgan. Shippen appealed to Congress to hold an inquiry (Gibson, *Dr. Bodo,* 213).

139. Bell, "Court Martial," 227–28, 232–34.

140. Ibid., 233; Gibson, *Dr. Bodo,* 278–79; *Pennsylvania Packet* December 12, 1780.

141. *Pennsylvania Packet,* September 2 to December 23, 1780.

142. Ibid., September 2, 1780.

143. Ibid., December 12, 1780.

144. Quoted in Gibson, *Dr. Bodo,* 264.

145. The type of prosecution we find in civil courts, for slander as an example.

146. Public prosecution would have granted the accused counsel, put the judge in a neutral position, and assigned prosecution to a public prosecutor who had the burden of proof. At the time of the Shippen court-martial, authority in the court room was shifting, so that the relative status of the judge, the accused, the complainant, and counsel were not stabilized. Carol J. Greenhouse, "Nature is to Culture as Praying is to Suing: Legal Pluralism in an American Suburb," *Journal of Legal Pluralism* 20 (1982): 17–35; Stephan Landsman, "The Rise of the Contentious Spirit: Adversary Procedure in Eighteenth-Century England," *Cornell Law Review* 75 (1990): 497–606; John H. Langbein, *The Origins of Adversary Criminal Trial* (Oxford: Oxford University Press, 2003); John H. Langbein, "Shaping the Eighteenth-Century Criminal Trial: A View from the Ryder Sources," *University of Chicago Law Review* 50 (1983): 1–136; William E. Nelson, *Americanization of the Common Law: The Impact of Legal Change on Massachusetts Society, 1760–1830* (Cambridge: Harvard University Press, 1975); Barbara Shapiro, *'Beyond Reasonable Doubt' and 'Probable Cause': Historical Perspectives on the Anglo-American Law of Evidence* (Berkeley: University of California Press, 1991).

147. Morgan letter to Samuel Huntington, March 28, 1780, Gibson, *Dr. Bodo,* 252.

148. Morgan letter to Huntington, November 22, 1779, ibid., 246.

149. Letter to Huntington, March 8, 1780, ibid., 253.

150. Quoted in ibid., 252.

151. Letter to Huntington, December 20, 1779, ibid., 250.

152. Letter to Huntington, March 28, 1780, ibid., 252.

153. Ibid., 253.

154. Letter to Huntington, November 22, 1779, ibid., 248.

155. Letter to Huntington, March 28, 1780, ibid., 252.

156. Letter to Richard Henry Lee, April 16, 1780, "Selections," 344.

157. Letter to Lee, April 16, 1780, "Selections," 345, Gibson, *Dr. Bodo,* 255.

158. Letter from Lee, May 7, 1780, "Selections," 346.

159. Ibid., 345, Gibson, *Dr. Bodo,* 255.

160. April 3, 1778, Gibson, *Dr. Bodo,* 249.

161. Gibson, *Dr. Bodo,* 249–50.

162. Letter to Huntington, December 20, 1779, quoted in ibid., 249.

163. Ibid., 250.

164. Ibid.

165. Letter to Huntington, March 28, 1780, Gibson, *Dr. Bodo,* 253.

166. Letter to Lee, April 16, 1780, Lee, "Selections," 344, Gibson, *Dr. Bodo,* 253–54.

167. Letter to Huntington, March 28, 1780, Gibson, *Dr. Bodo,* 25.

168. Letter to Lee, April 16, 1780, Lee, "Selections," 344, Gibson, *Dr. Bodo,* 254.

169. Ibid.

170. Letter to Huntington, March 28, 1780, Gibson, *Dr. Bodo,* 252.

171. *Pennsylvania Packet,* December 9, 1780.

172. Ibid., December 16, 1780.

173. Ibid., December 12, 1780.

174. As evidenced in the conduct of Cutting's testimony, Shippen, like Morgan, had elected to perform in a legal capacity in the court-martial, serving as his own defense counsel. Whereas both men, as well as Morgan's ally Rush, were physicians, all three of them exhibited considerable knowledge and skill in practical matters of the law. Such legal facility was in itself unremarkable since, as we have discussed, the education of physicians and lawyers followed the same general arts training and the function performed by each profession was not strictly demarcated. Moreover, many physicians, in particular for our purposes Rush, had either dabbled in the law before they committed to medicine or had actually considered the law as a profession.

175. *Pennsylvania Packet,* September 2, 1780.

176. Ibid., December 16, 1780.

177. Ibid.

178. Ibid., October 14, 1780.

179. Ibid., December 16, 1780.

180. Ibid., March 9, 1778.

181. Ibid., March 30, 1778.

182. Ibid., December 16, 1780.

183. Letter to Roberdeau, March 9, 1778, in Butterfield, *Letters,* 1: 204.

184. *Pennsylvania Packet,* November 18, 1780.

185. Ibid., December 16, 1780.

186. Ibid.

187. Ibid., November 18, 1780.

188. Ibid., November 28, 1780.

189. See Roger W. Shuy, *Language Crimes: The Use and Abuse of Language Evidence in the Courtroom* (Oxford: Blackwell, 1993).

190. Letter from Rush to Shippen, Butterfield, *Letters,* 1: 257.

191. *Pennsylvania Packet,* November 21, 1780.

192. Ibid., dated November 18, 1780.

193. Ibid., November 18, 1780.

194. Ibid.

195. Gibson, *Dr. Bodo,* 290.

196. Letter to Rush, May 27, 1780, quoted in Gibson, *Dr. Bodo,* 291.

197. Quoted in Gibson, *Dr. Bodo,* 291.

198. *Pennsylvania* Packet, December 23, 1780.

199. See ibid., November 21, 1780, dated November 18, 1780.

200. Ibid., December 16, 1780.

201. Ibid.

202. Gibson, *Dr. Bodo,* 279.

203. *Pennsylvania Packet,* September 2, 1780.

204. Ibid., December 23, 1780; Gibson, *Dr. Bodo,* 280.

205. Ibid.

206. Ibid., November 18, 1780.

207. Ibid., December 23, 1780.

208. Letter to Roberdeau March 9, 1778, Butterfield, *Letters,* 1: 204. It was important to Rush that Roberdeau, the member of Congress to whom the letter was addressed, think well of him, as a question of honor: "a regard to the honor of the Congress and my own character require that I should trouble you with the following facts. Judge after you have read them whether my charges against Dr. Shippen were founded in malice, and whether a 'want of harmony' was the cause."

209. *Pennsylvania Packet,* December 2, 1780.

210. Ibid., November 18, 1780.

211. Ibid., October 7, 1780.

212. Ibid., September 2, 1780.

213. Ibid., December 23, 1780. Of some interest here, Francis Hopkinson was John Morgan's brother-in-law. Bell, *John Morgan,* 195.

214. Francis Hopkinson, *Miscellaneous Essays and Occasional Writings* (Philadelphia: T. Dobson, 1792) 1: 152.

215. Ibid., 158.

216. Ibid., 157.

217. Ibid., 151.

218. Ibid., 152.

219. Ibid., 153.

220. Ibid., 155.

221. Ibid., 157.

222. Ibid., 154.

223. Bell, "Court Martial," 236.

224. Hopkinson, *Miscellaneous,* 1: 155–56.

Bibliography

PRIMARY SOURCES

Newspapers:

Aurora General Advertiser 1775———
Federal Gazette 1793———
Freeman's Journal 1781———
Pennsylvania Gazette 1765———
Pennsylvania Packet 1780———
Porcupine's Gazette 1797———
Rush-Light 1800———

Other Sources

A Citizen. *Fever; An Elegiac Poem Dedicated to the Citizens of Philadelphia by a Citizen.* Philadelphia: John Ormrod, 1799.

Addison, Alexander. *Reports of Cases in the County Courts of the Fifth Circuit, and in the High Court of Errors and Appeals, of the State of Pennsylvania.* Philadelphia: John Colerick, 1800.

Alexander, James. *A Brief Narrative of the Case and Trial of John Peter Zenger, Printer of the New York Weekly Journal.* Edited by Stanley Nider Katz. 1736. Reprint, Cambridge: Harvard University Press, 1963.

Allen, Richard. *The Life Experience and Gospel Labors of the Rt. Rev. Richard Allen To Which is Annexed The Rise and Progress of the African Methodist Episcopal Church in the United States of America.* 1794. Reprint, Nashville: Abingdon Press, 1960.

———. *A Collection of Hymns and Spiritual Songs.* Philadelphia: T. L. Plowman, 1801.

Baugh, Albert Ellery, ed. *The Writings of Thomas Jefferson.* Vol. 10. Washington, D.C., 1905.

Binns, John. *Binns' Justice, or Magistrate's Daily Companion. A Treatise on the Office and Duties of Aldermen and Justices of the Peace in the Commonwealth of Pennsylvania.* Edited by Frederick C. Brightly, 4th ed. Philadelphia: James Kay, Jun. & Brother, 1851.

Blackstone, William. *Commentaries on the Laws of England.* 4 vols. New York: E. Duyckinck, 1822.

Brackenridge, Hugh Henry. *A Hugh Henry Brackenridge Reader, 1770–1815.* Edited by Daniel Marder. Pittsburgh: University of Pittsburgh, 1970.

———. *Law Miscellanies: Containing An Introduction to the Study of the Law, Notes on Blackstone's Commentaries, Shewing the Law of Pennsylvania From the Law of England and What Acts of Assembly Might Require to be Repealed or Modified.* Philadelphia: P. Sterne, 1814.

———. *The Life and Writings of Hugh Henry Brackenridge.* Edited by Claude Milton Newlin. Mamaroneck: Paul P. Appel, 1971.

———. *Modern Chivalry, Containing the Adventures of Captain John Farrago and Teague O'Regan, His Servant.* Edited by Lewis Leary. 1792, 1793, 1797. Reprint, Albany: New College and University Press, Inc., 1965.

———. *Modern Chivalry.* Edited by Claude M. Newlin. 1815. Reprint, New York: American Book Company, 1937.

Brown, Charles Brockden. *Arthur Mervyn or, Memoirs of the Year 1793—A Romance.* 1799. Reprint, New York: The Library of America, 1999.

———. *Ormond; Or, The Secret Witness.* Edited by Mary Chapman. 1799. Reprint, Orchard Park: Broadview Literary Texts, 1999.

———. *The Rhapsodist and Other Uncollected Writings.* Edited by Harry R. Warfel. New York: Scholars' Facsimiles and Reprints, 1943.

Brown, Thaddeus. *An Address in Christian Love, to the Inhabitants of Philadelphia; on the Awful Dispensation of the Yellow Fever, in 1798.* Philadelphia: R. Aitken, 1798.

Butterfield, L. H., ed. *Letters of Benjamin Rush.* 2 vols. Princeton: Princeton University Press, 1951.

Caldwell, Charles. *Autobiography of Charles Caldwell, M.D.* Edited by Harriot W. Warner. 1855. Reprint, New York: Da Capo Press, 1968.

Carey, Mathew. *Mathew Carey: Autobiography.* 1833–1834. Reprint, Brooklyn: Research Classics, 1942.

———. *Observations on Dr. Rush's Enquiry into the Origins of the Late Epidemic Fever in Philadelphia.* Philadelphia: Mathew Carey, 1793.

———. *The Plagi-Scurriliad: A Hudibrastic Poem Dedicated to Colonel Eleazer Oswald.* Philadelphia: Mathew Carey, 1786.

———. *The Porcupiniad: A Hudibrastic Poem in Three Cantos Addressed to William Cobbett.* Philadelphia: Mathew Carey, 1799.

———. *A Short Account of the Malignant Fever Lately Prevalent in Philadelphia: With a Statement of the Proceedings That Took Place on the Subject, in Different Parts of the United States.* 4th ed. Philadelphia: Mathew Carey, 1794.

Carpenter, T. *A Report of an Action for a Libel Brought by Dr. Benjamin Rush Against William Cobbett in the Supreme Court of Pennsylvania, December Term, 1799, for Certain Defamatory Publications in a Newspaper Entitled Porcupine's Gazette.* Philadelphia: W.W. Woodward, 1800.

Cobbett, William. *The Democratic Judge: or, The Equal Liberty of the Press, as Exhibited, Explained, and Exposed, in the Prosecution of William Cobbett, for a Pretended Libel Against the King of Spain and his Embassador, before Thomas McKean, Chief Justice of the State of Pennsylvania.* Philadelphia: William Cobbett, 1798.

Cobbett, William. *Porcupine's Works; Containing Various Writings and Selections, Exhibiting a Faithful Picture of the United States of America; of Their Governments, Laws, Politics, and Resources; of the Characters of Their Presidents, Governors, Legislators,*

Magistrates, and Military Men; and of the Customs, Manners, Morals, Religion, Virtues and Vices of the People. 12 vols. London: Cobbett and Morgan, 1801.

Cobbett, William. *The Rush-Light.* 6 vols. New York: William Cobbett, February 15–August 30 1800.

Cole, G. D. H., ed. *Letters from William Cobbett to Edward Thornton Written in the Years 1797 to 1800.* London: Oxford University Press, 1937.

College of Physicians of Philadelphia Council Minutes. September 13 and 17, 1793.

Cresson, Joshua. *Meditations Written During the Prevalence of the Yellow Fever in the City of Philadelphia in the Year 1793.* London: W. Phillips, 1803.

Currie, William. *A Description of the Malignant, Infectious Fever Prevailing at Present in Philadelphia: With an Account of the Means to Prevent Infection, and the Remedies and Method of Treatment, Which Have Been Found Most Successful.* Philadelphia: Dobson, 1793.

———. *An Impartial Review of that Part of Dr. Rush's Late Publication Entitled "An Account of the Bilious Remitting Yellow Fever, as it Appeared in the City of Philadelphia."* Philadelphia: Dobson, 1794.

———. *Memoirs of the Yellow Fever, Which Prevailed in Philadelphia, and Other Parts of the United States of America, in the Summer and Autumn of the Present Year, 1798.* Philadelphia: John Bioren, 1798.

Dallas, Alexander J. *Reports of Cases Ruled and Adjudged in the Courts of Pennsylvania, Before and Since the Revolution.* 2 vols. Philadelphia: T. Bradford, 1790.

Deveze, Jean. *An Enquiry into and Observation Upon the Causes and Effects of the Epidemic Disease, Which Raged in Philadelphia From the Month of August Till Towards the Middle of December, 1793.* Philadelphia: Parent, 1794.

Elwell, John J. *A Medico-Legal Treatise on Medical Malpractice and Medical Evidence.* New York: John S. Voorhis, 1860.

Faugeres, Margaretta V. *The Ghost of John Young, the Homicide, Who Was Executed the 17th of August Last, for the Murder of Robert Barwick, a Sheriff's Officer.* New York, 1797.

Fielding, Henry. *An Enquiry Into the Causes of the Late Increase of Robbers and Related Writings.* Edited by Malvin R. Zirker. Middletown: Wesleyan University Press, 1988.

Fitzpatrick, John C., ed. *The Writings of George Washington from the Original Manuscript Sources, 1745–1799.* Vol. 33. Washington: US Government Printing Office, 1940.

The Foretokens of the Pestilence and Sickness Which Befel the Philadelphians, as It Was Warned to a Pious Inhabitant of the State, Many Years Ago, and Rewarned Again Some Time Past: Also, Signs and Tokens of Its Awful Approach, to Which is Added, a List of the Daily Burials. Philadelphia: Ormrod and Conrad, [1794].

Franklin, Benjamin. *Some Account of the Pennsylvania Hospital.* Introduction by Bernard Cohen. 1817. Reprint, Baltimore: Johns Hopkins University Press, 1954.

Freneau, Philip. *Newspaper Verse of Philip Freneau: An Edition and Bibliography.* Edited by Judith R. Hiltner. Troy: Whitston Pub., 1986.

———. *The Poems of Philip Freneau: Poet of the American Revolution.* Edited by Fred Lewis Pattee. 3 vols. New York: Russell and Russell, Inc., 1963.

[Green, Ashbel]. *A Pastoral Letter, from a Minister in the Country, to Those of His Flock*

Who Remained in the City of Philadelphia During the Pestilence of 1798. Philadelphia: John Ormrod, 1799.

Greene, Nathanael. "Letter of Nathanael Greene to Dr. John Morgan, 10 January 1779." *Pennsylvania Magazine of History and Biography* 43 (1919): 77–80.

Hall, John, and Samuel Clarkson, eds. *Memoirs of Matthew Clarkson of Philadelphia, 1735–1800.* Philadelphia, 1890.

Helmuth, J. Henry C. *A Short Account of the Yellow Fever in Philadelphia for the Reflecting Christian.* Philadelphia: Jones, Hoff, & Derrick, 1794.

Historical Record of the Bethel African Methodist Episcopal Church. New York: Carlton and Porter, 1864.

Hopkinson, Francis. *Miscellaneous Essays and Occasional Writings.* 3 vols. Philadelphia: T. Dobson, 1792.

Jones, Absalom, and Richard Allen. *A Narrative of the Proceedings of the Black People, During the Late Awful Calamity in Philadelphia, in the Year 1793 and a Refutation of Some Censures Thrown Upon Them in Some Late Publications.* 1794. Reprint, [Philadelphia: William W. Woodward]. In *The Life Experience and Gospel Labors.* Richard Allen. 1831. Reprint, Philadelphia: Independence National Historical Park, 1993.

Jones, Absolom. "A Thanksgiving Sermon." 1808. Reprint, *American Sermons: The Pilgrims to Martin Luther King, Jr.* New York: The Library of America, 1999, 538–45.

La Roche, R. *Yellow Fever Considered in its Historical, Pathological and Therapeutical Relations Including a Sketch of the Disease as It Has Occurred in Philadelphia from 1699 to 1854.* 2 vols. Philadelphia: Blanchard & Lea, 1855.

La Rochefoucauld-Liancourt, François de. *Travels through the United States of North America.* Vol 1. London, 1800.

Latrobe, Benjamin Henry. *View of the Practicality and Means of Supplying the City of Philadelphia with Wholesome Water.* Philadelphia: Zachariah Poulson, Jr., 1799.

Le Sage, Alain Rene. *Adventures of Gil Blas of Santillane.* Translated by Tobias Smollett. Philadelphia: J.P. Horn, 1749.

Lee, Richard Henry. "Selections and Excerpts from the Lee Papers." *The Southern Literary Messenger* 30 (May 1860): 344–46.

Linn, William. *A Discourse, Delivered on the 26th of November, 1795; Being the Day Recommended by the Governor of the State of New York To Be Observed as a Day of Thanksgiving and Prayer, On Account of the Removal of an Epidemic Fever, and for Other National Blessings.* New York: T. and J. Swords, 1795.

Lowell, Charles. *Authentic Report of a Trial before the Supreme Judicial Court of Maine, for the County of Washington. June 1824.* Portland: C. Lowell, 1825.

M. "The Republic of Beasts, A Fable." *Columbian Magazine* 2 (September 1788): 538–39; 602–5.

Marshall, William. *A Theological Dissertation on the Propriety of Removing from the Seat of Pestilence.* Philadelphia: David Hogan, 1799.

Mason, John Mitchel. *A Sermon, Preached September 20th, 1793: A Day Set Apart, in the City of New York, for Public Fasting, Humiliation and Prayer, on Account of a Malignant and Mortal Fever Prevailing in the City of Philadelphia.* New York: Samuel Loudon & Son, 1793.

McClelland, Milo A. *Civil Malpractice: A Treatise on Surgical Jurisprudence.* New York: Hurd and Houghton, 1877.

Minutes of the Proceedings of the Committee, Appointed on the 14th September, 1793, by the Citizens of Philadelphia, the Northern Liberties, and the District of Southwark, To Attend to and Alleviate the Sufferings of the Afflicted with the Malignant Fever Prevalent in the City and Its Vicinity. Philadelphia: City of Philadelphia, 1848.

Morgan, John. *A Discourse Upon the Institution of Medical Schools in America; Delivered at a Public Anniversary Commencement, Held in the College of Philadelphia, May 30 and 31, 1765.* Philadelphia: William Bradford, 1765.

————. *A Vindication of His Public Character in the Station of Director-General of the Military Hospitals, and Physician in Chief of the American Army.* Boston: Powars and Willis, 1777.

Nassy, David. *Observations on the Cause, Nature, and Treatment of the Epidemic Disease, Prevalent in Philadelphia.* Philadelphia: Mathew Carey, 1793.

"On the Multitude of Lawyers." *Massachusetts Magazine* 1 (December 1789): 792.

Plain Truth. *A View of the Absurd Practice, in the Yellow, or Bilious Fever, Addressed to the Inhabitants of Philadelphia.* Philadelphia: John Bioren, 1803.

Randolph, T. J., ed. *Memoir, Correspondence, and Miscellanies from the Papers of Thomas Jefferson.* Vol 4. Charlottesville: Gray and Bowen, 1829.

Reed, John. *A Modification of the Commentaries of Sir William Blackstone with Numerous Alterations and Additions, Designed to Present an Elementary Exposition of the Entire Laws of Pennsylvania.* 3 vols. Carlisle: George Fleming, 1831.

Rosenfeld, Richard N. *American Aurora a Democratic-Republican Returns: The Suppressed History of Our Nation's Beginnings and the Heroic Newspaper That Tried to Report It.* New York: St. Martin's Press, 1997.

Rush, Benjamin. *An Account of the Bilious Remitting Yellow Fever, as It Appeared in the City of Philadelphia, in the Year 1793.* Philadelphia: Thomas Dobson, 1794.

————. *An Address on the Slavery of the Negroes in America.* Philadelphia: John Dunlap, 1773.

————. *An Autobiography of Benjamin Rush: His "Travels Through Life" Together with His Commonplace Book.* Edited by George W. Corner. Princeton: Princeton University Press, 1948.

————. *Directions for Preserving the Health of Soldiers, Recommended to the Consideration of the Officers of the Army of the United States.* Lancaster: John Dunlap, 1778.

————. *Medical Inquiries and Observations.* 4th ed. 3 vols. Philadelphia: Johnson & Warner, 1815.

————. *Sixteen Introductory Lectures to Courses of Lectures Upon the Institutes and Practice of Medicine, With a Syllabus of the Latter.* Philadelphia: Bradford and Innskeep, 1811.

Smith, Horace Wemyss. *Life and Correspondence of the Rev. William Smith, D. D.* Vol. 1. Philadelphia: Ferguson Brothers & Co., 1880.

Spring, Samuel. *A Thanksgiving Sermon Preached November 29, 1798.* Newburyport: Angier March, 1798.

Stearns, Samuel. *An Account of the Terrible Effects of the Pestilential Infection in the City of Philadelphia, with an Elegy on the Deaths of the People.* 1793. Reprint, [Providence: William Child]. New York, 1794.

Thomson, Samuel. *Learned Quackery Exposed; Or, Theory According to Art, As Exemplified in the Practice of the Fashionable Doctors of the Present Day.* Syracuse: Lathrop and Dean, 1843.

Washington, H. A., ed. *The Writings of Thomas Jefferson, Being his Autobiography, Correspondence, Reports, Messages, Addresses, and Other Writings, Official and Private.* 4 vols. New York: John C. Riker, Taylor & Maury, 1854.

Webster, Noah. *A Brief History of Epidemic and Pestilential Diseases with the Principal Phenomena of the Physical World, Which Precede and Accompany Them and Observations Deduced from the Facts Stated.* 1799. 2 vols. New York: Burt Franklin, 1970.

―――. *Letters on Yellow Fever Addressed to Dr. William Currie.* Baltimore: Johns Hopkins University Press, 1947.

Winchester, Elhanan. *Wisdom Taught by Man's Mortality; Or the Shortness and Uncertainty of Life, the Certainty and Suddenness of Death, Considered a Discourse Adapted to the Awful Visitation of the City of Philadelphia, by the Yellow Fever, in the Year 1793.* Philadelphia: R. Fowell, 1795.

Wright, Henry. *A Sermon, Delivered October 9, 1793, at Bristol, at a Time Set Apart for Public Prayer and Humiliation by Several Christian Churches in the State of Rhode-Island, etc., On Account of the Distressing Sickness in the City of Philadelphia.* Warren: Nathaniel Phillips, 1794.

Secondary Sources

Altieri, Charles. "Judgment and Justice under Postmodern Conditions; or, How Lyotard Helps Us Read Rawls as a Postmodern Thinker." In *Redrawing the Lines: Analytic Philosophy, Deconstruction, and Literary Theory,* edited by Reed Way Dasenbrock. Minneapolis: University of Minnesota Press, 1989.

Anand, Sanjeez. "The Origins, Early History and Evolution of the English Criminal Trial Jury." *The Alberta Law Review* 43 (2005): 407–32.

Applegate, Howard Lewis. "The Medical Administrators of the American Revolutionary Army." *Military Affairs* 25, no. 1 (1961): 1–10.

Arnebeck, Bob. *Destroying Angel: Benjamin Rush, Yellow Fever and the Birth of Modern Medicine.* http://www.geocities.com/bobarnebeck/fever1793.html

Becker, Ann M. "Smallpox in Washington's Army: Strategic Implications of the Disease During the American Revolutionary War." *Journal of Military History* 68, no. 2 (2004): 381–430.

Bell, Whitfield J., Jr. "The Court Martial of Dr. William Shippen, Jr., 1780." *Journal of the History of Medicine and Allied Sciences* 19 (1964): 218–38.

―――. *John Morgan Continental Doctor.* Philadelphia: University of Pennsylvania Press, 1965.

Bender, John, and Michael Marrinan, eds. *Regimes of Description in the Archive of the Eighteenth Century* . Stanford: Stanford University Press, 2005.

Bewell, Alan. *Romanticism and Colonial Disease.* Baltimore: Johns Hopkins University Press, 1999.

Binger, Carl A. L. *Revolutionary Doctor: Benjamin Rush, 1746–1813.* New York: Norton, 1966.

Blake, John B. *Public Health in the Town of Boston, 1630–1822*. Cambridge: Harvard University Press, 1959.

Bloomfield, Maxwell. *American Lawyers in a Changing Society, 1776–1876*. Cambridge: Harvard University Press, 1976.

Bourdieu, Pierre. "The Force of Law: Toward a Sociology of the Juridical Field." *Hastings Law Journal* 38 (1987): 805–53.

———. *Outline of a Theory of Practice*. Translated by Richard Nice. Cambridge: Cambridge University Press, 1977.

Brock, Helen. "North America, a Western Outpost of European Medicine." In *The Medical Enlightenment of the Eighteenth Century*, edited by Andrew Cunningham and Roger French, 194–216. Cambridge: Cambridge University Press, 1990.

Brodsky, Alyn. *Benjamin Rush: Patriot and Physician*. New York: St. Martin's Press, 2004.

Burns, Chester R. "Malpractice Suits in American Medicine before the Civil War." *Bulletin of the History of Medicine* 43, no. 1 (1969): 41–56.

———. "Medical Ethics and Jurisprudence." In *The Education of American Physicians*, edited by Ronald L. Numbers, 273–89. Berkeley: University of California Press, 1980.

———. *Medical Ethics in the U.S. before the Civil War*. PhD diss. Johns Hopkins University, 1969.

Burns, Eric. *Infamous Scribblers: The Founding Fathers and the Rowdy Beginnings of American Journalism*. New York: Public Affairs, 2006.

Cash, Philip. "The Professionalization of Boston Medicine, 1760–1803." In *Medicine in Colonial Massachusetts, 1620–1820*, edited by Philip Cash, Eric H. Christianson, and J. Worth Estes, 69–94. Boston: Colonial Society of Massachusetts, 1980.

Cash, Philip, Eric H. Christianson, and J. Worth Estes, eds. *Medicine in Colonial Massachusetts, 1620–1820*. Boston: Colonial Society of Massachusetts, 1980.

———. "Eighteenth-Century Medicine and the Modern Physician." In *Medicine in Colonial Massachusetts, 1620–1820*, edited by Philip Cash, Eric H. Christianson, and J. Worth Estes, 26–32. Boston: Colonial Society of Massachusetts, 1980.

Chaden, Caryn. "Dress and Undress in Brackenridge's *Modern Chivalry*." *Early American Literature* 26, no. 1 (1991): 55–72.

Chinard, Gilbert. "Eighteenth-Century Theories on America as a Human Habitat." *Proceedings of the American Philosophical Society* 91 (1947): 45–52.

Clark, Mary Elizabeth. *Peter Porcupine in America: The Career of William Cobbett, 1792–1800*. PhD diss. University of Pennsylvania, 1939.

Cockburn, J. S., and Thomas S. Green, eds. *Twelve Good Men and True: The Criminal Trial Jury in England, 1200–1800*. Princeton: Princeton University Press, 1988.

Cohen, Daniel A. *Pillars of Salt, Monuments of Grace: New England Crime Literature and the Origins of American Popular Culture, 1674–1860*. New York: Oxford University Press, 1993.

Cohen, Dov, and Joe Vandello. "Social Norms, Social Meaning, and the Economic Analysis of Law: Meanings of Violence." *Journal of Legal Studies* 27 (1988): 567–84.

Cole, G. D. H. *Life of William Cobbett*. New York: Collins, 1924.

Conrad, Lawrence L, Michael Neve, Vivian Nutton, Roy Porter, and Andrew Wear. *The Western Medical Tradition: 800 BC to AD 1800.* Cambridge: Cambridge University Press, 1995.

Constable, Marianne. *The Law of the Other: The Mixed Jury and Changing Conceptions of Citizenship, Law, and Knowledge.* Chicago: University of Chicago Press, 1994.

Cooter, Roger. "'Framing' the End of the Social History of Medicine." In *Locating Medical History: The Stories and Their Meanings,* edited by Frank Huisman and John Harley Warner, 309–37. Baltimore: Johns Hopkins University Press, 2004.

Corner, Betsy Copping. *William Shippen, Jr.: Pioneer in American Medical Education.* Philadelphia: American Philosophical Society, 1951.

Cunningham, Andrew, and Roger French, eds. *The Medical Enlightenment of the Eighteenth Century.* Cambridge: Cambridge University Press, 1990.

Davidson, Cathy. *Revolution and the Word: The Rise of the Novel in America.* New York: Oxford University Press, 1986.

Davies, Terence C. "American Medicine During the Revolutionary Era." *Journal of the Medical Association of the State of Alabama* 6 (1976): 34–36.

Davis, Audrey P. *Medicine and Its Technology: An Introduction to the History of Medical Instrumentation.* Westport: Greenwood Press, 1981.

De Certeau, Michel. *The Practice of Everyday Life.* Translated by Steven Rendall. Berkeley: University of California Press, 1984.

De Ville, Kenneth Allen. *Medical Malpractice in Nineteenth Century America: Origins and Legacy.* New York: New York University Press, 1990.

Duffy, John. *Epidemics in Colonial America.* Baton Rouge: Louisiana State University Press, 1953.

———. *The Sanitarians: A History of American Public Health.* Urbana: University of Illinois Press, 1990.

Eckert, Jack. "In the Days of the Epidemic: The 1793 Yellow Fever Outbreak in Philadelphia as Seen by Physicians." *Transactions & Studies of the College of Physicians of Philadelphia* ser 5, 15 (1993): 31–38.

Edwards, Linden F. "Resurrection Roots During the Heroic Age of Anatomy in America." *Bulletin of the History of Medicine* 25 (1951): 178–84.

Ellickson, Robert C. *Order Without Law: How Neighbors Settle Disputes.* Cambridge: Harvard University Press, 1991.

Elliott, Emory. *Revolutionary Writers: Literature and Authority in the New Republic, 1725–1810.* New York: Oxford University Press, 1986.

Ellis, R. *The Jeffersonian Crisis: Courts and Politics in the Young Republic.* New York: Oxford University Press, 1971.

Engell, John. "Brackenridge, *Modern Chivalry,* and American Humor." *Early American Literature* 22, no. 1 (1987): 43–62.

Estes, J. Worth. "Therapeutic Practice in Colonial New England." In *Medicine in Colonial Massachusetts, 1620–1820,* edited by Philip Cash, Eric H. Christianson, and J. Worth Estes, 289–383. Boston: Colonial Society of Massachusetts, 1980.

Estes, J. Worth, and Billy G. Smith, eds. *A Melancholy Scene of Devastation: The Public Response to the 1793 Philadelphia Yellow Fever Epidemic.* Philadelphia: College of Physicians of Philadelphia, 1997.

Feeney, Joseph J. "Modernized by 1800: The Portrait of Urban America, Especially Philadelphia, in the Novels of Charles Brockden Brown." *American Studies* 23, no. 2 (1982): 25–38.

Ferguson, Robert A. "Yellow Fever and Charles Brockden Brown: Context of the Emerging Novelist." *Early American Literature* 14 (1979–80): 293–305.

———. *Law and Letters in American Culture.* Cambridge: Harvard University Press, 1984.

Fissell, Mary E. "Making Meaning from the Margins: The New Cultural History of Medicine." In *Locating Medical History: The Stories and Their Meanings,* edited by Frank Huisman and John Harley Warner, 364–85. Baltimore: Johns Hopkins University Press, 2004.

———. *Patients, Power, and the Poor in Eighteenth-Century Bristol.* Cambridge: Cambridge University Press, 1991.

Forsyth, William. *The History of Trial by Jury.* London: L. W. Parker, 1852.

Fox, Nick J. "Is There Life After Foucault? Texts, Frames and Differends." In *Foucault, Health and Medicine,* edited by Alan Peterson and Bryan S. Turner, 31–50. London: Routledge, 1997.

Friedman, Lawrence M. *Crime and Punishment in American History.* New York: Basic Books, 1993.

Garner, Bryan A., ed. *Black's Law Dictionary.* 7th ed. St. Paul: West Group, 1999.

Gibson, James E. *Dr. Bodo Otto and the Medical Background of the American Revolution.* Springfield: Charles C. Thomas, 1937.

Gieskes, Edward. *Representing the Professions: Administration, Law, and Theater in Early Modern England.* Newark: University of Delaware Press, 2006.

Gilman, C. M. "Military Surgery in the American Revolution." *The Journal of the Medical Society of New Jersey* 57 (1960): 491–96.

Gilmore, Michael T. "Eighteenth-Century Oppositional Ideology and Hugh Henry Brackenridge's *Modern Chivalry.*" *Early American Literature* 13 (1978): 181–92.

Goodman, Nathan. *Benjamin Rush: Physician and Citizen, 1746–1813.* Philadelphia: University of Pennsylvania Press, 1934.

Green, Thomas Andrew. *Verdict According to Conscience: Perspectives on the English Criminal Trial Jury 1200–1800.* Chicago: University of Chicago Press, 1985.

Greene, John C. *American Science in the Age of Jefferson.* Ames: University of Iowa Press, 1984.

Greenhouse, Carol J. "Nature is to Culture as Praying is to Suing: Legal Pluralism in an American Suburb." *Journal of Legal Pluralism* 20 (1982): 17–35.

Griffith, Sally F. "'A Total Dissolution of the Bonds of Society': Community, Death and Regeneration in Mathew Carey's *Short Account of the Malignant Fever.*" In *A Melancholy Scene of Devastation: The Public Response to the 1793 Philadelphia Yellow Fever Epidemic,* edited by J. Worth Estes and Billy G. Smith, 45–60. Philadelphia: College of Physicians of Philadelphia, 1997.

Hall, Kermit L. *The Magic Mirror: Law in American History.* New York: Oxford University Press, 1989.

Harkey, Joseph H. "The *Don Quixote* of the Frontier: Brackenridge's *Modern Chivalry.*" *Early American Literature* 8 (1973): 193–203.

Harley, David. "Honour and Property: The Structure of Professional Disputes in Eighteenth-Century English Medicine." In *The Medical Enlightenment of the Eighteenth Century*, edited by Andrew Cunningham and Roger French, 138–64. Cambridge: Cambridge University Press, 1990.

Harris, Jonathan Gil. *Sick Economies: Drama, Mercantilism, and Disease in Shakespeare's England*. Philadelphia: University of Pennsylvania Press, 2004.

Hastings, George Everett. *The Life and Works of Francis Hopkinson*. New York: Russell & Russell, 1926.

Hedges, William L. "Benjamin Rush, Charles Brockden Brown, and the American Plague Year." *Early American Literature* 7 (1973): 295–311.

Higginbotham, A. Leon. *In the Matter of Color, Race and the American Legal Process: The Colonial Period*. Oxford: Oxford University Press, 1978.

Holifield, E. Brooks. *Theology in America: Christian Thought from the Age of the Puritans to the Civil War*. New Haven: Yale University Press, 2003.

Holmes, Chris. "Benjamin Rush and the Yellow Fever." *Bulletin of the History of Medicine* 40 (1966): 246–63.

Horwitz, Morton J. *The Transformation of American Law, 1780–1860*. Cambridge: Harvard University Press, 1977.

Jelenko, C. "Emergency Medicine in Colonial America: Revolutionary War Casualties." *Annals of Emergency Medicine* 11, no. 1 (1982): 40–43.

Jones, Colin. "Plague and Its Metaphors in Early Modern France." *Representations* 53 (1996): 97–127.

Jordanova, Ludmilla. "The Social Construction of Medical Knowledge." In *Locating Medical History: The Stories and Their Meanings*, edited by Frank Huisman and John Harley Warner, 338–58. Baltimore: Johns Hopkins University Press, 2004.

Kafer, Peter. "Charles Brockden Brown and Revolutionary Philadelphia: An Imagination in Context." *Pennsylvania Magazine of History and Biography* 116, no. 4 (1992): 467–92.

Kahn, Paul W. *The Cultural Study of Law: Reconstructing Legal Scholarship*. Chicago: The University of Chicago Press, 1999.

Kilpatrick, Robert. " 'Living in the Light': Dispensaries, Philanthropy, and Medical Reform in Late Eighteenth-Century London." In *The Medical Enlightenment of the Eighteenth Century*, edited by Andrew Cunningham and Roger French, 254–80. Cambridge: Cambridge University Press, 1990.

Kleinman, Arthur. *Writing at the Margin: Discourse Between Anthropology and Medicine*. Berkeley: University of California Press, 1995.

Konkle, Burton Alva. *Joseph Hopkinson, 1770–1842: Jurist, Scholar, Inspirer of the Arts*. Philadelphia: University of Pennsylvania Press, 1981.

Kornfeld, Eve. "Crisis in the Capital: The Cultural Significance of Philadelphia's Great Yellow Fever Epidemic." *Pennsylvania History* 51 (1984): 189–205.

Landsman, Stephan. "The Rise of the Contentious Spirit: Adversary Procedure in Eighteenth-Century England." *Cornell Law Review* 75 (1990): 497–606.

Lane, John. "Jean Deveze (1753–1826? [sic]): Notes on the Yellow Fever Epidemic at Philadelphia in 1793." *Annals of Medical History* n.s. 8 (1936): 202–26.

Langbein, John H. "The Criminal Trial Before the Lawyers." *University of Chicago Law Review* 45 (1978): 263–316.

———. "The Historical Origins of the Privilege Against Self-Incrimination at Common Law." *Michigan Law Review* 92 (1994): 1047–85.

———. *The Origins of Adversary Criminal Trial* Oxford: Oxford University Press, 2003.

———. "Shaping the Eighteenth-Century Criminal Trial: A View from the Ryder Sources." *University of Chicago Law Review* 50 (1983): 1–136.

Lapansky, Phillip. "'Abigail, a Negress': The Role and Legacy of African Americans in the Yellow Fever Epidemic." In *A Melancholy Scene of Devastation: The Public Response to the 1793 Philadelphia Yellow Fever Epidemic,* edited by J. Worth Estes and Billy G. Smith, 61–78. Philadelphia: College of Physicians of Philadelphia, 1997.

Lupton, Deborah. "Foucault and the Medicalisation Critique." In *Foucault, Health and Medicine,* edited by Alan Peterson and Bryan S. Turner, 94–110. London: Routledge, 1997.

Lyotard, Jean François, and Jean Loup Thebaud. *Just Gaming.* Translated by Wald Godzich. Minneapolis: University of Minnesota Press, 1985.

———. *Peregrinations: Law, Form, Event.* Translated by Cecile Lindsay. New York: Columbia University Press, 1988.

Maier, Pauline. "Popular Uprisings and Civil Authority in Eighteenth-Century America." *William and Mary Quarterly* 3rd ser. 27 (1970): 3–35.

Malone, Wex. *Essays on Torts.* Baton Rouge: Paul M. Herbert Law Center, Louisiana State University Press, 1986.

Martin, Julian. "Sauvages's Nosology: Medical Enlightenment in Montpellier." In *The Medical Enlightenment of the Eighteenth Century,* edited by Andrew Cunningham and Roger French, 111–37. Cambridge: Cambridge University Press, 1990.

Martin, Wendy. "On the Road with the Philosopher and the Profiteer: A Study of Hugh Henry Brackenridge's *Modern Chivalry.*" *Eighteenth-Century Studies* 4 (1971): 241–56.

———. "The Rogue and the Rational Man: Hugh Henry Brackenridge's Study of a Con Man in *Modern Chivalry.*" *Early American Literature* 8 (1973): 179–92.

McFarland, Joseph. "The Epidemic of Yellow Fever in Philadelphia in 1793 and Its Influence Upon Dr. Benjamin Rush." *Medical Review of Reviews* 25 (1929): 627–74.

Meehan, Thomas R. "Courts, Cases, and Counselors in Revolutionary and Post-Revolutionary Pennsylvania." *Pennsylvania Magazine of History and Biography* 91, no. 1 (1967): 3–34.

Miller, Jacquelyn. "Passions and Politics: The Multiple Meanings of Benjamin Rush's Treatment for Yellow Fever." In *A Melancholy Scene of Devastation: The Public Response to the 1793 Philadelphia Yellow Fever Epidemic,* edited by J. Worth Estes and Billy G. Smith, 79–96. Philadelphia: College of Physicians of Philadelphia, 1997.

Miller, John C. *Crisis in Freedom: The Alien and Sedition Acts.* Boston: Little, Brown, 1951.

Modlin, Charles E. "The Folly of Ambition in *Modern Chivalry.*" *Proceedings of the American Antiquarian Society* 85 (1975): 310–13.

Mohr, James C. *Doctors and the Law: Medical Jurisprudence in Nineteenth-Century America*. Oxford: Oxford University Press, 1993.

Moss, Stephanie, and Kaara L. Peterson. *Disease, Diagnosis, and Cure on the Early Modern Stage*. Burlington: Ashgate, 2004.

Myrsiades, Linda. "A Language Game Approach to Narrative Analysis of Sexual Harassment Law in *Meritor v. Vinson*." *College Literature* 25, no. 1 (1998): 200–230.

Nance, William. "Satiric Elements in Brackenridge's *Modern Chivalry*." *Texas Studies in Language and Literature* 9 (1967): 381–89.

Nash, Gary B. *Forging Freedom: The Formation of Philadelphia's Black Community, 1720–1820*. Cambridge: Harvard University Press, 1988.

———. "New Light on Richard Allen: The Early Years of Freedom." *William and Mary Quarterly* 3rd ser. 46 (1989): 332–40.

———. "Poverty and Poor Relief in Pre-Revolutionary Philadelphia." *William and Mary Quarterly* 33, no. 1 (1997): 3–30.

Nathans, Heather S. *Early American Theatre from the Revolution to Thomas Jefferson: Into the Hands of the People*. Cambridge: Cambridge University Press, 2003.

Neilson, Winthrop, and Frances Neilson. *Verdict for the Doctor: The Case of Benjamin Rush*. New York: Hastings House, 1958.

Nelson, Dana D. "'Indications of the Public Will': *Modern Chivalry*'s Theory of Democratic Representation." *ANQ* 15, no. 1 (2002): 23–39.

Nelson, William E. *Americanization of the Common Law: The Impact of Legal Change on Massachusetts Society, 1760–1830*. Cambridge: Harvard University Press, 1975.

———. "Emerging Notions of Modern Criminal Law in the Revolutionary Era: An Historical Perspective." *New York University Law Review* 42 (1967): 450–82.

Novak, William J. *The People's Welfare: Law and Regulation in Nineteenth-Century America*. Chapel Hill: University of North Carolina Press, 1996.

O'Day, Rosemary. "The Anatomy of a Profession: The Clergy of the Church of England." In *The Professions in Early Modern England*, edited by Wilfrid Prest, 25–63. London: Croom Helm, 1987.

———. *The Professions in Early Modern England, 1450–1800: Servants of the Commonweal*. London: Longman, 2000.

Paster, Gail Kern. *The Body Embarrassed: Drama and the Disciplines of Shame in Early Modern England*. Ithaca: Cornell University Press, 1993.

Pelling, Margaret. "Medical Practice in Early Modern England: Trade or Profession?" In *The Professions in Early Modern England*, edited by Wilfrid Prest, 90–128. London: Croom Helm, 1987.

Pernick, Martin S. "Politics, Parties, and Pestilence: Epidemic Yellow Fever in Philadelphia and the Rise of the First Party System." In *A Melancholy Scene of Devastation: The Public Response to the 1793 Philadelphia Yellow Fever Epidemic*, edited by J. Worth Estes and Billy G. Smith, 119–46. Philadelphia: College of Physicians of Philadelphia, 1997.

Philip, Eric H. Christianson, and J. Worth Estes, eds. *Medicine in Colonial Massachusetts, 1620–1820*. Boston: Colonial Society of Massachusetts, 1980.

Porter, Roy. "The Eighteenth Century." In *The Western Medical Tradition: 800 BC to*

AD 1800, edited by Lawrence I. Conrad, Michael Neve, Vivian Nutton, Roy Porter, and Andrew Wear, 371–475. Cambridge: Cambridge University Press, 1995.

———. *Health for Sale: Quackery in England 1660–1850.* Manchester: Manchester University Press, 1989.

Posner, Eric A. *Law and Social Norms.* Cambridge: Harvard University Press, 2000.

Powell, John H. *Bring Out the Dead.* 1949. Reprint, Philadelphia: University of Pennsylvania Press, 1965.

Prest, Wilfrid. "Lawyers." In *The Professions in Early Modern England,* edited by Wilfed Prest, 64–89. London: Croom Helm, 1987.

———, ed. *The Professions in Early Modern England.* London: Croom Helm, 1987.

———. "The Professions and Society in Early Modern England." In *The Professions in Early Modern England,* edited by Wilfed Prest, 1–24. London: Croom Helm, 1987.

Rabban, David M. "Review Essay: The Ahistorical Historian." *Stanford Law Review* 37 (1985): 795–856.

Ranger, Terence and Paul Slack, eds. *Epidemics and Ideas: Essays on the Historical Perception of Pestilence.* Cambridge: Cambridge University Press, 1992.

Readings, Bill. *Introducing Lyotard: Art and Politics.* New York: Routledge, 1991.

Rice, Grantland S. "*Modern Chivalry* and the Resistance to Textual Authority." *American Literature* 67, no. 2 (1995): 257–81.

Richardson, Ruth. *Death, Dissection, and the Destitute.* London: Routledge and Kegan Paul, 1987.

Richman, Irwin. *The Brightest Ornament: A Biography of Nathaniel Chapman, M.D.* Bellefonte: Pennsylvania Heritage, Inc., 1967.

Robinson, Arthur Thomas. *Third Horseman of the Apocalypse: A Multidisciplinary Social History of the 1793 Yellow Fever Epidemic in Philadelphia.* Ph.D. diss. Washington State University, 1993.

Rosen, George. "The Fate of the Concept of Medical Police, 1780–1890." *Centaurus* 5, no. 1 (1957): 97–113.

———. *From Medical Police to Social Medicine: Essays on the History of Health Care.* New York: Science History Publications, 1974.

———. "Political Order and Human Health in Jeffersonian Thought." *Bulletin of the History of Medicine* 26 (1952): 32–54.

Rosenberg, Charles E. *The Cholera Years: The United States in 1831, 1849, and 1866.* Chicago: University of Chicago Press, 1987.

———. *Explaining Epidemics and Other Studies in the History of Medicine.* New York: Cambridge University Press, 1992.

Rosenberg, Charles E., and Janet Golden, eds. *Framing Disease: Studies in Cultural History.* New Brunswick: Rutgers University Press, 1992.

Rowe, G. S. *Embattled Bench: The Pennsylvania Supreme Court and the Forging of a Democratic Society. 1684–1809.* Newark: University of Delaware Press, 1994.

———. *Thomas McKean: The Shaping of an American Republicanism.* Boulder: Colorado Associated University Press, 1978.

Ryken, Leland. *Dictionary of Biblical Imagery.* Leicester: Inter Varsity Press, 1998.

Sambrook, James. *William Cobbett*. London: Routledge & Kegan Paul, 1973.

Samuels, Shirley. "Infidelity and Contagion: The Rhetoric of Revolution." *Early American Literature* 22, no. 2 (1987): 183–91.

———. "Plague and Politics in 1793: Arthur Merwyn." *Criticism* 27, no. 3 (1985): 225–46.

Sappol, Michael. *A Traffic of Dead Bodies: Anatomy and Embodied Social Identity in Nine-teenth-Century America*. Princeton: Princeton University Press, 2002.

Schor, Esther. *Bearing the Dead: The British Culture of Mourning from the Enlightenment to Victoria*. Princeton: Princeton University Press, 1994.

Schultz, Lucille. "Uncovering the Significance of the Animal Imagery in *Modern Chivalry*: An Application of Scottish Common Sense Realism." *Early American Literature* 14 (1979–80): 306–11.

Schwartz, Warren F., Keith Baxter, and David Ryan. "The Duel: Can These Gentlemen Be Acting Efficiently?" *Journal of Legal Studies* 13 (1984): 321–55.

Shapiro, Barbara. *'Beyond Reasonable Doubt' and 'Probable Cause': Historical Perspectives on the Anglo-American Law of Evidence*. Berkeley: University of California Press, 1991.

Shryock, Richard Harrison. *Medical Licensing in America, 1650–1965*. Baltimore: Johns Hopkins University Press, 1967.

———. *Medicine and Society in America, 1660–1860*. New York: New York University Press, 1960.

———. *Medicine in America: Historical Essays*. Baltimore: Johns Hopkins University Press, 1966.

Shuy, Roger W. *Language Crimes: The Use and Abuse of Language Evidence in the Court-room*. Oxford: Blackwell, 1993.

Silvette, Herbert. *Doctor on the Stage: Medicine and Medical Men in Seventeenth-Century England*. Nashville: University of Tennessee Press, 1967.

Sloane, David Charles. *The Last Great Necessity: Cemeteries in American History*. Baltimore: Johns Hopkins Press, 1991.

Smith, Billy G. *The "Lower Sort": Philadelphia's Laboring People, 1750–1800*. Ithaca: Cornell University Press, 1990.

Smith, James Morton. "The Aurora and the Alien and Sedition Laws, Part I: The Editorship of Benjamin Franklin Bache." *Pennsylvania Magazine of History and Biography* 77, no. 1 (1953): 3–23.

———. "The Aurora and the Alien and Sedition Laws, Part II: The Editorship of William Duane." *Pennsylvania Magazine of History and Biography* 77, no. 2 (1953): 123–55.

Spater, George. *William Cobbett: The Poor Man's Friend*. Vol 1. Cambridge: Cambridge University Press, 1982.

Starr, Paul. *The Social Transformation of American Medicine: The Rise of a Sovereign Profession and the Making of a Vast Industry*. New York: Basic Books, 1982.

Terdiman, Richard. "Translator's Introduction: The Force of Law: Toward a Sociology of the Juridical Field." *Hastings Law Journal* 38 (1987): 805–14.

Tucker, E. F. J. *Corum Paribus: Images of the Common Lawyer in Romantic and Victorian Literature*. Charleston: Citadel, 1986.

————. *Intruder into Eden: Representations of the Common Lawyer in English Literature 1350–1750*. New York: Camden House, 1984.

Turner, Bryan S. "From Governmentality to Risk: Some Reflections on Foucault's Contribution to Medical Sociology." In *Foucault, Health and Medicine*, edited by Alan Peterson and Bryan S. Turner, ix–xxi. London: Routledge, 1997.

Wallenborn, White McKenzie. "George Washington's Terminal Illness: A Modern Medical Analysis of the Last Illness and Death of George Washington." *The Papers of George Washington*. http://gwpapers.virginia.edu/articles/wallenborn/index.-html

Warden, G. B. "The Medical Profession in Colonial Boston." In *Medicine in Colonial Massachusetts, 1620–1820*, edited by Philip Cash, Eric H. Christianson, and J. Worth Estes, 145–57. Boston: Colonial Society of Massachusetts, 1980.

Warfel, Harry R., ed. *The Rhapsodist and Other Uncollected Writings by Charles Brockden Brown*. New York: Scholars' Facsimiles & Reprints, 1943.

Warner, John Harley. *The Therapeutic Perspective: Medical Practice, Knowledge, and Identity in America, 1820–1885*. Cambridge: Harvard University Press, 1986.

Watson, Patricia A. *The Angelic Conjunction: Preacher-Physicians of Colonial New England*. Knoxville: University of Tennessee Press, 1991.

Watts, Steven. *The Romance of Real Life: Charles Brockden Brown and the Origins of American Culture*. Baltimore: Johns Hopkins University Press, 1994.

Whittle, Amberys R. "*Modern Chivalry:* The Frontier Crucible." *Early American Literature* 6 (1971): 263–70.

Williams, Daniel E. "Gadding About Quack Like: The Science of Deception and the Practice of Physic in the Narrative of Henry Tufts." In *The Body and the Text: Comparative Essays in Literature and Medicine*, edited by Bruce Clarke and Wendell Aycock, 77–89. Lubbock: Texas Tech University Press, 1990.

Williams, Joan. "Critical Legal Studies: The Death of Transcendence & The Rise of the New Langdells." *New York University Law Review* 62 (1987): 429–96.

Williams, William H. *America's First Hospital: The Pennsylvania Hospital, 1751–1841*. Wayne: Haverford House, 1976.